Fiona Handyside is Senior Lecturer in European Film at the University of Exeter and received her PhD from Queen Mary, University of London. Previous publications include *International Cinema and the Girl: Local Issues, Transnational Contexts* (2015) and *Cinema at the Shore: The Beach in French Cinema* (2014) and her research has appeared in a number of journals such as *Continuum: Journal of Media and Cultural Studies, European Journal of Cultural Studies, Studies in French Cinema* and *Screen*.

'In this book, Fiona Handyside does not shirk from tackling the "thorny paradoxes" in Coppola's canon but rather weaves these issues into an insightful analysis of her films as both feminine and feminist. Written in beautiful prose, Handyside argues that the glittering, gilded cages in Coppola's films show us the light and the dark of girlhood culture.'

– Lucy Bolton, Queen Mary, University of London;
author of *Film and Female Consciousness: Irigaray,
Cinema and Thinking Women*

Sofia Coppola

A CINEMA OF GIRLHOOD

Fiona Handyside

I.B. TAURIS
LONDON · NEW YORK

Published in 2017 by
I.B.Tauris & Co. Ltd
London • New York
www.ibtauris.com

International Library of the Moving Image 39

HB ISBN: 978 1 78453 714 2
PB ISBN: 978 1 78453 715 9
eISBN: 978 1 78672 160 0
ePDF: 978 1 78673 160 9

A full CIP record for this book is available from the British Library
A full CIP record is available from the Library of Congress

Library of Congress Catalog Card Number: available

Printed and bound by TJ International Ltd, Padstow, Cornwall

Contents

List of Figures

Acknowledgments

This book would not have been written without the advice, enthusiasm, support and all round good cheer of my friend and colleague Danielle Hipkins whom I thank here. I've had the pleasure of teaching Sofia Coppola films on our shared 'girlhood' module and I would also like to thank the students who have provided such thoughtful responses to Coppola, and especially Katherine Bradshaw who keeps me up to date on all things Coppola related! The eagle-eyed Jen Barnes also kept me in the Coppola loop. Anna Coatman at I.B.Tauris provided early encouragement when I first suggested the project, and Maddy Hamey-Thomas a supportive editorial presence in the latter stages. Michael and Delphine were as always fun and generous hosts at their lovely apartment in the 18th when I spent a few days at the Cinémathèque française in Paris in November 2013 for Coppola research. Dom Holdaway kindly invited me to present a paper on some early Coppola research at a seminar on the female gaze held at Warwick in January 2014, which was an inspiring and enjoyable event. I was given the opportunity to refine my broader thoughts on girlhood and luminosity at a workshop in Paris organised by Ari Blatt and Ed Welch in July 2015, a delightful two days of discussion and reflection. Kate Taylor-Jones invited me to give papers on different aspects of my Coppola project at Bangor in March 2014 and at Sheffield in December 2015; I thank her for her hospitality, encouragement and insights. Jonathan Bramall made endless cups of ginger tea and coffee and was adept at suggesting alternative words when I was really stuck.

I'm always grateful for the love and support of family and friends, but especially now as I've completed this book during a difficult and turbulent time personally, as my family comes to terms with my mum's cancer diagnosis. We all love her very much, and it is to her, Marie Handyside, that I dedicate this book.

1

Sofia Coppola: Postfeminist [d]au[gh]te[u]r?

'One is not born, but rather becomes, a woman.'[1]

'Explicitly and implicitly, women are instructed by their environment (from the school room to the women's magazine) in how to "become" a woman – a task that is never completed and subject to constant revision.'[2]

'[My films are] sort of about a lonely girl in a big hotel or palace or whatever, kind of wandering around, trying to grow up.'[3]

Postfeminism and Girlhood

For feminist theory and politics, the question of how a baby comes to identify first as a girl and then as a woman is of crucial importance. As the quotes above show, feminist theorists such as Simone de Beauvoir and feminist film scholars such as Hilary Radner figure this identification as a complex process of becoming – a becoming that film director Sofia Coppola names as both a 'wandering around' and a 'trying to grow up', her phrasing capturing the lack of direction, ambivalence and difficulties for girls becoming women. In a society in which gender difference is attributed cultural and sociological as well as biological meaning, the frameworks which guide the process of learning which gender one is have the power to either reinforce or overcome prejudice, inequality and oppression. For girls, feminism seeks to provide positive role-models to enable them to feel proud of their gender identity rather than constrained by it. However, it also has the more negative task of identifying how a patriarchal system can still oppress girls and women. Early feminist film theory that emerged in the 1970s developed in response to both these traditions, with on the one hand the so-called 'positive images' criticism calling for aspirational and non-stereotyped images of women in film, epitomised by the cultural studies/sociological work of Molly Haskell and

Marjorie Rosen, and on the other critical accounts of cinema itself as a tool used to idealise and objectify women that needs to be rethought in a non-patriarchal way, associated especially with the psychoanalytic methods of Laura Mulvey and Claire Johnston.[4] These theorists had a direct impact on film-making, what Mulvey described as theory's 'utopian other'.[5] Feminist possibilities in film oscillate between two poles of a radical avant-garde committed to destroying visual pleasure and creating a non-patriarchal counter-cinema, and a more entertainment-led narrative approach intended to record the realities of women's lives and agitate for social change.

Since the heady days of the first Festival of Women's films, held in 1971, the identity and context of women's film-making has changed enormously, to the extent that it can no longer be labelled 'utopian' or 'feminist'. Partly, this is because there are simply more women film-makers, with directors such as Andrea Arnold, Catherine Breillat, Kathryn Bigelow, Nancy Meyers, Nora Ephron, Sally Potter, Jane Campion, Agnès Varda, Isabel Coixet, Diane Kurys and Lucrecia Martel testifying to the range of films produced across nations, and in commercial, art-house and subsidised cinema.[6] Such a narrative of female progress would seem to chime perfectly with the dominant cultural mode of postfeminism and its diffusion in the cinematic sphere. This holds that the demands of feminism, for example for a specific support for, and encouragement of, female filmmakers, are not necessary, as women have succeeded in making films, demonstrating that we now live in an era of gender equality. Hollywood also makes films that target a female audience. Far from being either avant-garde or social realist, it is a 'chick' postfeminist sensibility that informs such paradigmatic films 'for women' as *Bridget Jones' Diary* (Maguire, 2001), *The Devil Wears Prada* (Frankel, 2006) and *Sex and the City: the Movie* (King, 2008).[7] Generally speaking, the postfeminist takes for granted the goals and gains of second-wave feminism as concerns women having the right to paid employment and the vote, but rather than rejecting femininity, delights in such 'feminine' pursuits as shopping, wearing make-up, and pursuing (usually) heterosexual romance. Rosalind Gill defines the postfeminist film as one in which there are recurrent themes, tropes and constructions centred on the (female) body and its need for constant surveillance and discipline, the dominance of the makeover paradigm, a marked sexualisation of culture, and the awkward entanglement of feminist and anti-feminist ideas.[8] For Hilary Radner, this sensibility owes less to the solidarity and sisterliness of the 1970s feminist movement than a parallel movement which grew up alongside it. She labels this 'neo-feminism', which she sees as having had far more impact on the postfeminist cultural landscape than feminism, particularly in its emphasis on the individual.

Both feminism and neo-feminism argue for women's right to financial autonomy and self-determination, but whereas feminism placed this within the context of state interventions and social justice, neo-feminism is more closely aligned with neoliberalism, the dominant ethos of the twenty-first century. Neoliberalism assumes that empowered individuals can exercise choice and agency to reach their goals, and takes no account of institutional constraints. While Radner states that Gill's definition of the traits of postfeminist film is an accurate analysis of the content of many films aimed at women, she explains the importance of under-standing these films as neo-feminist rather than (or as well as) postfeminist is that they allow us to see how while they have picked up on some of the second-wave's rhetorical devices, such as the right of the individual feminine subject to self-determination, they are not so much hostile as *indifferent* to the social and political concerns that set feminists apart from a general group of female strivers attempt-ing to achieve the ideals of neoliberalism. Neo-feminism, she posits, is only very tangentially a consequence of feminism, but rather shares neoliberalism's concern with consumer culture as one of the dominant means through which a woman 'can affirm her identity and express herself', thus constituting 'a very attractive version of feminine culture in terms of the needs and designs of the media con-glomerates that dominate the contemporary scene.'[9]

For Radner, films that are neo-feminist dominate what she labels Conglomerate Hollywood's notion of films that are aimed at a female audience.[10] They repeat a significant number of traits: a charismatic female star as the focus of the diegesis, often portraying a professional working woman; an emphasis on fashion and con-sumer culture; the disappearance of chastity as a 'feminine virtue'; romance as a significant theme; the 'do-over' [makeover] as a solution to seemingly insur-mountable problems. Radner dubs these 'girly films', in order to underline their close relations to a feminine ideal that is represented through 'girlishness' as a mode of appearance and a way of being. Although as Radner explains, girlishness is not necessarily correlated to biological age, its importance as a signifier of the feminine ideal indicates just how important the figure of the girl is in neo-feminist and postfeminist culture.[11] For feminist discourse, the girl is a problematic figure. As Catherine Driscoll explains:

> feminist practices [...] are still dominated by adult models of subjectiv-
> ity presumed to be the end-point of a naturalised process of develop-
> ing individual identity that relegates [...] roles, behaviours, practices
> to its immature past. As a future-directed politics, a politics of trans-
> formation, girls and the widest range of representation of, discourses
> on, and sites of becoming women are crucial to feminism. Yet feminist

3

> discussions of girls rarely engage with feminine adolescence without
> constructing girls as opposed to […] the mature, independent woman
> as feminist subject […] shaping a dominant feminist address in norms
> of independence, agency and originality that while liberatory for some
> also works to restrict and homogenise the category of women.[12]

In contrast, youth and girlishness are prized within postfeminist culture, and
while this obviously could work to infantilise and belittle adult women, it can
also enable a more open and flexible approach to what Driscoll labels 'the sites of
becoming women'. Radner explains that reclaiming the figure of the girl and girlish pursuits underlines the unwillingness of (many) women to reject femininity.
A neo-feminist paradigm offers a way to retain femininity even as its definition
evolves with rapid social and economic change.

In postfeminist popular culture, the figure of the girl is hypervisible. Identified
as beginning with the emergence of 'girl power' in the 1990s, which co-opted a
certain version of liberal feminism and sold it to young girls as attractive and
empowering, the girl has become an increasingly visible figure in popular culture.
Sarah Projansky argues that thinking about girls is not a new cultural phenomenon, but rather that it 'draws on a long standing tradition of focusing cultural
attention on girls as problems, as victim of social ills, as symbols of ideal citizenship, and as all round fascinating figures.'[13] What is new is an intense and sustained focus on girls, often characterised as 'new girl heroes' or 'icons': as well
as the Spice Girls band, the 1990s also saw for example Nickelodean's ground-
breaking series *Clarissa Explains it All* (1991–94) which initiated a new trend
in children's TV programming for female heroes, challenging the logic that said
children's shows with girl leads could not be successful and rippling out to such
figures as Buffy, the Vampire Slayer; Sabrina, the Teenage Witch; Princess Merida
in Disney's *Brave* (Andrews, Chapman and Purcell, 2012) and Katniss Everdeen in
The Hunger Games franchise (Ross, 2012+). As Projansky comments, 'the current
proliferation of discourse about girls literally coincides chronologically with the
proliferation of discourse about postfeminism.'[14] Projansky attributes this to five
main factors: first, both postfeminism and girlness can be seen as part of a focus
on youthful femininity in culture; second, this cultural obsession with girlhood
could be seen as backlash against a certain 1980s version of feminism associated
with serious business women and 'power-dressing' – girls haven't yet learned they
can't have a career and a family and retain a 'sense of fun'; third, postfeminism
itself is intensely invested in girlhood as what Diane Negra and Yvonne Tasker
characterise as a site of transcendence and escape from adult pressures, so that
girlhood becomes a highly attractive space for all postfeminist women, regardless

of age;[15] fourth, turning to girls is a way to keep postfeminism fresh and interesting, within the context of a corporate commodity culture; lastly, as the girls visible in the media today are the daughters of postfeminists themselves, anxieties about their future becomes a way to debate the very terms of postfeminism itself. Many of the ways popular culture represents girls and girlhood work through questions about postfeminism and its effects on the gendered organisation of present and future society.

A Postfeminist Cinema of Girlhood: Sofia Coppola

In this book, I suggest that one of the most dynamic and insightful bodies of work to address the figure of the girl in contemporary cinematic culture, and her role as lynchpin in neo-feminist/ postfeminist debates concerning agency, subjectivity and empowerment, has been produced by the film maker Sofia Coppola (b. 1971). Coppola's films consciously address the difficult job of growing up female, and attempt to carve out new spaces for the expression of female subjectivity that embraces rather than rejects femininity. The vulnerable, childlike and abject associations of girlhood are not denied, but held in careful counter-balance with forthright examination of its pleasures and possibilities, although just how precarious this balancing-act is illuminated through the contradictions of Coppola's own authorial persona. A key question this book addresses is the extent to which this acknowledgement of vulnerability and feeling, alongside a celebration of pleasure in girlhood, is enabled by privilege. A further point to consider is how the films enable access for audiences to a point of identification with this essential ambivalence of girlhood. In such a way, the films are postfeminist in their embrace of femininity, but also offer an apparatus to gain critical purchase upon its repeated motifs of sex, travel, shopping and makeovers as empowerment pure and simple.

Rather than developing a counter-cinema feminist aesthetic of 'destroying pleasure', Coppola invents a quintessentially postfeminist aesthetic which takes femininity seriously and offers sustained, intimate engagements with female characters. The recurrent themes and motifs of her films – celebrity culture; fame; power; fashion; travel – are central questions of the postfeminist age. Girls and women are encouraged to celebrate their equal access to paid employment, political representation, sexual enjoyment and the outside world, thanks to feminism, while simultaneously considering the movement passé, outmoded and irrelevant to their twenty-first-century lives. All Coppola's films pay close attention to the experiences of girls and young women (her youngest protagonist is 11, her oldest 25 – notably played however by an 18 year-old, giving her a remarkably youthful appearance). Her debut short, *Lick the Star* (1998) explores the petty rivalries and jealousies among a gang of school-girls; her first feature, *The Virgin Suicides* (2000), concerns a beautiful group of teenage sisters; *Lost in Translation* (2003) features a young newly-wed abroad and lonely who bonds with a much older man in a chaste May-December romance; *Marie Antoinette* (2006) is a sympathetic biopic of the teenaged queen; *Somewhere* (2010) recounts the activities of an eleven year-old daughter of a movie star; *The Bling Ring* (2013) is the study of a group of high school girls (and one boy) involved in celebrity burglaries. Even in this brief précis of her output, her films' sympathetic engagement with the experiences, dilemmas, fantasies and desires of girls and young women shines through. Indeed, so strongly is Coppola identified with youthful femininity that this becomes an optic through which all her cultural interventions are read. In what could potentially be seen as evidence of auteurist excess, but equally speaks to the niche Coppola has carved out in the popular cultural landscape for herself, her curation of a photography exhibition in Paris in 2011–2012 is analysed as a feminisation of that most stereotypically homoerotic and male centric of photographers, Robert Mapplethorpe. Coppola avoided his best known work, instead featuring series of horses and portraits of children and women (Patti Smith, Marisa Benson). A wonderful black-and-white photograph of a young woman, Lisa Lyon, wearing a bikini and a snorkel speaks to Coppola's project in challenging stereotypical views of femininity; Lyon's bikini clad body is in contrast to her direct, serious, confrontational gaze mediated through her diver's mask. As Jean-Max Colard writes, 'the director has managed to appropriate Mapplethorpe's photographs for herself, to slip some of her own personal universe into them, both her fiction and possibly even her self-portrait. This is how to talk about yourself through the work of another.'[16]

Of course, Sofia Coppola's auteur status and image is not just informed by her films and allied cultural work. She grew up in the cinema, and her image and its meanings have been codified practically from her birth. She first appeared on screen as a baby boy, Michael, at the culmination of *The Godfather* (1972), her father, Francis Ford Coppola's, critically acclaimed film based on the novel by Mario Puzo. She is baptised on-screen, in a sacred ceremony marking the importance of birth and the continuity of family both within the story world of *The Godfather* and within the 'real world' of the Coppolas. Within the complex narrative of *The Godfather*, s/he unknowingly provides a vital service for her uncle and literal godfather Michael Corleone, as the baptism provides him with an alibi while his 'soldiers' are out murdering the family's enemies during the ceremony. Of course, she also unwittingly provides a service for her father, available to 'perform' for him in the film which would make his career. Her involuntary transvestite performance nicely captures the paradoxes and privileges of her position within global contemporary cinematic culture. On the one hand, she is welcomed, both on and off-screen, into a highly influential family, bound not only by ties of blood but also loyalty and business. On the other hand, she is marked from the very start as being from this family, contained by its meanings, and established firmly as a scion. The fact that she performs as a boy further complicates the meanings of her initial foray into the cinema, suggesting access to the power and agency of the image-making apparatus contains within it conflicts for women, and recalling Laura Mulvey's famous thesis (developed when Coppola was three years old) that women's enjoyment of the cinema pushes them into a masculine position. Coppola is baptised as a boy in a film that belongs to the mildly counter-cultural New Hollywood Cinema of the 1970s, which was heavily indebted to European models of the male auteur. From the very start, she inhabits paradoxes and crosses boundaries that are usually assumed to be watertight – male and female, auteur and popular cinema, European and American. Coppola is both heavily marked by Italian ethnicity and European influences but placed firmly at the heart of Hollywood, allowed access to the father's power and influence, but at the price of losing her own agency and becoming (like) a son.

The contradictions and tensions of Coppola's position, in place from her first cinematic appearance as an infant, are addressed within and subtly inform her work as filmmaker. She is one of the most critically acclaimed directors working in cinema today. She won an Academy award for Best Original Screenplay in 2004 for *Lost in Translation* and in 2010 she became the first ever American female director (and only fourth American ever) to win the Golden Lion at the Venice Film Festival for *Somewhere*. She was at the time only the third woman ever, and the first ever American woman, to be nominated for an Oscar for Best Director (again in 2004 for *Lost in Translation*), and she has won two Golden Globes (Best Motion Picture – Comedy or Musical for *Lost in Translation*, 2004 and Best Director, Motion Picture, also for *Lost in Translation*, 2004). Her most recent film, *The Bling Ring* opened the *Un Certain Regard* section at the Cannes film festival. Serious film critics in high profile newspapers generally praise her work, locating in it the key auteurist elements of originality and signature style. Lynn Hirschberg in the *New York Times*, the key opinion former for the US East Coast market, describes her as 'the most original and promising young filmmaker in America'. The influential French cultural magazine *Les Inrockuptibles* sums up her style on its home page for all articles about her as 'hazy, faded, and jewelled with moments of grace that belong only to her'.[17] Her films also enjoy a measure of commercial success commensurate with their positioning within the production and distribution circuits of what has been labelled 'Indiewood' or American 'smart' cinema, of which more anon. *Lost in Translation* was considered one of the indie-hits of the 2003–4 season, which performed extremely well at the box-office in terms of screen average takings (on its opening weekend it took a screen average of $40,221, an absolutely exceptional amount). Such critical and commercial success is unusual for a female film director, for the number of female directors working within the anything approaching the mainstream of American film production remains strikingly low. Martha Lauzen's annual report *The Celluloid Ceiling* shows that in 2010 women comprised just seven percent of directors of the top 250 grossing films in the USA, a decline in two percentage points from 1998.[18]

Yet, despite this critical and commercial success, Coppola is frequently associated not with her own films and professional achievements but those of her father. In an interview on the *Late Show* with David Letterman, broadcast 13 Feb 2004, promoting *Lost in Translation*, for which she had just become the first ever American woman to be nominated for an Oscar for Best Director, Coppola is mainly asked about what it was like being on the set of *Apocalypse Now* (Francis Ford Coppola, 1979), her disastrous acting appearance in *The Godfather 3* (Francis Ford Coppola, 1990), whether her father gives her advice, and if he visited on the set of *Lost in Translation* in Japan. Similarly, when she is interviewed by Anna Praderio on the occasion of being awarded the Golden Lion at Venice, Coppola is asked about *his* recently awarded Oscar for Lifetime Achievement. More acerbic commentary dismisses her as vapid and shallow, a beneficiary of nepotism and as a girl who is dependent upon her father for her profession. A sympathetic article by Sam Adams in *Indiewire* quotes film reviews for *The Bling Ring* which dismiss Coppola as 'a pampered Hollywood Princess' or 'using cinema as therapy to deal with her own guilt-trip for being brought up into Hollywood opulence.'[19] As Adams concludes, it is not as if Coppola's moneyed upper-middle class upbringing is unusual in Hollywood, or that other children of directors and film critics don't become directors themselves, such as Jason Reitman, the son of director Ivan Reitman, or Noah Baumbach, son of film critic and novelist Jonathan Baumbach. (Equally, having a famous well-connected film director father is no guarantee of authorial credibility as Zoe Cassavetes, Jennifer Lynch and even Sofia's brother Roman have found out). It is hard to avoid concluding that Coppola's gender is significant in the accusations of frivolity and nepotism, as she is cast as a spoiled 'daddy's girl'. Peter Vonder Haar claims she is given her money by 'Daddy' (to refer to funds received from the production company American Zoetrope) and Dana Stevens writing in *Slate* compares her to the dreadful Veruca Salt from Roald Dahl's *Charlie and the Chocolate Factory*: '[Coppola] is the privileged little girl whose father, a nut tycoon, makes sure his daughter wins a golden ticket.'[20]

As Caitlin Yuneun Lewis neatly summarises for us:

> the clearly contrasting views of Coppola's filmic practice – one that she is an innovative feminist film-maker articulating important issues of contemporary womanhood, the other that she is a shallow, spoiled daughter of privilege who spends excessive amounts of her father's money on frivolous girlishness – highlight a contrast that reflects the contemporary dilemmas of femininity that are at work in all aspects of her stardom. Rather than being feminist, anti-feminist, or even quasi-feminist, Sofia Coppola is strongly located in the current climate of postfeminism.[21]

While Lewis identifies Coppola with postfeminist culture mainly through the critical reception of her films and her broader 'star director' persona, Todd Kennedy and Amy Woodworth both identify a distinctive feminine or postfeminist aesthetic at work in her films.[22] For Kennedy, Coppola's films are important above all because of their reformulation of the gaze. He explains that 'Sofia Coppola has developed an aesthetic that simultaneously evokes foundational gaze theory, comments upon postfeminist concerns about consumption as a feminine ideal, and attempts to reverse macho tropes from the 1960s and 1970s male auteur movement, which includes her father.'[23] In his argument, *Marie Antoinette* figures as Coppola's masterpiece, developing an aesthetic that asks the audience to identify and sympathise with the 'naked, vulnerable' object of the gaze, not those who gaze upon her. The more difficult critical reception of this film is because, unlike the male narrators of *The Virgin Suicides* or Bill Murray's Bob in *Lost in Translation*, there is no proxy for a male gaze which can intercept and forestall the pain of this identification with the abject and vulnerable sides of femininity. For Woodworth too, Coppola's work provides an opportunity to revisit the vexed question of the male gaze and its formulation in feminist film theory. She explains that 'these tasks are important because as scholarship turns towards issues of postfeminism, it seems scholars spend more time discussing character and plot than film form.'[24] She too credits *Marie Antoinette* as having a 'fully-realised feminine aesthetic based on Coppola's careful use of the camera for mediating Marie Antoinette's experience without objectifying her.'[25]

Other significant interventions on Coppola's individual films also demonstrate her importance for feminist film scholarship, such as Lucy Bolton's stirring argument that *Lost in Translation* offers us a vision of female subjectivity and interiority that resonates with Luce Irigaray's call for a new feminist philosophy or Diana Diamond's bracing intervention that demonstrates the significance of costume to *Marie Antoinette*'s aesthetic and thoroughly rejects the equation of clothing with superficiality.[26]

Over the course of this book, I concentrate mostly on Coppola's films, but it is important for us to remember that these films are part of a broader authorial persona. Partly, this is based on other work Coppola carries out, as she directs music videos, designs fashion items and even curates photographic exhibitions. It is, of course, also based on the lustre and significance of her name. As well as being able to offer a more complete picture of all the diverse elements of Coppola's postfeminist authorship, my book also argues that, while her films are highly expressive and articulate interventions, they are also symptomatic of the narrow constraints that contain her. As I discuss in the opening of chapter 2, Coppola gives her name within a 'girlish' signature, using curlicued hand-written type scripts or referring to herself in bright pink lettering as a 'rich bitch' in self-aware, witty credit sequences that nevertheless suggest her name is both advantage and limiting, forever placing her as a scion of the Coppola family.

Coppola's films undertake multiple border-crossings, suggesting the globalised condition of the postfeminist girl. While these have positive connotations of contact zones and cosmopolitan mixing, enabling a sympathetic meeting of difference (especially via international film culture), they also place girls into vulnerable positions where their identities are under erasure, as in Marie Antoinette's crossing from Austria to France, or the Bling Ring's invasion into celebrity homes in the hope they could become (like) the celebrity in question. The films enact a constant tension between exterior and interior, public and private, which I especially explore in chapter 3. Bree Hoskin intriguingly suggests that this topographical consistency maps onto Coppola's interest in the adolescent, marking this as yet another way Coppola's films are quintessentially youthful: 'adolescence might be seen as a time when there is a fantasised inversion of boundaries. To put it very simply: we exist on a terrain where what is inside finds itself outside (acne, menstrual blood, rage) and what should be visibly outside (heroic dreams, attractiveness, sexual organs) remains resolutely inside and hidden.'[27]

Home and outside both remain desperately ambivalent spaces, with Coppola's protagonists both yearning for, and fearing the consequences of, escape. Her characters frequently find themselves in the interstices, unsettled in both the home and the outside word and dwelling momentarily in an uncomfortable middle ground between the two. For example, The *Virgin Suicides* culminates in the surviving four of the Lisbon sisters grounded by their mother and forced to remain in the family home and Lux/Kirsten Dunst rebels by climbing up onto the roof. As they are holed up in one of their bedrooms, the neighbourhood boys find a way to communicate with them, playing records to them down the telephone. The film suggests the porosity of borders between inside and outside, here enabled by technology. This technological blurring of the difference between a private and a public existence reaches its apogee in *The Bling Ring*'s protagonists use of internet sites and social media to 'follow' stars (a legitimate, indeed desired loss of privacy for the star) but also to be able to break into their homes when they are away (an illegitimate and taboo loss of privacy for the star). Media scholars Alice Marwick and danah boyd (sic) argue that 'networked media is changing celebrity culture, the ways that people relate to celebrity images, how celebrities are produced, and how celebrity is practiced.'²⁸ Social media sites such as Twitter create new ways of circulating and creating celebrity. Celebrity management is no longer a one-way relation of institutional management and careful media presentation, but a two-way process of interaction and 'performed intimacy.'²⁹ *The Bling Ring* reveals how the crimes are rooted in a digital culture which gives unprecedented access to celebrity lives: Marc/Israel Broussard digs up Paris Hilton's address from a professional website and visually locates the property using Google Earth. Furthermore, the group then use social media to post photographs of themselves, so that perform themselves as if they were celebrities. Digital culture erodes the border between celebrity and wannabe, screen life and real life. In a different mode, Charlotte/Scarlett Johansson seems discontent with the familiarity of her marriage but unsure of herself as she ventures out into the exotic and enticing world of Kyoto temples and Tokyo sushi bars, lost in the transition/translation between the two.

Coppola's films offer a particular perspective on the possibilities of the transnational, from her complex multinational production deals (described in more detail below) to her portrayals of the cosmopolitan girl. While, as Ana Moya argues, films that picture women travelling abroad and experiencing new potential lifestyle choices 'represent the way in which the female subject at the turn of the millennium may seek empowerment through cosmopolitanism', Coppola's portrayal of the tourist is far more ambivalent, seeing travel as a way of getting lost as much as one finding oneself.³⁰ Furthermore, her films, unlike *The Godfather* trilogy that made her father's name and in which she appeared on-screen, do not function as a reflection upon her Italian-American ethnicity, other than perhaps via a theme of melancholia and nostalgia, a Mediterranean 'spleen' that infects the protagonists of *The Virgin Suicides* (notably the girls are surrounded by the ritualised objects of the Catholic faith) and *Lost in Translation* (where the inevitable foreignness and loss of the émigré is projected onto the utter alienation of being outside of the Europeanised West).[31] The echoes of Coppola's Italian-American background can be found in the references to Fellini, the Italian films she watched with her father and her own 'voyage to Italy' enacted in *Somewhere*, but Coppola's ethnicity in no way accents her films as an expression of a diaspora in the way we may understand with films by her father, Martin Scorsese, Brian de Palma or Michael Cimino. More generally, the films navigate the complexity of the pull of home and the familiar against the lure of the exotic and the enthralling through their interest in the banal everyday life of the celebrity, and conversely the infiltration of celebrity culture into the everyday, which speaks to an utter confusion of the private and the public spheres. Such a dialectic invites us to read the films both as acute appraisals of contemporary cultural mores and a quasi autobiographical comment on the complexities of Coppola's own position as Italian-American celebrity daughter and stylish cool fashion icon as well as director.

Authorship and Iconoclasm: Questions of Form

The films repeatedly return to the fraught question of whether and how femininity can be reconciled with power and agency, whether this is in the context of the high-school gang, the failing marriage, or the politics of late-eighteenth-century Versailles. The passionate response Coppola's films have within contemporary internet girl culture, especially the reprisal of her debut feature, *The Virgin Suicides*, discussed and given a new soundtrack on the girl site Rookie, speaks both to the relevance of her portrayal of girls and young women and its relative scarcity.[32] In this way, both by the very fact of their existence, and their interest in issues of concern to feminist film theorists, Coppola's films offer an important and significant body of work from which to interrogate the possibility for (relatively) mainstream female-focused film in the twenty-first century, beyond the 'girly film' of Conglomerate Hollywood such as *Legally Blonde* (Luketic, 2001), *Mean Girls* (Waters, 2004), *The Devil Wears Prada* (Frankel, 2006) and *Bride Wars* (Winick, 2009) and 'quality' programming associated with popular postfeminist culture such as *Sex and the City*, *Desperate Housewives* and *Mad Men*. Coppola's films, concerned as they are with the position of girls and women within the privileged and affluent world of neoliberal postfeminist cultural norms, turn to similar themes, spaces and issues as these films and television programmes, such as ambivalences of female friendship and the appeal of 'girly' femininity (discussed in chapter 2), the lure of the domestic setting (discussed in chapter 3) and the highly visible role of fashion and the dangers of excess (discussed in chapter 4). I draw on important insights from such commentators on this postfeminist popular visual culture as Hilary Radner, Alison Winch, Diane Negra, and Rebecca Munford and Melanie Waters, but I also compare Coppola's formal strategies to those deployed by avant-garde feminist directors Chantal Akerman and Agnès Varda. I would thus argue that Coppola's work straddles two differing, indeed possibly conflicting, definitions of postfeminism. On the one hand, her films participate in postfeminist cultural norms (interested in femininity, questions of female agency and power, and showcasing friendship, girliness, fashionable clothes and beautiful homes). On the other hand, they also draw on a significant feminist critical inheritance, showing her films as literally postfeminist (as in being able to learn from these interventions of feminist filmmakers from the 1970s, rather than disavowing them), and thus display a particular interest in questions of form that tend to be unusual in most female focused films. For Chantal Akerman, creating a new subject position for women in film must go beyond content. Women filmmakers must 'look for formal ways to express who they are and what they want, their own rhythms, their own way of looking at things.'[33] What is particularly helpful in Akerman's statement is the understanding not only of the importance of form as well as content, key though that is, but also an avoidance of a prescriptive approach to what this form might be. For Teresa de Lauretis, feminist aesthetics must be plural, as she writes, 'radical change requires a delineation and a better understanding of the difference of women from Woman, and that is to say as well, *the differences among women*.'[34]

Woodworth argues that Coppola's films may seem politically ambiguous, 'as her questionable framing of women's faces and bodies dances a fine line between duplicating and effectively exploiting the way various social observers [...] view women. Furthermore, her use of traditional images of women [...] sunbathing in *The Virgin Suicides*, applying make-up in *Lost in Translation*, soaking in the bathtub (repeatedly) in *Marie Antoinette* – raises interesting questions about how feminist filmmakers can change the effect of conventional close-ups.'[35] While I concur with Woodworth that Coppola frequently redeploys close-ups to offer us a sympathetic account of feminine interiority, a reading also offered by Bolton in relation to *Lost in Translation*, I would also claim that there is a deliberate, radical and so far critically undiscussed iconoclasm in her work which partly explains her desire to show us beautiful passive women, only to complicate that vision, recalling perhaps the violence of the suffragettes who repeatedly attacked works of art featuring beautiful nude women to protest the conditions of ordinary women.[36] Coppola privileges conventionally beautiful, white, fair-haired, young female film stars – Kirsten Dunst, Scarlett Johannsson, Elle Fanning, Emma Watson – and her films frequently explore the private lives of those who are iconic, from the 'queen bees' of high school in *Lick the Star* and *The Virgin Suicides* to celebrities and princesses in *The Bling Ring* and *Marie Antoinette*. Coppola's use of traditional images of women enumerated by Woodworth, and her predilection for girls in repose (sunbathing, soaking in bathtubs, lying in bed) references high art conceptions of the female form from Velaquez's 1647–1651 'The Toilet of Venus' to American photorealist work by John Kacere. The latter is a source acknowledged by Coppola as inspiration for the opening shot of *Lost in Translation*, which features a fade-up from black to a medium close-up on Johansson's rear clad in transparent pink pastel underwear. As Geoff King notes, this opening shot is emblematic of *Lost in Translation*'s ambiguous status within the wider cinematic spectrum of production. 'It offers on the one hand, an "obvious" point of appeal, in its potentially erotic dimension and the proximity of bodily spectacle to the camera, although this is combined with what might be considered to be more "subtle" aesthetic qualities and an "artistic" point of reference.'[37] Part then of Coppola's ability to be iconoclastic comes from the position of her films within the ecology of global cinema which allows them to use deliberately slow pacing, often reinforced by locked down camera positions and attention to repetitive rituals and everyday activities. This disrupts the voyeuristic gaze at the women's body as pure spectacle, for as Coppola makes viewers aware of time passing (or indeed, not passing), the very weight of time pulls these women from being pure empty iconic spectacle and into the material matter of history itself (echoing indeed Mulvey's calls for a feminist cinema that would 'free the look of the camera into its materiality in time and space').[38]

Her iconoclasm can also be linked to her deliberate use of anachronistic detail, so that the 1970s suburbia of *The Virgin Suicides* has a resolutely contemporary sound track from Air alongside period music as such as 10cc's 'I'm Not in Love' or Carole King's 'So Far Away.' The temporal disjunction is, of course, far clearer between the eighteenth-century setting of Versailles and its postpunk soundtrack featuring Gang of Four, Bow Wow Wow and Siouxsie and the Banshees as well as the period opera pieces Marie Antoinette enjoys. Such a deliberately playful and anachronistic approach is also carried over into the mise-en-scène, particularly the fashion, as I discuss in more detail in chapter 4. Pam Cook summarises such an approach to the historical film as one of travesty, which she links to the postmodern mixing of styles she associates with an iconoclastic use of fashion:

travesty, a common device in theatre and literature, irreverently wrests its source material from its historical context, producing blatantly fake fabrications that challenge accepted notions of authenticity and value. It brazenly mixes high and low culture, and does not disguise its impulse to sweep away tradition. In the case of historical fictions, travesty collapses boundaries of time and place through pastiche, emphasising that history is in the eye of the beholder, whether group or individual. Travesty is playful, but it can have a serious purpose: to demonstrate that the past is always viewed through the filter of the present, and represents the vested interests of those who reinvent it. [...] One of the key vehicles for travesty and pastiche is fashion [...] Fashion engages in dialogue with history; at its most adventurous and provocative, it achieves the status of both graphic and performance art – witness the iconoclasm of, say, Vivienne Westwood or Jean-Paul Gaultier.[39]

Fashion also allows Coppola to add a third iconoclastic device to her filmmaking practice. Attention to the material textures of clothing is part of the way she undermines a purely visual approach to femininity through a haptic approach to filmmaking, her camera playing over fabric enabling the tactile sensuality of varying textures of silk and fur. Her films also feature soundtracks that feature evocative and empathetic use of music, and linger on both the preparation and consumption on food, so that altogether films become charged with attention to touch, hearing and taste as well as sight in the experience of girlhood.

Coppola's films thus use cinematic aesthetics to take the time to understand how it *feels* to be a girl. This emphasis on the inchoate, embodied and disordered world of emotions recalls Radner's comment that part of the appeal of neo-feminist rhetoric for women may be its attention to the ineffable and the inexplicable nature of emotion as a prized rather than despised part of the feminine world. As Radner explains:

feminism [...] perhaps actually began with the Enlightenment, when the capacity for rational thought became increasingly the sign and the pretext for humanity, and, eventually citizenship. One of the most important legacies of second-wave feminism has been the interrogation of the place occupied by the rational and the exploration of different kinds of epistemologies. Neo-feminism did not reason with women; it appealed to their emotions and feelings. By attempting to understand the emotions that drive girly culture, it will become perhaps possible to think about the role feminism might play in the twenty first century [...] a feminism that does not situate femininity as one dimension in

15

the play of gender and identity within the broad terrain of neoliberal-ism will continue to fail.[40]

Within the logic of Radner's argument, Coppola's development of a feminine film aesthetic that attends to the shifting *emotions* of girlhood and its cultural manifestations is a good starting-place for envisioning a new feminist politics, as is her conviction that 'film is not only a visual medium but also an emotional one.'[41]

Locating Authorship: Agency and Gender

The question of agency and femininity clearly informs the content of Coppola's films, and I develop this argument in chapter 2, but here I contend it is also key to our understanding of her unique position as postfeminist auteur. How much do Coppola's films offer us a singular female-authored vision of the world, uncompromised by the demands of Conglomerate Hollywood and 'girly' films? To what extent can Coppola reconcile her need for professional autonomy with the cachet and usefulness of her acknowledged position as Francis Ford Coppola's daughter? To what extent does our knowledge of Coppola's private life influence our understanding of the films, especially as her private persona blends into the topics of the films? The very name, Coppola, speaks to the contradictory nature of Coppola's particular authorship, placing her films literally as well as metaphorically under the name of the father, but also inviting them to be read as part of the 'Coppola' brand. Coppola's authorship thus oscillates between two very different models, both of which envisage the question of director agency and gender in varied ways. On the one hand, much of the commentary and criticism on the films, and their repeated themes and motifs, invite an auteurist reading which seeks to understand them as a unified, coherent body-of-work, and my book is clearly indebted itself to this approach as it seeks to interpret commonalities between the films. On the other, Coppola herself is constructed extra-textually, outside the films, as a celebrity, and the unity comes not from the films themselves but from the power and significance of the Coppola name as marketing and branding device. Timothy Corrigan explains that contemporary discourses of authorship have deviated from analysis of text into a 'cult of personality' that makes directors into stars and situates itself in publicity and advertisement. Discussing the auteur Alexander Kluge, Corrigan argues that he has a 'specific cultural strategy' in which

> a politics of agency takes its place as much in an extra-textual as in a textual business, more exactly as a 'semi- textual' practice where Kluge

admits to performing himself as an image of the writer/producer/film-maker but primarily as a strategy for eliciting certain relations with his audience. In a crucial sense, Kluge's writing of a self in today's national/international film industry situates itself between the more social and political work surrounding the films (his involvements with government policies or television networks) and the reception of his film practice (whose material textuality refuses to be the authority for its reading).[42]

In the very different context of Indiewood or American 'smart' cinema, of which more shortly, Coppola also offers us a performed image, here of the postfeminist director. All of Coppola's 'writing of the self' in her media image and film publicity is shaped by notions of chic, girlish femininity, from the decision to market her film of *Marie Antoinette* in hot pink packaging for the DVD, her advertisements for Louis Vuitton and Marc Jacobs, her editing of Paris *Vogue* in July 2005, her appearance as Australia *Vogue* cover star in August 2013, her direction of supermodel Kate Moss in the White Stripes Video 'I Just Don't Know what to do with Myself', to her travel guide to Paris (dedicated entirely to shopping and visiting cafés, rather than any mention of high art and culture, and the shops recommended are for flowers, vintage clothing, antique jewellery, beauty products, children's clothes, designer clothes and perfume [with the light relief of one quirky address for taxidermy requirements!]).[43] Coppola offers us an image of authorship not so much as individual genius as a market-place positioning which draws together strands from fashion, music, travel, photography and film to offer a vision of a certain highly desirable, aspirational lifestyle. While Corrigan senses in Kluge's fragmentation, diversification and multiplication a political desire to disperse authorship as authority and play up its material conditions, Coppola's equally fragmented, diverse and multiple body of work illuminates the complex accommodations that must be made for activities traditionally marked as girly or feminine to be recuperated into the 'high art' world of the feminist film-auteur.

To borrow Corrigan's useful distinction, the Romantic traditional approach toward agency (as talent or genius) emphasises authorship in the production of films, his view of auteurism as a form of commerce authorship in the critical reception of them. In the first mode of authorship, Coppola's gender marks her as unusual, given the historical link between authorship and masculinity as I will explain below, and her choice of subject matter alone marks her films as having feminist agency. In the second mode of authorship, Coppola's position is more complex. Her film making becomes part of a much broader celebrity persona which is also linked to advertising, travel, music and fashion, and Coppola's image is one of cool, refined femininity. Coppola oscillates then between an institutional authorship predicated on production values that harks back to European art-cinema models while simultaneously feminising them, and a twenty-first-century celebrity brand version of authorship that borrows from stereotypically 'feminine' interests of fashion and domesticity and moves them into the 'masculine' world of cinema.

Indeed, Coppola might be considered one of the most visible film directors working today in terms of image. Such visibility allows us to analyse Coppola as a celebrity director. She is unusual and notable among directors for her fame and visibility outside of specialist film magazines. To give just one paradigmatic example, on the release of *The Bling Ring* in the UK in July 2013, Coppola featured on the cover of *Red* magazine, a mainstream magazine aimed at women in their 20s-40s rather than a specialist film journal, or even the film section of a newspaper. It would be more usual for the star of the film to be the face used in film promotion in this kind of publication. Furthermore, the magazine cover uses the following strapline: 'Sofia Coppola: Oscar-winning mother and movie-maker', suggesting to us one of the reasons it is her celebrity image rather than that of her stars that has appeal. As well as having directed five feature films, Coppola has also acted in some films, and more recently has become involved in advertising, posing with her father for Louis Vuitton and promoting the Marc Jacobs perfume range. Fragrance adverts are also more usually associated with film stars and supermodels than film directors, but Coppola straddles between the worlds of film and couture fashion. She is embraced as a style icon, featuring for example on the August 2013 cover of Australian *Vogue*, being featured as one of Louis Vuitton's six timeless 'muses' at an exhibition in summer 2013 in Tokyo, and having indeed had a Vuitton bag named after her (she also designed a fashion range herself, MilkFed, which is marketed in Japan). This is a very obvious reason her face would be rather more known than that of many directors. However, *Red* magazine's cover heading speaks to another aspect of Coppola's celebrity persona, and one that is far less discussed generally: she is a working mother. Her ability to achieve professional success while also being a mother and projecting an image of girlish charm speaks to a highly contentious postfeminist dilemma. In Coppola's case, she reconciles the demands of having a highly successful career and being a mother, as we are told in a mere six words. As such, she operates at this moment as a literal poster girl for what is posed as a key postfeminist question: can women really 'do it all'?

As Richard Dyer has famously explained, star personas are important as they do cultural and ideological work in managing social tensions and contradictions.[44] Dyer's influential theory of stardom as a semiotic system that articulates larger ideological and political relations has paved the way for the study of celebrities. However, as Diane Negra and Su Holmes explain, in contrast to a 'star' who navigates between on-screen and off-screen personas, a celebrity connotes a 'representational structure' that is framed by a person's 'private life or lifestyle.'[45] It is usually the celebrity's private life that functions as a screen upon which larger social anxieties are played out. In their introduction to the inaugural issue of the journal *Celebrity Studies*, Su Holmes and Sean Redmond note that a celebrity 'exists at the core of many of the spaces, experiences and economies of modern life.'[46] Graeme Turner discusses celebrities as situated in, and productive of, what he calls 'para-social' relations: relationships constructed via the mass-media rather than face-to-face contact.[47] The magazine image of the private individual Coppola as successful director, glamorous muse and working mother, offers us a para-social relation to an idealised performance of postfeminist femininity that is at the heart of Coppola's celebrity appeal.

Diane Negra and Su Holmes point out that fame is gendered.[48] They argue that celebrity studies has been dominated by men, and there have been very few feminist interventions. However, given that the celebrity is structured through an emphasis on lifestyle, and it is women who are primarily associated with the domestic and the private, celebrity culture is itself gendered. Celebrity culture produces and is ensconced within larger social issues concerning gender relations. While Coppola has clearly achieved significant success in terms of her career, her celebrity image authenticates the tenacious postfeminist ideal of the woman whose career can be seen as expressive of her innate femininity. With her work's close links to the areas of girlhood and fashion, Coppola's privileged celebrity auteur image demonstrates women can indeed have it all, as long as they remain within the prescribed arena of the feminine. While *Red*'s cover headline labels Coppola as 'Oscar-winning mother and movie-maker' (the word order hinting that her Oscar is for her maternal skills as much as her films!), the copy in the magazine highlights Coppola's association with the privileged yet feminine world of high fashion, summing up her achievements as 'An Oscar, an IT Bag, Marc Jacobs on speed dial…'. The image chosen to accompany this text reinforces Coppola's association with privilege, whiteness and girlishness. The photograph shows her from the elbow up. She is stood behind a window, and the image is shot in soft-focus, so that it is slightly blurred and there are light reflections in front of her face. She is wearing a soft-pink dress with a pink and silver sequin encrusted collar. The small text at the bottom of the photograph informs us that this viscose, acetate and sequin dress is available for £1,330. The delicacy, softness and pinkness of the photograph (Coppola also wears a light blusher and a nude pink lipstick) mitigates any 'masculinity' that could possible accrue to Coppola's choice of profession and considerable success within it, and her choice of expensive, light-coloured clothing lets us know she is most definitely a 'yummy mummy' not struggling to cope with baby sick or a toddler's sticky hands.[49]

In contrast to this highly feminised celebrity image, the award recognition and critical commentary on Coppola's films clearly locates Coppola as an auteur in the 'romantic' and masculine sense of the director as presiding talent (genius?) whose personal, artistic vision is communicated to us via her or (much more usually) his films. This position, largely developed through the group of young men associated with *Cahiers du cinéma* in the 1950s, especially François Truffaut and Jean-Luc Godard, argues that the film should be the unique personal vision of its director, who above all communicates via mise-en-scène. It is a polemical position, developed not only in order to grant cinema that same high art status as painting or literature, but also to attack what these critics saw as the hidebound conventions of the *cinéma de qualité*. Both Godard and Truffaut saw film-making as a personal expression; Godard promoting film as a way of filming friends, lovers and parents;[50] Truffaut explaining that the numbers of viewers a film has is in direct proportion to the number of friends its director has.[51] For Godard and Truffaut, the film is the expression of the individual, and the politique des auteurs stresses the importance of their agency in getting the film made, even as it neglects to mention what kind of technological and institutional infrastructure is needed to facilitate this. They also make gendered assumptions: they envisage the director as a (young) man, hanging out with his friends, watching male friends' films and treating such subjects as beautiful girls to fall in love with.

Coppola's films are analysed as the result of a singular, artistic vision and would thus seem to testify to her position as masculine auteur. However, through her own investment in the personal story, and the attention she plays to the experiences of girls and young women rather than adolescent boys and young men, Coppola feminises this figure, rather as photographs of her work to 'feminise' the image of her professional success through her pink clothing and dreamy, hazy out-of-focus aesthetics. This sense that Coppola feminises the role of director is reinforced in the anecdote repeated across media that her father told her she needed to say 'action' more forcefully, from her diaphragm, when he visited her on-set. Coppola laughs about such advice, claiming, 'I may say it differently, but I still get what I want', giving directorial authority a different voice as well as vision.[52] However, Coppola's films could be seen as a more aggressive intervention into the male-dominated world of the auteur. Indeed, her short *Lick the Star* can be seen as a very self-conscious feminist decon- struction of powerful male figures.[53] Its very title is a playful invocation of a desire to kill the figure of the powerful male, as 'lick the star' is revealed to be an anagram for kill the rats, an allusion to the plan by a group of High School girls to poison male students with rat poison (inspired by the poisoning plot of Virginia Andrews's cult classic *Flowers in the Attic*, a book being read by all the girls in the clique). The plot falls apart when the girls cannot remain united and instead turn on their leader and former 'queen' Chloe/Audrey Heaven. The film has suggested from the start that the girls' struggle for power will be com- promised by their own internal divisions and rivalries, when it begins with the narrator Kate/Christina Turley telling us that 'I was dreading going back. Missing school's like a death wish' because of the changed status of girls within friendship groups during one's absence. 'A lot can happen in a few days. When Sam was out with the 'flu, everyone decided she was a big lesbian and she spent the rest of the month eating lunch in the library.' Coppola's film does not ide- alise female solidarity, then, and the film finishes with Chloe alone reciting a self-penned poem that only the audience (but not her fellow pupils) get to hear.

However, the film does also punish characters who attempt to objectify women, even if only momentarily. The scene where Chloe slaps a boy after he lifts her skirt and says 'Cute panties. Little Mermaid, huh?' when they walk past him in the school corridor, then complains 'I can't believe him', before murmuring 'lick the star', could be seen as a riposte to numerous shots where men get to 'accidentally' see women's legs and pants, such as The Girl/Marilyn Monroe standing over the grate in *The Seven Year Itch* (Wilder, 1955), and most pertinently here Antoine Doinel/Jean-Pierre Léaud's fascinated glimpse at his mother's legs while she changes her stockings in *Les 400 Coups/The 400 Blows* (Truffaut, 1959). As Kennedy explains, '*Lick the Star* appears largely as homage to and inversion of François Truffaut's *Les 400 Coups*.'[54] Having so vehemently declared the need for personal film-making in the pages of *Arts* and *Cahiers*, Truffaut realised this vision with *Les 400 Coups*, a film that placed his alter-ego, Antoine Doinel, onto the screen. Coppola borrows Truffaut's high school set- ting, and even has similar events occur within her narrative. Just as Truffaut's film features a sequence where boys gradually run away from their gym teacher, so Coppola also includes a scene where pupils sneak away during a class run. Kennedy also comments on the similarity of the opening and closing shots of the respective films. 'In so doing, Coppola invokes the foundational masculine auteur film in order to construct a film fundamentally concerned with young women's lack of agency and voice, and the manner in which they are exploited and determined by the male gaze [...] Coppola posits a feminine authorship that asks her audience to identify with the gaze of powerless women.'[55] As we will see throughout the book, Coppola's strategic references to gender inversions of the European art-house classics of male auteurs (not just Truffaut, but also Fellini and Antonioni) combines with her borrowing the attentiveness to the minimalist gestures of everyday life explored by female auteurs such as Chantal Akerman and Agnès Varda in order to reconfigure her auteurist heritage. She demonstrates her claim to auteur status through the ease with which she deploys a great knowledge of film history, referencing and recalling cinephilic moments, but places them into a postfeminist context where great attention is paid to the previously neglected or objectified figure of the girl.

Production Contexts

Coppola's films occupy a very particular position within the ecology of American cinema, associated with prestige and art rather than the mass-appeal and entertainment end of the market, which allows for the development of a very personal aesthetic that is also associated with the romantic figure of the auteur. Her films belong to Indiewood and American 'smart' cinema, the former referring to the particular funding arrangements of the films, and the second their overall tone. The two are in practice interlinked, as lower budget films tend to have a different aesthetic and feel than those with higher budgets. Coppola's funding arrangements for her projects vary according to their size and scale. Her most mainstream project in terms of budget and funding was *Marie Antoinette*, her only film to date financed by a major Hollywood studio – Columbia Pictures – though even this project was the result of co-distribution deals with France's Pathé and Japan's Tohokushinsha Film. As Christina Lane and Nicole Richter explain:

> the director has always shown skill in cultivating hybrid production and distribution deals with an eye toward the global market. She has also drawn on the resources of Francis Ford Coppola's American Zoetrope [...] Her debut *The Virgin Suicides* came about through merged financing from American Zoetrope and the small, Los-Angeles based Muse Productions [...] *Lost in Translation* and *Somewhere* have also benefitted from an innovative model that draws support from Pathé, Tohokushinsha, and Zoetrope, while relying heavily on a home base at James Schamus's Focus Features.[56]

Within the current American system of a few dominant global media players created by waves of studio acquisitions and mergers, labelled 'Conglomerate Hollywood' by Thomas Schatz, Coppola has deftly navigated a way to draw on multiple funding structures and maintain her autonomy. Drawing on the funds of her father's production company, American Zoetrope, for her first three films lead to accusations of nepotism, but could also be read more generously as an indication of the way the family and the personal provides some kind of necessary buffer against the relentless changes and impersonal business decisions of globalised capitalism, of which Conglomerate Hollywood is such a striking example. The fact that this buffer is dependent on a privilege – whether of talent or personal connection or both – demonstrates the way that Coppola's films are symptoms of the inequalities that structure contemporary society, in their very material ground as well as their themes and aesthetics. (It is intriguing to note that thematically, Coppola's films are very ambivalent about families, from the reference to Andrews' incest and death pulp novel *Flowers in the Attic* in *Lick the Star* to the ditsy, clueless mother in *The Bling Ring*.)

Geoff King argues that Coppola's funding arrangements for her films, where she often has studio involvement through their smaller, speciality arm (Focus Features is the speciality distributor of NBC Universal, a major Hollywood conglomerate) but also puts together complex packages involving multiple funders means her films do not qualify for the label 'independent' in the purist industrial sense. Rather, he locates them in the 'Indiewood' category, where studios come on board at a relatively late stage, as a significant but crucially not the only funding source, and can help market and distribute the film. King explains that as Hollywood studios have moved toward greater investment in the 'specialty' part of the cinematic spectrum, films emerge that borrow from both mainstream cinematic practices (the presence of film stars, for example) but also are positioned as more 'alternative' or 'difficult' (playing with generic expectations or having a relatively slight and downplayed narrative framework).[57] Coppola's films' funding allow her to retain a large degree of personal control at the production stage, allowing her for example to resist budgetary pressure to shoot *Lost in Translation* on digital video, and permitting greater scope for improvisation 'that would have given a studio "several cases of the heebie-jeebies" if it had been in sole control of the production.'[58]

There is an interesting point for debate that emerges here. Lane and Richter write that 'in an environment governed by brand-based franchises, sequels and remakes, Coppola's films – which are more lyrical, poetic and character-driven – have succeeded not necessarily through counter-strategies of financing but rather by exploiting and aggressively co-opting economic structures.'[59] Lane and Richter thus identify Coppola's films as opposed to the commercial cinema's financially motivated compulsion to repeat and suggest that their funding strategies gives her films an alternative aesthetic of individuality and singularity (indeed, the strikingly singular release may be a pre-condition of the kind of production deals Coppola negotiates). The irony here, of course, is that they name a repetition within this singularity – of lyricism, character and poetry – and such repetition is necessary for an auteurist approach (certainly, over the course of the book, attention will be paid to these characteristics of Coppola's films). However, asked in interview if she thought *Marie Antoinette* was the culmination of a trilogy, Coppola responded 'when I finished this movie, I definitely looked at the fact [...] that there's a connection between the themes of my films. I feel like this is sort of the final chapter of something I was working on – it's the next step of a girl's evolution.' In the same interview, asked if there would be a fourth film featuring a female character who's already a women, providing a sense of continuity, Coppola replies, 'no, I mean for me it feels like the three films fit together in something I was thinking about in that phase of my life... I feel like now I'd like to go in another direction.'[60]

Woodworth identifies images of reclining young women as the recurrent thread across the films, and argues that the characters of Lux Lisbon, Charlotte and Marie Antoinette/ Kirsten Dunst share a 'spiritual kinship', and she thus labels Coppola's first three films a postfeminist trilogy.[61] R. Barton Palmer undertakes a complex discussion of whether Coppola's first three films can be considered a trilogy, or if they should be considered as singularities linked only by Coppola's authorship. He argues that the trilogy form is associated with authorship, anyway, as in *The Godfather* trilogy which made Coppola's father's reputation, or illustrious arthouse examples such as Michelangelo Antonioni's trilogy on alienation in modernity formed by *L'Avventura* (1960), *La Notte* (1961) and *L'Eclisse* (1962). Unlike the sequel or the remake, the trilogy as form is inherently linked to film artistry, and as the Antonioni example shows, does not necessarily have to repeat characters between films. Rather than a cynical cashing-in, the trilogy form enables sequelisation to be thought in creative ways that enables resonance and growth rather than 'mere' repetition and exhaustion. He argues that, despite the notable pressure within the codes of Indiewood cinema for the singular, quirky release, to the extent that Coppola shifts genres for each new film (in the cases he discusses, from literary adaptation to romantic comedy to historical biopic) 'Coppola's first three films do lend themselves in some respects to being read as interconnected, so much so that they might be (and indeed have been) considered a trilogy: not a multiplicity of interdependent texts joined by complex transtextual bonds [...] but rather complex variations on a theme with deep personal, even autobiographical meaning for their screenwriter/director.'[62] The overall pattern Palmer identifies is that of feminine degradation, most notably in Marie Antoinette's dramatic fate, but also on a smaller domestic scale of the sisters' suicides in *The Virgin Suicides* and Charlotte's return to a loveless marriage in *Lost in Translation*; these are all girls who get 'lost' in the awkward transition from adolescence to adulthood. As he acknowledges, this is a trilogy that is 'a product more of reception than production and distribution' and which 'responds interestingly to the ways in which the classic studio model, with its industrially determined forms of multiplicity, has been transformed, even as its appeal persists into the contemporary phase of New Hollywood (at least among the cognoscenti).'[63] Palmer concludes that the desire to read Coppola's first three films as forming a trilogy can be seen as a way of confirming her status as auteur, as the trilogy format has a specific role within the independent/commercial sector Coppola works in.

> What needs explanation is the desire on the part of critics to promote the first three of Coppola's works as a Young Girls trilogy, a suggestion to which the director responded positively. In part this seems a traditionally neo-romantic, authorialist move designed to further the received view of Coppola as an auteur, with the director unconsciously [...] 'speaking herself' not only through projects based on her original ideas, but also through those she has adapted from other sources.[64]

Shaping Coppola's work post-facto into a trilogy navigates between the paradoxical desire for singularity and uniqueness befitting the status of her film as auteur-driven art rather than Conglomerate Hollywood franchise and the meaning rich multiplicity necessary for that very authorial status to be granted.[65] Intriguingly, Palmer suggests that other trilogies could also emerge, identifying *The Virgin Suicides*, *Lost in Translation* and *Somewhere* as versions of the male melodrama, as all three films offer sympathetic portraits of men puzzled, frustrated or frightened by the elusive nature of the feminine, a reading that Anna Rogers supports with her argument that, while it is not erroneous to remark upon Coppola's interest in female experience this should not mask 'the fact that *The Virgin Suicides* is actually a film about male adolescent desire whilst the crises addressed in *Lost in Translation* is equally a male mid-life one and that of a young female.'[66] (The sense that a male mid-life crisis may indeed be more immediately visible in *Lost in Translation* is underlined by Charlotte's wry question to Bob, asking him if he has bought a Porsche yet.) Certainly, the marketing of *Lost in Translation* and *Somewhere* emphasises the presence of Bill Murray and Stephen Dorff as much as, if not more than, that of Scarlett Johansson and Elle Fanning. Such an emphasis makes *Marie Antoinette* more of an outlier, with its very limited insight into or sympathy for Louis XVI. We could possibly trace a third 'fetish objects' trilogy, with *The Virgin Suicides*, *Marie Antoinette* and *The Bling Ring* all interested in role of beautiful objects, from crucifixes to shoes to haute couture. Coppola's films also navigate between examining groups or even 'gangs' of girls (*Lick the Star*, *The Virgin Suicides*, *The Bling Ring*) and the lonely, isolated individual girl (*Lost in Translation*, *Marie Antoinette*, *Somewhere*), reflecting cultural ideas that adolescent delinquency and deviance is fostered in gang culture, as I discuss in my comments on female friendship in chapter 2. All this to say that we should not reify Coppola's films into one trilogy without any connections to her previous or subsequent work, but that we should be aware of fruitful connections that can be made within groups of texts, and that such a search for meaning functions as a marker of distinction within Coppola's production context. Pam Cook intriguingly suggests that rather than corralling them into fixed sets, we could see Coppola's films as 'an incomplete serial oeuvre motivated more by the director's personal creative journey than by narrative or genre constraints.'[67] She claims this sense of incompleteness is bolstered by Coppola's habit, now almost a trademark, of not finishing her sentences in interviews, but simply trailing off. Such a conclusion reinforces the authorial agency of Coppola's films while also marking them as incomplete, in process. This would strengthen their associations with postfeminist culture, for, as Projansky has astutely explained, 'the postfeminist woman is always in process, always using the freedom and equality handed to her by feminism in the pursuit of having it all (including discovering her sexuality) but never quite managing to reach full adulthood, to fully have it all.'[68] She also remarks that this sense of process makes the ideal postfeminist woman an eternal adolescent, so that we could argue that Coppola's oeuvre itself becomes adolescent in the sense that it is constantly being redefined and has no definitive status.

Within this independent/commercial sector, Coppola could be considered alongside such directors as Quentin Tarantino, Steven Soderberg, Wes Anderson, Todd Solondz, Alexander Payne, Ang Lee and Spike Jonze, all of whom have made films with speciality, niche producers and who cultivate a careful distance from the industry that serves them. They do not pursue anything like a group aesthetic, constituting nothing a like a wave and certainly not sharing any kind of manifesto (unlike for example Dogma) but nevertheless their films can be considered as united by a sensibility and a certain tone that critiques bourgeois taste. This sensibility is identified by Jeff Sconce as belonging to 'smart cinema'. Sconce explains that 'smart cinema' is highly disparate in terms of narrative and aesthetics, but 'suggest[s] an interesting shift in the strategies of contemporary "art cinema", here defined as movies marketed in explicit counterdistinction to mainstream Hollywood fare as "smarter", "artier" and more "independent" (however questionable and manufactured such distinctions might actually be).[69] There is a world of difference between the clinical polish of *Ice Storm* (Lee, 1997), the matter-of-fact surrealism of *Being John Malkovitch* (Jonze, 1999) and the sweet sentimentality of *Ghost World* (Zwigoff, 2001) but all share being placed by 'marketers, critics and audiences in symbolic opposition to the imaginary mass-cult monster of mainstream, commercial, Hollywood cinema [...] not quite "art" films in the sober Bergmanesque art-house tradition, nor "Hollywood" in the sense of 1200 screen saturation bombing campaigns, nor "independent" films according to DIY outsider credo, "smart" films nevertheless share an aura of "intelligence" that distinguishes them.'[70]

Although it may seem that these films are thus defined mainly by what they are not, and the audiences that choose to watch them as part of a politics of taste, nevertheless, Sconce asserts, 'engaging this smart sensibility in recent American cinema [...] requires attention to both the sociocultural formation informing the circulation of these films (the "smart" set) and a shared set of stylistic and thematic practises (a "smart" aesthetic).'[71] Aesthetically speaking, these films tend to use coherent time-space structures associated with classical Hollywood style, avoiding the spatial and /or temporal confusion associated with directors such as Fellini, Resnais or Bergman; on the other hand, they eschew the intensified continuity editing and frenetic pace of contemporary mainstream film, favouring long-shots, static composition and sparse cutting which gives rise to a rather blank, detached tone. If the art-film self-consciously employed the jump-cut as a style statement, the shot of choice for these films is the static tableau.

Sconce identifies these films with the post-boomer generation, the so-called Generation X, 'smart, highly-educated men and women born in the 1960s and 1970s, who missed out on the post-war US gravy train of unlimited economic growth and opportunity enjoyed by the baby-boomers who preceded them.'[72] These Gen-Xers reject the hippy idealism and social consciousness of their parents, seeing it as having failed to bring any social justice, but they simultaneously refuse to 'sell out' to corporate culture themselves. Disdainful of the hippy past, dismayed by the materialist yuppy present and wary of a bumpy future without the generous pensions and welfare enjoyed by their parents, this generation's preferred mode is ironic disengagement. The media coverage of the new generation of film directors often commented on their troubled relationship with the consecrating function of 'film school'. Unlike the directors of New Hollywood, these directors were autodidacts or drop outs, creating subcultural cachet through their rebel status, from Quentin Tarantino's legendary video store education to PT Anderson dropping out: it is worth noting in this context that Coppola did not complete her education in the Fine Art program at Cal Arts, but dropped out, a fact she happily acknowledges in interview with alumna Mason Richards on BlackTree TV.[73]

It is excusable that Sconce does not name Coppola in his roster of smart directors, as she had only released one film, *The Virgin Suicides*, when his article was published in 2002. He does not, however, comment on the fact that despite all the stylistic and generational shifts in film aesthetics and director positions he brilliantly adumbrates, there is not a single female director on his capacious list. Coppola conforms in many ways to Sconce's descriptions. Generationally, she belongs to Gen-X, and is friends with directors on Sconce's list such as Wes Anderson (it was Anderson who helped her secure Bill Murray's participation in *Lost in Translation* – Anderson had cast him in a similar quirky role in *Rushmore* (1998)). Her style, as I have commented elsewhere, is marked by long shot durations and locked down camera positions leading to static tableaux. Furthermore, her films make use of downplayed narrative frameworks, so that, for example, Marie Antoinette's execution is subtly hinted at by a fade-to-black. *Lost in Translation*, for all that it provoked controversy for its own depiction of Japan, takes time to evoke the impressions, feelings and experiences of its characters' interactions with Japan and its landscape, as in a three minute long, dialogue-free sequence where Charlotte visits Kyoto. She wanders the gardens and sees a traditional bridal party, elements that reinforce the film's thematic interest in her unhappy marriage and hint at her state-of-mind, but mainly the emphasis is on mood and atmosphere. Coppola implicitly contrasts her film's slowness to the crass speed of Hollywood by contrasting Charlotte's quiet, thoughtful character to the shallow, annoying, loud Kelly/Anna Faris. Kelly is in Tokyo to promote her action film *Midnight Velocity* in which she co-stars with Keanu Reeves, an obvious playful reference to *Speed* (de Bont, 1994), the quintessential opposite to Coppola's minimalist pacing and atmospheric details (it seems no accident that the film enjoyed by Bob and Charlotte in their hotel room is *La Dolce Vita*, rather than a Hollywood film). For Rogers, such an attention to detail, slowness in pacing and emphasis on mood and atmosphere lends Coppola's films a 'European' feel. She argues that, similarly to Gilles Deleuze's comments that the classical cinema's character of action has been replaced in many European art-films by a protagonist who cannot act, the 'seer' of modern cinema, so Coppola too foregrounds characters who are incapacitated in some way – numbed, shocked, jetlagged, disconnected.[74]

Somewhere draws together these observations on slowness and the influence of European art-house aesthetics. Its lead male character, Johnny Marco/Stephen Dorff recalls for me David Bordwell's classic comments on the lost hero of the European art-house: 'the Hollywood protagonist speeds directly towards the target; lacking a goal, the art-film character slides passively from one situation to another [...] the hero often shudders on the edge of breakdown.'[75] *Somewhere's* opening shot marries the sense of an aimless protagonist with a deliberate slowing down of pace and a provocative challenge to the audience. We see a two minute static tableau shot of a black Ferrari completing laps around a desert racetrack, its driver literally zooming fast but getting nowhere. Its engine roar dominates the soundtrack, underlining the futility of the power being expended. Finally, Johnny Marco completes his laps, drives into frame in medium shot, gets out of his car and walks to its front, before we fade to black. This opening repays a sustained comparison with that of *La Dolce Vita*, an important intertext for this film, as it demonstrates clearly how Coppola plays on the similarities and differences in tone and style between the European art-house and the American smart cinema.

La Dolce Vita famously opens with a spectacular sequence of Marcello/Marcello Mastrioanni in a helicopter, accompanied by the photographer Paparazzo, trailing another helicopter which is delivering a statue of Christ to Rome. We see images of the helicopter flying over an ancient Roman aqueduct, then building sites, before swooping over a building where four women are sunbathing on the roof. One of the women says 'It's Christ! Where are they taking him?' comically (but possibly also blasphemously) aligning this gleeful ride over Rome with the second coming. The helicopter hovers over the roof, and the women gather in a row to shout up at the helicopter's inhabitants. In a series of shot-reverse shots, they exchange snippets of information, and Marcello signals he would like their telephone number, conversation drowned out by the din of the constantly-whirring helicopter blades. *Somewhere* opens with a two minute static shot of a race track in a desert described above. There are obvious similarities – both films are carefully delineating setting and character, and doing so through a particularly ostentatious mode of transport that speaks of masculinity, wealth and individualism – but more striking are the differences. For all its playful mocking of Christ's presence in Rome, Fellini's film still seems to suggest a possibility of spiritual salvation and some attempts are made at human contact. In contrast, Johnny is completely alone in an arid desert, devoid of any possibility of meaning. Fellini's opening sequence is typical of a European art-house film, inviting multiple layers of interpretation, its self-conscious use of symbolic imagery and dynamic camera work announcing a strong authorial presence. In contrast, Coppola's opening sequence sets up the film as smart cinema, with the overly long static shot and lack of dialogue challenging the viewer, disrupting expectations of a mainstream aesthetic and remaining coolly observational of and removed from her character's predicament.

Such an opening, with its explicit denial of any spiritual encounter or renewal in the desert (the preferred Biblical location for just such events) aligns Coppola's film with another trend Sconce identifies in American smart cinema, which is to say its overall shift from the broader concerns with social justice and morals that animated earlier art-house films to a focus on the private, the intimate and the familial. Art cinema's concern with questions of subjectivity, institutions, power and representation (especially in its more explicitly political versions such as Z [Costa-Gavras, 1969] or Tout va bien (Godard and Gorin, 1974]) is replaced with a concentration, often with ironic disdain, on the personal politics of emotional dysfunction in the white middle-classes. It is here that I think we can trace Coppola's explicitly feminine and postfeminist take on the American smart cinema, a twist neglected in Sconce's account. Coppola's concentration on the private sphere, to the extent that she often concentrates on the private lives of those who live in the public eye, such as celebrities, socialites and royalty, means she focuses entirely on the emotional and personal at the expense of the structural and institutional (this is perhaps most obvious in her retelling of Marie Antoinette's story with little allusion to the wider political context of her actions, a decision that provoked some criticism).[76] Sconce relates this retreat to the private as part of American smart cinema's post-boomer cynicism, but Coppola's films relate this more general loss of faith in ideology to a specific loss of faith in the collectivist politics of feminism. In this way, we can see her adoption of the very male dominated smart aesthetic, with its emphasis on a world-weary masculinity (encapsulated above all by Bill Murray) as demonstrating how postfeminism is part of much broader social changes that impact upon everyone. Rather than postfeminism being simply 'about women', we can see here how it develops out of what Angela McRobbie defines as disarticulation.

Articulation is the process by which various progressive social movements (trade unionism, feminism, civil rights, gay and lesbian rights) come together and forge connections and alliances. They enter into what sociologists Ernesto Laclau and Chantal Mouffe called 'a chain of equivalence', making for a radical democratic pluralist politics of the struggle for social justice. In the UK under the auspices of modernisation and in the US under the impetus of neoliberalism, these chains have been undone or 'disarticulated', largely through a discourse that claims economic politics as neutral, a pure matter of technique and expertise. Under attack from economic politics that dismantle the welfare state in the name of either desirable progress or pragmatic necessity, identity politics has tended to retreat into single causes and to attempt assimilation into the mainstream (from gay marriage to 'equality feminism') as a matter of survival. 'This in turn sees a further disarticulation of leftist movements characterised as irresponsible or anachronistic and their replacement by neoliberal versions of equality, diversity and tolerance.'[77] The personal, white, privileged worlds Coppola examines are very specifically inhabited by girls to whom Coppola pays great attention, but their crisis are played out against a broader backdrop of a disarticulated culture that mitigates against connections across gendered, raced and class divisions. In the face of such a society, retreat to the domestic space, the comforts of home, or an attempt to fashion a new glamorous identity through fashion, seems an entirely logical legitimate response. It is not so much that Coppola and her female protagonists no longer enact collectivist feminist values, it is more that such collectivities fracture in the face of a society which promotes the model of the citizen as an active entrepreneur of the self. As such, Coppola's films offer a specifically feminine and indeed, potentially feminist, understanding of the ironic detachment Sconce identifies within the American smart cinema.

As part of the personal control and creative input she exercises, Coppola writes her own screenplays. While three of these have been adaptations (from a novel, a historical biography and an article in *Vanity Fair* magazine), two of them have been original screenplays, and of course, she won the Oscar for her *Lost in Translation* screenplay. The fact that the films originate with Coppola's writing inscribes them into the auteurist tradition that has its background in the French New Wave and Andrew Sarris' concept of the 'auteur theory'. Certainly it invites autobiographical readings of the films based on original screenplays, with *Lost in Translation* considered to be partly about Coppola's own 'early twenties crisis' and failing marriage (she divorced Spike Jonze, allegedly the model for Giovanni Ribisi's nervy performance as Charlotte's remote husband, two months after the film was released) and *Somewhere* about her experience of growing up with a famous father. There are further resonances from Coppola's life experience in the films, with *Lost in Translation* based on her frequent travels to Japan promoting her clothing line and the Telegatti awards ceremony in *Somewhere* based on memories of attending similar ceremonies with her father. Commentators also read *Marie Antoinette* as a kind of parallel for her own life of luxury. The *New York Times*'s account of the film's production and French reception is entitled 'French Royalty as seen by Hollywood Royalty' and attributes the film's mixed reception at the Cannes Film festival to a sense it was more about Sofia Coppola than its eponymous subject: 'others wondered aloud if Ms Coppola's sympathetic portrait of her heroine as a poor little rich girl had more to do with her own experience as a child of Hollywood child and privilege.'[78] Even *The Virgin Suicides* can be read through the lens of Coppola's lifestory: Pam Cook suggests that its 'dark themes of youthful alienation, obsession, senseless cruelty and death' can be traced to 'the traumatic effect on Coppola of the 1986 speedboat accident in which her beloved elder brother Gian-Carlo was killed.'[79] This is an angle Coppola has acknowledged: ' "Gio was that kind of enchanting older brother who would take me on adventures and treat me like an adult," Sofia recalled. "Gio and my other brother, Roman, did everything together. I was in Napa with my mother when Gio died. It was a heartbreaking time. You never really get over something like that." Sofia paused, then went on to say: "I think some of that sadness went into *The Virgin Suicides*. I think I'm always drawn to projects that help me understand something about myself." '[80]

Small wonder that in a glowing review of *Lost in Translation*, Elvis Mitchell suggests that her films are 'a kind of ongoing metaphorical autobiography.'[81] The point is not so much how truthful such assertions are, but rather how, especially given the visibility of Coppola's childhood and family, the films reinforce her celebrity status not just through their success but through the perception, supported in the press, that their subject matter can reveal more to us about Coppola and her world (rather as we might assume that we could 'know' an actor through a character they play – indeed, even more so in some ways given Coppola's agency as the producer of the image).

The sense that Coppola resurrects traditional auteurist ways of working alongside a contemporary celebrity status is reinforced by her method of repeatedly working with the same or similar crews from film-to-film. This also works to bolster autobiographical and family-based readings. She always works with her brother, Roman Coppola. He worked as second unit director on *The Virgin Suicides*, *Lost in Translation* and *Marie Antoinette*, and as producer on *Somewhere* and *The Bling Ring*. She cast her cousin, Jason Schwartzman, as Louis XVI in *Marie Antoinette*. She works with people who also worked with her father, such as sound designer Richard Beggs, who won an Oscar for his sound design on *Apocalypse Now*. She also works repeatedly with the same trusted people in key roles: Lance Acord is cinematographer on *Lick the Star*, *Lost in Translation*, *Marie Antoinette* and a White Stripes video; Harris Savides is cinematographer on *Somewhere* and shares the credit (with Christopher Blauvelt) on *The Bling Ring* (he had to leave the film early due to his illness); Sarah Flack has edited

Lost in Translation, Marie Antoinette, Somewhere and *The Bling Ring*; and, given the importance of music to Coppola's films' mood and tone, it is significant that she has worked with Brian Reitzell, who plays drums with the French electronic group Air, as music producer on all of her films, with the exception of *Somewhere* (famously it was Reitzell who persuaded Kevin Shields from My Bloody Valentine to contribute two new compositions to *Lost in Translation*, 'City Girl' and 'Are You Awake?').[82] As King explains, 'repeated use of the same collaborators, in what remains a largely collaborative medium, is another more qualified mark of the auteur and one that has particular currency in the case of Coppola, who has benefited from connections with a network of film-related and other creative individuals, including but not limited to associates of her father.'[83] A real sense of how interconnected and synergistic Coppola's network is emerges in the account (from 2003) of her 'smart mob' (an echo of Sconce's descriptive category), which reports back from the set of a video shoot where Robin Conrad is teaching Kate Moss how to pole-dance in a basement at the Mercer hotel and is worth quoting at length:

> This is where the Coppola all-cool-worlds-collide element kicks in: most video directors aren't friends, the way Coppola is, with the owners of the Mercer. They haven't known Kate Moss since they were both teenagers, as Sofia has, and they don't pour champagne on the set from the family vineyard, which Coppola was doing now. The champagne, named Sofia, was created by her father, and the label reads, in part: 'revolutionary, petulant, reactionary, ebullient, fragrant, cold, cool.' 'Her dad wrote that,' said Zoe Cassavetes, Sofia's great friend, as she poured herself a glass. Cassavetes – the daughter of John Cassavetes, the groundbreaking director, and Gena Rowlands, his wife and a star in some of his best films – met Sofia about 12 years ago, when they were both in a *Vogue* photo shoot. [...] After meeting Zoe, Sofia told her she was going to appear in a video for the Black Crowes, and Zoe ended up tagging along. They have been on sets together ever since. Around the same time – the early 90's – Cassavetes and Coppola met Marc Jacobs. Jacobs, in turn, had just met Kim Gordon and Thurston Moore of the seminal New York post-punk band Sonic Youth. They, in turn, were working with Spike Jonze, who was shooting skateboard footage for a music video of theirs. There was lots of hanging out, Jonze met Coppola and the rest is history: Coppola had found her network and her husband (she and Jonze married in 1999), who would become, with *Being John Malkovich* and then *Adaptation*, a celebrated young

director himself (with some help along the way from the Coppola family and network).[84]

Coppola's network, with its fusion of people working in fashion, music, photography and film, echoes the way that her films engage with the intermedial nexus of contemporary culture. They offer a vision of directorial agency that shores up some stereotypical if paradoxical views of the feminine – Coppola's soft voice versus her steely determination; her serving of cucumber sandwiches and cold champagne on set where she films a girl pole-dancing. Such a network, dating back to her schooldays, also boosts the image of Coppola's girlishness, as her work seems an extension of her social and romantic life rather than divorced from it (another blurring of the private and public we can see as a theme of her films). Cook reads this collage as follows: 'the close connections between her life, persona and films are essential to the fabrication of the Sofia Coppola brand that operates across different media to promote her work and, crucially, give it a distinctive identity. This identity is directly, and deliberately, opposed to that of the patriarch, Francis Ford Coppola.'[85] While I agree with Cook that Coppola's image is based on the paradoxes of the postfeminist subject – passive and active; girly but determined; trivial pursuits and serious intent; fragility and drive; naturalness and artifice; – she does not rebel against her father. Indeed, the method of forming a close collaborative network is taken directly from his working methods, and she is also closely aligned with her brother. Coppola may be forging her own path, but she remains very much a younger sister and a beloved daughter: her films are made by a girl – a powerful, agentic girl, but a girl nevertheless.

Girls' Worlds

Coppola's films are also remarkably attentive to the importance of place and its impact on emotions and their expressions. She places characters into settings that continually blur the line between private and public (hotels, palaces, swimming pools, bars, social media) so as to emphasise the contradictions and restrictions of a culture that celebrates successful public femininity to the extent it leaves precious little room for private expression of feelings of inadequacy, failure or anger. Lux's asphyxiated cry 'I can't breathe in here!' when her mother keeps her in their suburban home in *The Virgin Suicides* would seem to apply to all of her female characters. Her characters live in a space of almost permanent display, as in the fetishised, frozen performances of eating and dressing at Versailles for the assembled crowd of courtiers, or the entirely glass-fronted house belonging to Audrina Patridge in *The Bling Ring*. Here, emotions can't be expressed as they are unseemly and enfeebling. On the other hand, characters are locked away in total exclusion, as in the Lisbon girls in their bedroom, or *The Bling Ring* in prison. Here, emotions may be expressed, but they have no chance of being encountered and taken seriously by another. The subject lives in a contradiction of either total, invasive visibility, with no access to private space, or total, cloistered seclusion, with no access to a functioning public sphere. So important is place to Coppola that she films on location, achieving the coup of *Marie Antoinette* being the first film ever to be filmed at Versailles, and filming *The Bling Ring* in Paris Hilton's Beverly Hills mansion, a material trace of her remarkable levels of access which I discuss in chapter 3. Through insisting on filming on location rather than in studio sets, Coppola draws our attention to the way place produces our experience of the world. She frequently shows us the private and homosocial spaces of femininity: the bathroom and the bedroom of the Lisbon sisters; the girls' locker room at the R.L.S. high school; the dressing of Marie Antoinette in her bedroom; the ikebana (flower-arranging) classes at the Hilton in Tokyo; Paris Hilton's closet and nightclub. She thus opens up places normally associated with the privacy of femininity and carefully examines how these operate as places of creativity and self-expression, but also tend to be associated with feminine rivalry, bitchiness and competition. There is no sense that the female homosocial space can offer the opportunities for social advancement associated with such classic sites of male homosociality as public school, the church and the armed forces.

Coppola's films are unconsciously symptomatic of the problems and contradictions of postfeminism for girls and women. While her films celebrate the feminine, and carve out a space for expression of feminine subjectivity, they remind blind to the extent to which this is a restricted, privileged and elitist view. Coppola's girls and women may travel, but they remain safely within cosseted white worlds. They may use fashion as a means of expression, but this is elitist fashion that restricts and imprisons. It is noticeable that the two films that most closely investigate fashion as expression, *Marie Antoinette* and *The Bling Ring*, both end with their female protagonists in prison. Coppola's films seem peculiarly judgemental and wary of sex (one very significant way they veer away from the themes and tone of the more typical postfeminist or neo-feminist film as discussed by Gill and Radner). While she features the consumption and makeovers that typify the Hollywood girly film, her films remain remarkably chaste. *The Virgin Suicides*, as its title suggests, remains in awe of the purity of the female adolescent. Charlotte and Bob in *Lost in Translation* do not consummate their relationship, and the film contrasts their bonding through watching *La Dolce Vita* favourably to Bob's one-night stand with the red-haired nightclub singer – we are left in no doubt as to what the more appropriate activity for bed is. Similarly, in *Somewhere*, Cleo/Elle Fanning's gelato feast and watching dubbed *Friends* episodes tucked up in bed with Dad is far preferable to his one-night stand with an Italian showgirl. Throughout, the film insists on the contrast between Cleo's innocence and the anomie and anonymity of sex in the world of the celebrity. For *Marie Antoinette*, the consummation of her marriage is vital to securing her position in the Royal Court in Versailles. Her brief fling with the Swedish count Van Fersen/Jamie Dornan is the closest any Coppola film comes to hinting that sex could be a pleasurable activity for women, but the film concentrates far more on sexual intercourse's relationship to consumption and power. Sex is a means to acquire political power rather than linked to desire. By the time of *The Bling Ring*, consumption seems to have replaced sex as the target and goal of the deepest fantasies of Coppola's protagonists.

Coppola's postfeminist auteur status allows her to carve out a space of transcendence and evasion, but her films paint a picture of eternally-extended girlhood that demands protagonists remain dutiful daughters. Rather than taking a chronological approach, I study the recurrent ways Coppola's films express femininity as a series of thorny paradoxes: simultaneously privileged and oppressed, private and public, materialistic and engaged, desiring and blocked. Coppola's films are products of a postfeminist moment, but given their auteur credentials, are able to self-consciously tarry with their blindspots and impasses rather than forcing the problems into a hasty narrative closure. Radner explains that studying popular Hollywood film's articulation of the postfeminist cultural formation through a feminist lens is important because 'cinema is perhaps the most logical area in which to analyse dominant trends in popular thought, because feature-length films provide a dense articulation of the contemporaneous discursive formation in which a film participates – formations that it may reproduce, modify and critique.'[86] Whilst concurring with Radner that the feature film remains a privileged moment for the expression and contestation of dominant ideology, I would add that attending to a set of films identified with the singular signature of the female auteur enables a complementary set of ideas to be debated. Coppola's films engage with many similar topics to those found in more typical postfeminist and 'girly' films, such as the makeover and the love of fashion and style, the pursuit of romance and the pains of adolescence, but here they are contrasted with relative narrative openness, minimalist aesthetics and a close attention to texture and tone, as well as a reversal of the gaze discussed by Kennedy and Woodworth. Indeed, in some quarters, postfeminism and auteurship may seem to be in utter contradiction, as the former is associated with the mass-entertainment of Conglomerate Hollywood and its narrow repetitive strain of themes 'for women', and the latter with film as art and individual personal statement. It is worth remembering at this point that, as far as the original French founders of 'auteur theory' are concerned, the genius of the director resides in his (sic) ability to produce profoundly personal works *despite* working in the industrialised studio system of Hollywood. I would not want to return to their excess of romanticised view of the artistic genius, but rather to stress that auteurship and genre are not opposed to one another, but are both systems that allow a capitalist film-production system to manage its need for innovation, creativity and difference (in order to prevent old audiences from getting bored and to encourage new audiences) and security, guarantees and similarity (in order not to alienate audiences and to encourage repeat viewing habits). Coppola plays with genre forms, having made variants on the romantic comedy (her central couple don't get together at the end), the historical biopic (which deliberately included anachronism) and a crime mystery (in which we know the outcome before the start of the film). She flits in and out of genre without being constrained by it, another way of confirming that her films belong to the 'specialty' prestige and art-house end of studio film-making identified with auteur cinema in twenty-first-century Hollywood.

This book has three chapters that examine Coppola's films under rubrics that are crucial to postfeminism, looking at (in turn) luminosity and aesthetics of girlhood; the complex construction of home; and fashion as expression of the 'feminine' self. In each chapter, I also demonstrate how each topic is influenced by the form as well as the content of Coppola's filmmaking, showing how her depiction of girlhood and postfeminist culture draws on the tools of cinema for its power. My second chapter focuses on Coppola's cinematography and examines the dominant visual construction of girlhood and its associations with sparkle and luminosity. Drawing on a variety of theorists of girlhood, I show how Coppola's films articulate an intricate and complex portrayal of girls. I suggest that Coppola's love of celluloid is a way of retooling light, and I demonstrate how she creates portraits of girls that are both rebellious and feminine. This paradox comes at a cost, however, and Coppola's girls, in order to retain their idealised qualities, must become as white as possible, a whiteness that leads to disembodiment and death. My third chapter offers a chronotopic reading of Coppola's films, concentrating on how Coppola depicts space and time through her editing. I demonstrate how Coppola's use of space inscribes privilege into the very materiality of her films as she manages to film in locations that others simply would not be able to access. Coppola's films privilege what I name 'the exploded home' chronotope, as she depicts a variety of spaces that have all exploded domestic space. Within this space, the temporality is one of repetition and ritual. I suggest that her characters are thus in a state of post-traumatic shock, wondering around the rubble of spaces that have been caught in the force-field of feminist politics but unable to fashion any kind of new site to move forwards but caught in eternal circles. My fourth chapter turns to questions of mise-en-scene and in particular the attention Coppola's films play to dress as a form of self-expression. I argue that fashion becomes key to Coppola's negotiation of her auteur identity and embodies some of its tensions and paradoxes. I conclude that a stiletto heel is the perfect metaphor for Coppola's performance of authorship as it is marked as feminine; it symbolises girlish rebellion and high end consumer culture; but it also constrains and restricts. In all three chapters, concentrating on different aspects of cinema (cinematography, editing, mise-en-scene) and preoccupations of postfeminist culture (girls, homes, fashion) nevertheless what shines through is the way that all these lead to a blockage, a stasis. These are characters whose solution to boredom and ennui is other versions of more of the same: more parties, more shoes, more champagne. The only reproduction is repetition, and there is no room for the energy and life-giving force of difference.

In this world, sexual desire itself is a problem. The girls seem to be unable to grow into sexual beings, as there are no possibilities offered for an expression of adult female sexuality. Mothers are either invisible (*Somewhere, Lost in Translation*); goofily neglectful (*The Bling Ring*) or utterly overbearing (*The Virgin Suicides, Marie Antoinette*). Fathers in contrast are benign, often highly passive figures (*The Virgin Suicides, Somewhere, The Bling Ring*). Sex is a problem in this family, either repressed or used as a political tool. Any attempt to grow-up, claim agency and power, and above all escape the benign but constraining patriarchal father, whether through the acquisition of goods, the loss of virginity, or leaving enclosing interior spaces to get out in the world, is severely punished and ends tragically in three of Coppola's five films. In the two films which have more hopeful endings, *Somewhere* and *Lost in Translation*, the girl remains close to her father figure, and thus forever a daughter. Cleo and Charlotte both explore their cities in ways that evoke the liberatory figure of the flaneuse, the woman on the street who is free to explore.[87] They enter such (adult) male-encoded spaces as casinos, sex bars and arcades, but their movement is facilitated by a much older male guide, tempering any transgressive or subversive potential in their movement across the city. Both girls remain associated with sexual innocence in comparison to older, highly sexualised women who seduce the father figure, and their relationships with him are seen as more authentic and meaningful because of this.

In this way, for all that they are films produced within the film-festival, speciality division 'prestige' end of the global film market, and thus contained within its need for singular, auteur-driven projects, they construct a Girl World remarkably similar to that found in popular, genre-driven teen films that are usually viewed as 'cinematic fluff.'[88] As Kathleen Rowe Karlyn explains, films that concentrate on female desire – whether for goods, sex or power – usually construct their heroines as 'unruly', as desire is forbidden to girls and women. Desire unfolds in a specially created space, a 'Girl World' (Rowe Karlyn borrows the term from the film *Mean Girls* (Waters, 2004)). It is worth quoting her definition at some length:

> Girl World refers to a liminal time and space between childhood and adulthood where girls rule. [...] When cultural producers recognised the untapped potential of teen girls as consumers, Girl World found expression in a full range of contemporary Girl Culture texts.[... Girl World is characterised by] girls flexing their muscles as they begin to leave childhood behind and test the waters of womanhood. They experiment with Femininity with a capital F, from fashion to girliness to romance, all mediated through popular culture. They experience close connections with each other through shopping, gossip and makeovers [...] Most threateningly, Girl World lets girls experience the taboo emotion of anger. Girls let themselves get mean. What matters most is girls, who begin to learn about social power by exercising it over each other. At the same time, Girl's World fantasies are manufactured and constrained by the ideologies of a patriarchal, postfeminist culture, and as girls experiment with social hierarchies, the results largely mirror the adult world. [...] Today, happy endings for young women may no longer assume marriage, at least right away, but in the teen-girl films unruly Girls leave Girl World behind for a femininity that is less focused on other girls and the self than on gracefully acquiescing to a social order that is still largely defined by patriarchy and capitalism. And so, postfeminist films tell the stories of daughters still more identified with their fathers than their mothers.[89]

Coppola's directorial persona is one founded on a notion of inheritance from her father, whether that is discussed in terms of talent by admiring critics, or denounced as nepotism by her detractors. Her films are literally and figuratively placed under the name of the father. In keeping with the emphasis on the father (figure) as emotional touchstone for the protagonist, mothers remain rather more problematic figures, alternatively haranguing, vengeful, neglectful or foolish. Furthermore, Coppola's films explore issues of generational conflict and ambivalence and matters of inheritance in other ways too. Her films enact a complex meeting of past and present, most notably in the notorious historically inaccurate *Marie Antoinette*'s Versailles which used an MTV aesthetic to capture Marie Antoinette's frenetic consumption. Beyond this playful mashup, Coppola incorporates history into her films in various ways: the period setting of *Marie Antoinette* and *The Virgin Suicides*; the use of flashbacks and retroactive, regretful voiceover in *Lick the Star* and *The Virgin Suicides*; the references to European art-cinema film history, especially *La Dolce Vita*, in *Lost in Translation* and *Somewhere*; and her own past through the autobiographical references peppered in the films. Through this constant enfolding of past and present, Coppola's films disturb conventional linear narrative, although they do so in a fairly mild and contained way (these films are no *Last Year in Marienbad* (Resnais, 1961), despite the proliferation of hotels!) This disturbance speaks to ways in which Coppola's films could move beyond the limitations of Girl World sketched above. Coppola takes us back to a pre-feminist past, a time of (depending on the film) sexual double standards (*The Virgin Suicides*); European art-house male-dominated film cultures, with women as beautiful objects (*Lost in Translation*, *Somewhere*); and women as mere breeders, tasked with providing sons and heirs (*Marie Antoinette*). Through bringing together past and present in these films, Coppola doesn't suggest an easy transition from a pre-feminist past into a postfeminist present, but creates an understanding of social and cultural progress as involving loops, digressions and stumbling blocks, as well as positive transformation. Nevertheless, she does show that girls and women's lives have changed, and her films are at their most hopeful when they find a way to give back to girls the voices that were traditionally denied them in the cinema. Coppola shows us that woman can be bearer of the look; the challenge is to find a way to make her also a bearer of the voice. The question remains as to how privileged one has to be to be given an opportunity to speak.

Coppola offers a vision of twenty-first-century film authorship, thoroughly embedded within in and highly critical of celebrity culture. She offers us a paradigm for thinking about how film with a pronounced authorial signature offers a different perspective on postfeminist culture than the popular genre-driven pieces more readily associated with postfeminism. Her films are simultaneously highly aestheticised, beautifully constructed and deeply intelligent comments on the pressures and pleasures of girlhood, and symptoms of postfeminism's own deeply engrained exclusions of race, class and sex. How does a postfeminist culture envisage the role of the female director? (How) can the female director express her and her characters' contradictory, embodied, emotional response to feminist and postfeminist desires? Coppola's work extends the fraught question of the very possibility of female authorship, in a form theorised as inherently patriarchal, and asks what it means to be making films from a position where femininity is experienced as possibility and punishment, pleasure and pain.

2

Luminous Girlhoods: Sparkle and Light in Coppola's Films

'In the changing social, economic, political and globalizing context of the new millennium, where "girl power" has become a marketing tool and a branding of girlhood, it is important to look anew at the relations between girlhood, power, agency and resistance.'[1]

'The Marc Jacobs "girl" (and they always say "girl") is not going to suffer. "She's like 'I bought a nice dress, I'm going to wear it tonight.' She's the awkward little sister." It makes sense that Jacobs has settled on Sofia Coppola as his muse. [She is…] "young and sweet and innocent and beautiful. The epitome of this girl I fantasize of."'[2]

'I had a teacher when I was in college, and he was the first person who liked my photos and said, "The way you look at girls is your own way of seeing." He was the first person who really gave me the confidence to try something.'[3]

Authoring Girlhood: The Signature Aesthetic of the Coppola Film

Coppola's films' dominant aesthetic is that associated with the contemporary visual construction of girlhood. While Chapter 1 worked to place Coppola into the complex debates concerning the why and wherefores of female authorship within a globalising postfeminist context, here I concentrate on a reading of how Coppola deploys the apparatus of cinema to create a light-filled, ethereal image of girlhood that dazzles and sparkles. Her films, as her discussion quoted above reveals, offer a unique vision of girlhood. Coppola's construction of girlhood is highly imbricated with the broader cultural questions of girlhood and agency that emerge in the contemporary post girl-power era, while she herself is cast by fashion designer Marc Jacobs as the ultimate girl.

42

Coppola's girl images are luminous, drenched in sun-light and featuring jewellery, glittery shoes, sequins and shimmering silks. She references iconic painterly, photographic and filmic images of girls, from pre-Raphaelite paintings to celebrity paparazzi shots. Her mise-en-scene is cluttered with objects and designs linked to contemporary girl culture in its various guises, including unicorns, rainbows, meadows, flowers, doodles, dainty delicate cakes and macarons, shoes, coloured wigs, beautiful (often white, pink or floral) party dresses and jewellery, and her characters participate in such stereotypically girlish activities as pole dancing, ice-skating, dancing and tea parties.

Furthermore, Coppola 'girlifies' her authorial signature, beginning with the title graphics for her first feature film, *The Virgin Suicides*. The credit sequence follows an exchange in a hospital bay between the psychologist Dr Hornicker/ Danny De Vito and Cecilia/Hanna Hall, a 13-year-old girl who we've seen lying in a bath of bloody water following a suicide attempt. Hornicker asks 'what are you even doing here, honey? You're too young to even know how bad life gets', to which Cecilia responds in a deadpan tone, while filmed in medium close-up, 'obviously, doctor, you've never been a 13 year-old girl.' Having established its faith in the specificity of the subjective experience of girlhood in this exchange, the film begins its credit sequence. Extra-diegetic electronic music plays as the camera pans along a suburban street before moving up to a sky and filming bright afternoon light filtered through the trees. The trees fade and a dissolve introduces an image of a blue sky filled with fluffy white clouds over them. The title 'The Virgin Suicides' appears, in a script that mimics hand-writing, with small white hearts replacing the dots over the 'I's. Then the screen fills with variants on the hand-writing style, with *The Virgin Suicides* written variously in bubble-writing, block capitals, with lightning style zig-zags and so on. The hand-written titles, still projected against an image of the sky, are interspersed with assorted girlish doodles, such as a rose, hearts, clouds, a caterpillar, a girl's head and two unicorns. The image clearly references a school exercise book or jotter, the kind that's scribbled in to fill the time during a boring class (see Fig 2.1). The scene dissolves so that it superimposes a golden sunset and a girl's (Lux Lisbon) face, in close-up over the images of the clouds and sky. She winks at the camera, the action highlighted by a jingle on the soundtrack.

The conjunction of a girl's face, a girlish script which reproduces hearts in its writing of the self, and sun-drenched ennui is replicated in *Somewhere*. The first fifteen minutes of the film establish its protagonist's, Johnny Marco's, state of boredom and apathy. He drives his fast Ferrari in circles around

Fig. 2.1. The *Virgin Suicides* credit sequence

a race track; he attends a party in his hotel suite; he falls down some stairs and breaks his arm. This desultory series of activities culminates (but definitely does not climax!) in him watching a pair of blonde twins, Bambi/Kristina Shannon and Cindy/Karissa Shannon, perform a pole-dancing routine while dressed as sexy tennis-players (tiny white skirts and a white and green bikini top accessorised by tennis rackets and wrist bands). This is the second dance routine Johnny has watched in his hotel room, adding to the layers of repetition: the identical twins in their matching outfits (Johnny mistakes Cindy for Bambi, so interchangeable are they); the mirrors reflecting the dancers; the twirling around the pole. The scene finishes on a close-up of Bambi popping a bubble of gum in Johnny's bemused face before cutting to black, almost as if Johnny has passed out (not that unlikely as he was drinking whisky while watching the performance). The screen remains black and we hear the distant noise of traffic, then some distinctive scratching, before images flood back in and we see what is making the noise: a pen. We see a close-up of Johnny's plaster cast and a black pen drawing a heart and then signing Cleo in a curvy script (see Fig 2.2). We can see some blonde hair in the corner of the frame: Cleo is introduced as signature *before* we see her face. The camera then pans up Johnny's arm to his face burrowed into the pillow and his messy hair. The reverse shot shows us a close-up on Cleo, her face leaning forward toward the camera/Johnny, and she is surrounded by light as he looks up at her and she is framed by the window. The traffic noise has been replaced on the soundtrack by bird song. 'Hey Cleo' says Johnny, as she leans forward to hug him.

Fig. 2.2. Cleo signs her Dad's cast

Coppola mobilises the motif of the girl signature, showing a girl naming herself. We see a similar, deeply poignant moment in *Marie Antoinette* which reinforces the significance of the girl signature in Coppola's films. While clearly Coppola was not aiming for mimesis in her deliberately playful and anachronistic representation of life at Versailles, she nevertheless chooses to replicate the famous marriage contract between Marie Antoinette and her husband, the dauphin. A close-up shot shows us the bottom of the document, signed with a flourish by both Louis, her father-in-law, and Louis Auguste, her husband (the fact that two men sign this contract shows its dual function as sealing both a national and a personal alliance). We see Marie Antoinette's hand clasping a quill and signing her name in the bottom right-hand corner of the frame. As she draws a line across the two 't's of her name to complete her signature, a large ink blot appears, dripping down the velum (see Fig 2.3). The signing has taken place in silence, exaggerating the scratching sound of pen against velum: as the ink spills, so a trumpet sounds and we cut back to the extravagant wedding ceremony and a hall filled with courtiers. The close-up on the contract interrupts the wedding spectacle to offer us a different image of the girl: her image as signature. The childish writing and the ink blot, replicating as they do the historical original (and this replication gaining in significance within the postmodern pastiche of the Coppola Versailles), speak to us of the *historic* Marie Antoinette's relative lack of education, trepidation and youth.[4] However, the very fact of its repetition across films and its girlish style makes the *cinematic* Marie Antoinette another Coppola girl and adds to the paradoxes of

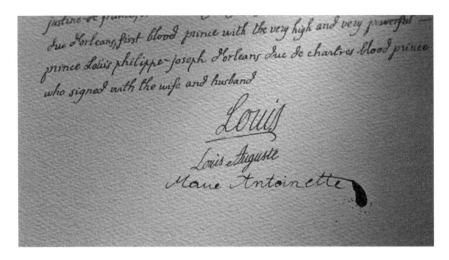

Fig. 2.3. Marie Antoinette's marriage certificate

the signature within a reading that sees it as a comment on more contemporary cultural problematics. On the one hand, it is a demonstrable moment of agency, recognising the self as subject and bringing a certain kind of legal subjectivity into existence. On the other hand, the signature is not really an operation of free-will, but added to a document that has been framed by male adult others in order to corral Marie Antoinette into a useful political function as wife of one King and mother of another, metaphorically illustrating the larger webs of constraint under which girls and women enact their agency and empowerment.

As Janet Staiger reminds us, names are never innocent in auteur theory – indeed Michel Foucault's very concept of 'the author function' relies on the permanence and significance of the name. It is through the author's name that the texts they have created gain their identity and create the textual organisation category of the author. The name is how we apprehend the role of the author as a heuristic device to understand the relations between certain texts. Staiger further claims that names have particular importance for female directors. First, the move away from auteur theory and to poststructuralist accounts which deny the author agency can 'seem like a plot' to remove women's names from the field of cultural production just at the point that they are finally being acknowledged in significant numbers; second, she justifies feminist interest in female authorship precisely as a question of names and naming: 'What matters whose speaking? […] It matters, for example, to women who still routinely lose their proper name on marriage, and whose signature – not merely their voice – has not been worth the paper it's been written on.'[5] Women's names are always already under erasure in patriarchy, taken from the father in anticipation of being replaced by that of the husband. The multiple scripts and scribbles that comprise the credit sequence of *The Virgin Suicides* cannot help but recall the teen girl habit of practising a variety of potential future signatures including the surname of whomever is the recipient of the latest crush. In contrast, Cleo marks her space on her father's cast, signs her name and asserts her identity. This takes on an especial weight if we consider Cleo's name to be a deliberate reference to Agnès Varda's film *Cléo de 5 à 7* (1962), a seminal feminist film which shows us two hours in the life of a Parisian singer/Corinne Marchand. While we believe her name to be Cleo, both due to the title of the film and the fact this is what characters in it call her, when she encounters a sympathetic solider, Antoine/Antoine Boursellier, in the park, she reveals to him that this is a stage name and her true name is Flore. This unleashes a poetic monologue from Antoine, as he riffs on the various connotations of the two names: 'Florence, Italy, the Renaissance, Botticelli, a rose. Cleopatra: Egypt, the Sphinx, the asp, a tigress.' Varda's Cléo attempts to locate her own identity from within the plethora of meanings generated by the feminine ideal: in contrast, Coppola's Cleo is sure of herself and her place in the world, able to confidently place her name into the fabric of the film, at the price of course of not becoming anything other than the singular 'Cleo', the lack of surname keeping her out of the feminist politics of marriage and her potential loss of status as her father's daughter.

Cleo's power to assert her girl identity in this way partly comes from her position of class and race privilege, confirmed for us in our introduction to her I described above: on her movie star father's bed, surrounded by a halo of light, her blonde hair falling into the frame. We get some acknowledgment in a typical witty way from Coppola of how the power of the girl name depends on privilege though the credit sequence of her next film after *Somewhere*, *The Bling Ring*. Rather than naturally owning the privileges of alpha-girl luminosity, The Bling Ring have to steal them. Leaving a tangible signature behind in this context would be extremely risky and foolish. The signature here reverts back from the girl character to Coppola herself. The credit sequence features a series of shots of glittering, sparkling objects and bright flashing lights: shoes covered in sequins; celebrities posing on the red carpets; celebrities trying to escape the paparazzi; popping camera flashbulbs; gleaming costume jewellery; diamond-encrusted brooches; gilded make-up cases. The 'bling' of the title is repeatedly asserted for us as the credits showcase how luminosity figures in creating the aesthetics of celebrity, with its dependence on flash photography and flaunting of wealth through glittering product. Most notable for its tongue-in-cheek humour however is the shot which names Coppola as director. The camera pans slowly hovering just over a collection of jewellery laid out on a reflective surface, so that light gleams and bounces off it. These jewels have papers nestled in them that read 'evidence' and therefore tell us that these are stolen goods. As the camera pans over a glittering necklace that spells out 'rich bitch' in pink capitals, the credit 'written and directed by Sofia Coppola' appears on the screen, displayed that so the words 'rich bitch' precede Coppola's name (see Fig 2.4). Coppola of course is such a 'rich bitch' she can afford to stay out of the light and doesn't need the sparkly goods to affirm her celebrity status. Unlike the (often) black hip-hop stars from whom the term 'bling' as slang for jewels originates, and whose pursuit of wealth comes from a context of systemic racial prejudice and a sense that celebrity culture is one of few escape routes from poverty, Coppola comes from an (ethnic) white background of cultural and economic privilege that means she doesn't need to proclaim her financial success in obvious ways and can avoid the extremes of celebrity culture. The girl's signature power relies on often invisible and innate class and race privilege that is for once made clear here. Through these self-conscious naming devices, Coppola invokes her authorial persona as a self-aware, self-fashioning construct that speaks to us from the space of girl culture.

Coppola's attention to girlhood and its visual parameters is part of a broader obsession with this figure in contemporary popular culture. The girl is an accessible way to debate the legacies of feminism, the possibilities of becoming for the female subject and the persistence of gendered understanding of the self. In a neoliberal capitalist world, the young girl, seemingly the most pliable and flexible of

Fig. 2.4. *The Bling Ring* credit sequence

subjects, represents an ideal, ready to see herself as an individual project to be brought to perfection using all the consumerist technologies available to her. On the other hand, youth has long been understood as a time of resistance to dominant ideologies. Girls offer a complex take on the pleasures and pitfalls for all of us in a society that glamorises celebrity, shores up notions of individual agency and offers bountiful rewards and punitive retribution within a system that tells us having it all is within our grasp (and that if we fail it is simply that we didn't reach hard enough). Coppola's films demonstrate the extent to which girlhood is a visual construction, associated with luminosity and sparkle, and her films' recurrent deployment of sunlight, lens flare, haze and glow creates a politics of dazzling girlhood. Furthermore, she showcases the aesthetics of girlhood, investigates the way it circulates as a series of idealised images and does not offer any easy conclusions. The sheer appeal of girlhood as a time of fantasy, evasion and escape is held in tension with its precarious, vulnerable and abject qualities. Although visually dominated by luminescence, Coppola's films also venture into narratively darker territory, particularly when they show us girls navigating friendships. Coppola's visual construction of girlhood as luminous and sparkling is thus placed in tension with a narrative attention to unhappiness, boredom and anxiety. Coppola's films thus offer a resistant aesthetic that repurposes light and gives it a much broader affective tone and range than the persistent cultural insistence that 'when the Young Girl gives into her own insignificance, she still manages to find glory in it, because she is "having fun."'[6]

Between Light and Dark: Regulating Girlhoods

Concentrating on her two films that show us groups of girls – *The Virgin Suicides*, *The Bling Ring* – this chapter argues that, while all Coppola's films display a girlified authorial signature, her films that show us groups of girls offer us the most complex and ambivalent exploration of girl culture. This is because it is in the spaces of female adolescent friendships that girls work through what it means to be a girl in our contemporary social formation. Friendship creates a useful bridge between the singularity of the individual and the anonymity of the social. It is in the company of other girls that the possibilities and constraints of girl culture are writ large. As Felicity Colman explains, 'friendship contains the possibility of becoming not the other, but becoming self-sentient. I become aware of my own desires, of what I *do not* desire, of what I *do aspire to*, through my interactions with my friend.'[7] Within Coppola's homosocial girls' worlds, we see the gamut of group behaviours, from support, love and enjoyment of each other's company, to rivalry, jealousy and betrayal. We see the joy and sustenance friendship can provide, from Marie Antoinette's pained goodbye hug to her group of attendants at the Austrian border to the joyful abandon of the girls in Paris' nightclub room in *The Bling Ring*.[8] Coppola does not romanticise friendship, however, and bitchy cliques of girls operate in *Lick the Star*, *Marie Antoinette* and *The Bling Ring*.

It is worth pausing here to reflect upon the ambivalence accorded to female friendship within Coppola's films, given its significance to contemporary cultures of girlhood. Indeed, Alison Winch discusses how the 'female friendship film' identified by Karen Hollander as an important element in Hollywood production in the 1980s and 1990s has shifted into 'the girlfriend flick.' The change of name is important as it brings together the intense focus on female friendship and support in these films, with men often relegated to benign or hapless bystanders, and an emphasis on maintaining girlish, youthful femininity through consumption and constant body surveillance. Such surveillance is performed via a 'girlfriend gaze', a regulation of the body that operates in an analogous way to Foucault's panoptican. Groups of female friends form 'affective networks of control which constitute a gynaeoptican where the many girlfriends survey the many girlfriends.'[9] Winch pays particular attention to *Mean Girls* (Waters, 2004), arguing that while its bullying clique of 'the Plastics' may be somewhat caricatured (it is, after all, a comedy), it nevertheless demonstrates the powerful dynamics of adolescent girl friendship groups as they regulate through forces of belonging and exclusion, 'a loving meanness' that animates girl culture more broadly. Drawing on psycho-sociological ethnographic research on adolescent girl friendships, Winch comments that experiences in childhood and adolescence – 'the threshing floor of friendship' – regulate girls' performance of gender into adulthood: 'feminine identities, shaped in the playgrounds and private spaces of adolescence, are still susceptible to, and shaped by, girlfriends in older life.'[10] The search for inclusion, participation and comfort does not dissipate in adult life; rather, it partly explains the need for and appeal of the girlfriend film, which women often watch in groups, imitating the processes of female intimacy and sharing off-screen that are being depicted on-screen. Media such as girlfriend films, alongside women's magazines, celebrity culture and internet sites dedicated to weddings, fashion, beauty and slenderness, can imitate these dynamics, creating spaces that have a tone and feel of intimate concern and friendly guidance but also harshly condemn 'sluttish' behaviour, 'matchy-matchy' clothing, or 'out-of-control' eating. Friendship in adolescence between girls is often formed within close-knit peer groups, outside of the influence of the mother, but the sisterly solidarity associated with certain kinds of feminist thought here becomes a space for the performance of 'normative cruelties' which discipline feminine behaviour. Conflict in girlfriend culture, and in its representation in the girlfriend film, is resolved through the childhood fantasy of 'being good friends'.[11] It's noticeable here, for example, that *Mean Girls* has to take an over-determined and fantasy style approach to its resolution of girl conflict. First, it uses adult intervention aimed at calming slut shaming when the teacher Ms. Norbury, played by Tina Fey, who also scripted the film and thus has a privileged voice, tells the girls 'you all have to stop calling each other sluts and whores. It just makes it OK for guys to call you sluts and whores'. Second, it creates a highly unlikely narrative of inclusion and belonging when Cady/Lyndsey Lohan breaks her tiara into pieces and distributes it to everybody at prom, so all can share in the prize of popularity and acceptance. Third, it suggests that teens outgrow the regulative normative cruelties of female friendship, with Cady declaring that leaving Junior High allows her to be 'normal'. Yet the continued importance and significance of girlfriends in popular postfeminist culture and the continued dynamics of advice, concern and criticism show that the joys and scars of adolescent friendship continue into adult life; a truth that *Mean Girls* perhaps unconsciously acknowledges as the teacher who attempts to maintain a female self outside of the these discourses is invisible, a nobody (Ms. Norbury). Consequently, sexual and social hierarchies among girls and women are maintained through girlfriend culture, but subsumed under a sentimentalised and idealised view of female relations where regulation is glossed as loving friendship.

Coppola acknowledges the rivalries and bitchiness of the female friendship clique, especially in *Lick the Star* with its high school setting and portrayal of a 'queen bee' inviting direct comparisons with *Mean Girls*, as the latter film's script is based on Rosalind Wiseman's self-help book *Queen Bees and Wannabies: Helping Your Daughter Survive Cliques, Gossip, Boyfriends, and Other Realities of Adolescence*.[12] In both *Lick the Star* and *Marie Antoinette*, Coppola demonstrates how gossip is an important tool of social regulation of the adolescent girl body, especially in preventing it from 'getting above itself'. Coppola herself draws attention to the similarities between *Lick the Star* and *Marie Antoinette*, particularly in their use of feminine bitchiness.

> There's obviously a link with my two earlier films [...]I have to finish making stories about lonely, melancholic girls who put off adulthood. In *Marie Antoinette* with its tales of palace plots, there's also an echo of my first short about girls at high school, the competitiveness, the gossip ... I made Du Barry a real bitch.[13]

In *Lick The Star*, the brief credit sequence finishes with Chloe, 'the queen of 7th grade' opening a classroom door. We cut to a classroom, Kate (the narrator) in the middle of the frame in medium shot at her desk. The only other visible human object is another hand at the bottom left of the frame, but we hear multiple voices on the soundtrack, which is mixed to enable us to hear different conversations. In the background, we hear a girl's monotonous chanting voice, clearly reading out loud from a pre-prepared script. Two girls lean in to talk to each other and their faces obscure Kate. 'She's never going to be a model', they whisper, while we hear the background voice say 'I'm going to be a model.' As the camera leaves the girls' faces to focus on Chloe walking into the room and choosing which desk to sit at, forcing another girl out of her seat, we continue to hear the whispered conversation. 'I mean, please. Really […] that sweater […] her taste in clothes is unbelievable.' We see a long shot of the classroom, with the teacher and the girl giving the talk at the far end. 'Chloe, maybe you can tell us what you thought of Andrea's speech', suggests the teacher. We return to a close-up on Chloe, who in a dead-pan voice replies, 'I laughed. I cried', ironically displaying her utter lack of interest. In the middle of the sequence, the camera has panned around the floor and desks of the classroom where Chloe and her whispering friends are sitting, focusing in on a tattoo of a star, a girl reading *Flowers in the Attic* and a folder with 'Lick the star' written on it in cursive script. This sets up Kate's curiosity. She does not know what 'lick the star' means, as she has become an outsider because she has been away from school for a week after her father accidentally ran over her foot. Gossip is thus used to create the divide between the inside and the outside, those in the know and those in ignorance, and concentrates above all on criticising looks.

Coppola uses similar devices to show the role and impact of gossip in *Marie Antoinette*, perhaps allowing us to read Marie Antoinette's treatment at Versailles as not that different from that of the new girl at school and giving further weight to Amanda Dobbin's argument that *Marie Antoinette* and *Mean Girls* can sustain comparison. At the first communal dinner party we see, as opposed to the official dining ritual where Marie Antoinette and the Dauphin eat alone in front of their courtiers, Coppola brings dialogue high up into the sound mix, so that we can hear multiple whispered conversations.[14] The sound of several overlapping conversations means that no dialogue is easily attributed to a single character, so that speech becomes a cacophony of information that seems almost autonomous. The camera tracks around the dining table, sometimes focusing on the characters who are gossiping together, but sometimes paying attention to the food, or the objects of their discussion. Within this fluid movement, there are frequent cut-ins to Marie Antoinette, who is unable to join in this chatter: tellingly the only time we hear her speak is when she has to ask who the King's mistress is. The scene finishes with a cut from a close-up on Marie Antoinette in pink silk to a medium-long shot of three anonymous courtiers, all discussing her, as if the camera had momentarily held their perspective. Over the image of the close-up, we hear one woman's voice say, 'she's delightful. I think she looks like a little piece of cake,' and then on the three in longer shot the response, 'be interesting to see how long she lasts' before we cut to the next sequence. While clearly in the context of this hermetically sealed world, where the gossip we have just heard is purely concerned with sexual rumours and discussions of appearance, the reference to seeing how long she lasts refers simply to Marie Antoinette's powerful position in court, by cheekily aligning this with the mention of cake, Coppola's film draws on our extra-historical knowledge about how gossip, scandal and rumours became a particular vicious and gendered way to punish Marie Antoinette for her girlish ignorance and frivolities.[15] Despite the vast difference in historical context between Versailles and high school, Coppola demonstrates how in both environments groups use gossip to reinforce the difference between insiders and outsiders, and in particular shows how girls are judged in terms of appearance and sexual behaviour through it. Friendship becomes necessary for survival: it is when alone that one becomes most vulnerable to the attacks of gossip.

Most significantly, Coppola avoids the kind of neat narrative resolutions which mark *Mean Girls* and other girlfriend films, overcoming the tying of friendship to sentimentality and idealisation. Rather, she keeps the darkness, difficulty and struggle of the friendship in view. *Lick the Star* concludes with the deposed queen bee writing a poem that states 'everything changes/nothing changes/the tables turn/and life goes on'. She tucks the paper her poem is written on into a copy of Jean Stein's *Edie: An American Biography*, inviting us to speculate that she sees her individual tale of bullying and victimisation as part of a wider commentary on American cultural life and its practices. Its concluding sentiment that the removal of one queen bee to be substituted by another is symbolic of how what seems revolutionary ('everything changes') actually means the continuation of a harsh girlfriend culture ('nothing changes') undermines *Mean Girls*' rather facile happy ending that Cady deposing Regina/Rachel McAdams will mean the re-writing of girl meanness. Such darkness in female friendships is articulated in the suicide pact of the Lisbon sisters and the selfishness and self-absorption of the Bling Ring, undercutting the sentimentality that accompanies much representation of girlfriends in girl culture and indeed the dominant luminosity of Coppola's own aesthetics. Coppola leaves girl culture's normative cruelties more visible, demonstrating to us how powerful fear of exclusion and the desire to belong can be as drivers of behaviour. This finds perhaps more extreme expression in *The Virgin Suicides* and *The Bling Ring*. Here the dynamics of the girl friendship group are both filtered to some extent through boys' imaginary. Indeed, the films highlight the closed nature of the female friendship group through the narrative device of having a boy's voiceover narrating the dynamic of the group for us, holding the viewer at one remove. In the case of *The Virgin Suicides*, the voiceover is retrospective, and its provenance is unclear – it could belong to any of the four boys who spent a summer spying on the Lisbon girls. The film insists on the gendered divisions of their lives, and the boys' access to the girls is strictly regulated by Mrs. Lisbon/Kathleen Turner. There's no way they can access the group other than through ephemera. In the case of *The Bling Ring* Marc, whose voiceover we hear, is permitted access to the group, through the controlling dynamic of his infatuation with Rebecca/Katie Chang. He attempts to join in with the girls, but worries that they will be caught, and looks foolish when he tries on Paris Hilton's heels. He remains the odd, gawky outsider figure who never really quite fits into the whole group. The film emphasises the gendered logic that keeps him outside of the girl group dynamic as its penultimate sequence shows us Marc in his orange LA county prison uniform shuffling and hand cuffed to his fellow older male prisoners as he makes his way to a coach. In contrast, the only other character we see after the court sentencing is Nicki/Emma Watson, but she is on a chat show, wearing fashionable clothes, neatly made-up, promoting her website and talking about sharing a cell with Lindsay Lohan. She is able to sustain her image and her girl connections in a way unavailable to the boy. Furthermore, as both films narrate the female friendship group through a male narrator, we can only imagine that some of the peer pressure that animates the group – toward a suicide pact or to keep robbing houses – is not witnessed, even if implied.

We do sometimes see adolescent female friendship as a site of freedom and jouissance, a liberty of mind and body, as these friendships finally also encourage letting go of the feminine norms of submitting to oppression, and exercising will-power and restraint. Ironically, however, this feeling of freedom is generated within the strict confines of the clearly demarcated realms of teen girl friendship culture: school classrooms, bedrooms, dressing rooms, fields and meadows, and nightclubs. The movement of the friendship group in terms of negotiations of desire and aspiration are subject to the immediate and certain imposition of a range of laws, but nevertheless, as Colman writes, 'it is autopoietic and autoproductive', with strong affective bonds.[16] These are girls who, while constructed as spectacular and embracing the sparkling attributes of girl culture, also behave as delinquent failures: suicidal, drug-abusing, stealing. Notably, the other attribute of rebellious delinquent girlhood, premature sexualisation, is mainly avoided. In *The Virgin Suicides*, the bloody mess of female adolescence is disavowed. In *The Bling Ring*, as Coppola explains, the pursuit of goods replaces sexual desire. 'Yeah, I didn't feel like sex excited them. It was about the stuff – and dressing sexy and getting attention in clubs, and maybe being discovered. But it was never about sex. It was about being sexy to get where they wanted to go.'[17]

This is a girlhood that refuses to grow up into womanhood, rejecting normative narratives of adult responsibility, and entering into what Judith Jack Halberstam calls queer time: 'a perverse turn away from the coherent narrative of adolescence – early adulthood – reproduction – child-rearing – retirement – death.'[18] As such, queer time challenges both hetero and homo normativities, functioning as a 'critique of the careful social scripts that usher even the most queer among us through major markers of individual development and into normativity.'[19] These girls skip the stages, moving from adolescence to literal/ social death without entering into adulthood. They offer us an image of girlhood that is rebellious while remaining girlish, avoiding the association of resistance within cultural studies and popular feminist writing to masculine behaviours and attire.[20] They challenge the metaphors of growth and development that mark most films concerned with adolescence, the coming-of-age movies. These girls refuse to come, to arrive at a final destination. In this way they show up the gendered nature of these framings of experience, for as Halberstam explains 'if adolescence for boys represents a rite of passage (much celebrated in Western literature in the form of the *Bildungsroman*) and ascension to some version (however attenuated) of social power, for girls adolescence is a lesson in restraint, punishment and repression.'[21] In *The Virgin Suicides*, this gendered experience of adolescence is made all too visible. The film insists in the contrasting homosocial worlds of the neighbourhood boys and girls, the mise-en-scène of their bedrooms and costuming reinforcing traditional gendered divisions. As Colman says, 'for empathetic viewers, *The Virgin Suicides* affords an acknowledgment of the dire constraints on identity through social mores and standards for teenage girls. […] What are the girls' motives for death? Their movement toward becoming adolescent has been stilled, and the fatigue with their position as women living within an ideology of oppression causes the cessation of the transversal crossing of life.'[22] If *The Virgin Suicides* shows girls opting for death over the repression of female adolescence, in *Marie Antoinette* and *The Bling Ring* adult 'womanly' responsibility is refused through a wilful embrace of superficiality and frivolity. In both films, girlishness is a desirable image to be captured and projected through fashion and cosmetics (of which more in chapter 4). The protagonists favour becoming-image over

becoming-woman. It seems then that girlhood can avoid the repressions and constraints of adult femininity, continuing to retain power and desirability. This ability comes though at the price of its own embrace of futility, immaturity and death,
and its attendant lack of political weight and sexual expression. This is a girlhood
that while constantly reproducing itself as a series of copies fails to find a way to
sustain itself beyond the stilled, superficial image; and that gains power within
the highly limited parameters of its own demise. Thus while I sense resistance in
Coppola's cinema of girlhood, it is finally in the very absence of lines of flight out
of their numbing, restrictive and repetitive lives that Coppola's girls most clearly
show the need for a new kind of feminist politics beyond the horizon of the films
themselves.

Contemporary Girlhood: Spectacle, Luminosity, Sparkle

As Marnina Gonick, Emma Renold, Jessica Ringrose and Lisa Weems note,
there is a 'current proliferation of images and narratives of girls and girlhood
in popular culture.'[23] In a similar vein, Sarah Projansky argues that 'since
approximately 1990, girls have appeared often and everywhere in U.S. media
culture.'[24] She supports this claim by tracking the number of girls to appear on
the cover of mass market magazines such as *Newsweek* and *Time*, and analysing
the most discussed of the 'literally hundreds of films featuring girls as central
characters' released in US cinemas in the period 2000–2009. This sense that
girlhood is hypervisible in the contemporary popular cultural formation needs
to be nuanced: historical studies demonstrate to us that the figure of the girl
has acted as a lightning rod for broader cultural anxieties in other periods.
Carol Dyhouse's study of young women in twenty and twenty-first-century
Britain shows how 'modern British history is packed with horror stories about
girls' and that 'attention to representations of girlhood in British social history and popular culture shows clearly that the changes in young women's lives
since Victorian times have been accompanied by anxiety and social unease.'[25]
Similarly, Projansky finds that 'girls have appeared in U.S. media culture repeatedly over the past two centuries in ways that work through cultural anxieties
about any number of social issues.'[26] Examples include age-of-consent laws in
the early 1900s; anxiety about girls as babysitters as labourers or nurturers; the
1950s teenage 'bobby-soxer', a girl who sought heteronormative romance but
disrupted home life in (to adults) incomprehensible ways. Clearly, then, the
claim that the representation of girlhood is new does not stand up to historical scrutiny. Furthermore, although the box-office behemoth *Frozen* (Buck and

Lee, 2013) has received much attention as the first Disney film to feature two young female leads, Anna and Elsa, Frances Gateward and Murray Pomerance's study of American cinema demonstrates the significance of the teen girl for this cultural form throughout the twentieth century. Taking into account inflation, six of the ten top grossing US movies of all time have teenage girls as their main protagonist. These are *Snow White and the Seven Dwarves* (Cottrel, Jackson et al, 1937); *Gone With the Wind* (Fleming, 1939); *The Wizard of Oz* (Fleming, 1939); *The Sound of Music* (Wise, 1965); *Dr. Zhivago* (Lean, 1965); *Titanic* (Cameron, 1997). The latter example also demonstrates the power of the teen girl audience, whose repeated visits to the cinema to see *Titanic* fuelled a teen fan culture and prompted recognition of their significance as a market.[27] Indeed, for Kathleen Rowe Karlyn, in its depiction of a rebellious upper-class girl, Rose/Kate Winslet, determined to defy her mother and marry the working-class boy she has fallen in love with, *Titanic* 'was among the first films identified with Girl Culture, and it valorized a model of unruly femininity that spoke to teen girls.'[28]

Now, a decade into the twenty-first century, the convenient figure of the girl – already adept at standing in for myriad social concerns – surfaces to work through anxieties about the way we live now: in particular, what is perceived as a shallow, crass celebrity culture obsessed with looks. Girls are seen as dupes, in danger of 'premature sexualisation' or severe body image issues as they show worrying tendencies (for parents, schools and governments) to admire and wish to emulate models or popstars.[29] At the same time as girls can be portrayed as naïve victims, psychologist and TV pundit Oliver James has likened girls' situation to that of canaries down the mine, whose unhappiness in the face of impossible expectations for looks and lifestyle should warn others of their impending fate under 'selfish capitalism.'[30] Anita Harris argues that the contemporary girl functions as an idealised citizen for the neoliberal global economy: a flexible, pliant, enthusiastic, energetic participant in commodity consumption and eager to acquire not only goods but also the cool cultural cachet peddled by globalised corporate multimedia conglomerates. She argues that whereas in the nineteenth century, adolescence was regulated and controlled in attempts to fashion the future of the nation/ Empire, in the twenty-first century 'it is young women, rather than youth in general who are now the subjects of this scrutiny and regulation [...] At the beginning of the twenty-first century, the creation of the contemporary social order and citizenship is achieved in part within the space of girlhood.'[31] Tiqqun's radical 'trash theory' of the Young-Girl understands the exemplary value of girlhood to consumer society, arguing that the Young-Girl rather than being a gendered concept, is 'the model citizen as redefined by consumer society since World War 1, in explicit response to the revolutionary menace [...] all the old figures of patriarchal authority, from statesmen to bosses to cops, have become Young-Girlified, every last one of them, even the Pope.'[32]

Coppola's close attention to the experiences of actual girls, and the micro shifts in girlish mood and feeling that occur in her films, nuance and give specificity and individuality back to this generalised figure. In popular culture, the state and processes of girlhood reflect and project the values of neoliberalism and our generally ambivalent and conflicted attitude towards its social, cultural and political impact. Whereas frequently we may concentrate on the negative pressures of neoliberalism's push to manage ourselves, a self-starting view of girlhood echoed in Coppola's range of girls, from ice-skating Cleo to self-styling Rebecca, Coppola's films force us also to acknowledge the sheer fun of self-indulgence that consumerist society permits, from Marie Antoinette's shopping spree to late night drives with friends in Beverly Hills. Coppola's films enter into critical engagement with cultures of girlhood and how girlhood is represented in the contemporary media. They do this through two main strategies this chapter will now discuss: first, through challenging the binary oppositions that structure how we think about girls, to embrace instead girlhood as ambivalent and contradictory; second, through resisting the digital and redeploying aesthetics of sparkle and luminosity. They thus offer a particularly subtle reading of girl culture, as the insights of theorists Sarah Projansky, Angela McRobbie and Mary Celeste Kearney show how digital culture, mutability, luminosity and sparkle are key to how we understand contemporary girlhood.

Projansky argues that media fascination with girlhood builds on both the accessibility and immediacy of digital culture and the intensification of a culture of celebrity that attracts through spectacle and sparkle. Although the concept of celebrity is certainly not new (a point eloquently made by Coppola in *Marie Antoinette*) what has changed is the sheer accessibility and ubiquity of the celebrity, now operating in the ever increasing vastness of a mediascape where images circulate freely, repetitively and non-sequentially. Given that the media's fascination with celebrity and girls is intensifying at the same time, and that both figures mobilise concern with contemporary neoliberal lifestyles and their emphasis on the individual and questions of identity, then girls (all girls) function in some ways as celebrities, and girlhood is essential to understanding celebrity culture. Projansky fleshes out this argument by describing a process she terms 'the spectacularization of girlhood in turn-of-the-twenty-first century media culture.' By invoking the term spectacle, she means several things. First, girls are construed as objects of the media gaze and on display in film, television, on the internet, in magazines and so on. Second, some of these media girls are spectacular, as in fabulous: exemplars of the energetic, compliant girl identified by Harris. Third, some of these media girls are scandals as 'media wait with bated breath – paparazzi seek out and produce – the moment of a celebrity girl's fall.'[33] These ambivalent representations combine fascination and derision, pulling together girlphilia and girlphobia, and are used to frame possibilities and constraints not just for the high-profile celebrities, but all girls, everywhere. Spectacle and celebrity are not synonymous for Projansky; rather she explains that spectacularization is a 'discursive and economic strategy of turn of the twenty-first century celebrity culture easily applied to girls.'[34] She concludes that

> to say that media spectacularizes girls in celebrity culture is to emphasize the intense publicness of contemporary girlhood: the way in which girls are readily available to us, similar to the way every aspect of a celebrity's life is fair game for discussion, evaluation and consumption [...] Analysis of the spectacularization of girls can help us better understand how both celebrity culture and public girlhoods function.[35]

Angela McRobbie's work on girlhood offers further insights into the surveillance and disciplinary techniques that characterise modern girlhood and its formation within a celebrity-focused, highly visual and increasingly digital media culture. According to McRobbie, gender equality has been mainstreamed, in particular in terms of education and employment, so that girls are exhorted to be newly visible beneficiaries of an ostensibly egalitarian meritocracy.[36] If in the 1990s girlpower suggested girls *could* be active, in the post girlpower period of the 2000–2010s, they are now *expected/demanded* to be fully actualised, highly successful agentic subjects, able to benefit from all the opportunities allegedly offered to them, and held personally responsible for any failures to live up to these expectations. Those who succeed in this task are labelled 'top girls' by McRobbie, and what was once a feminist discourse of collective female endeavour for empowerment and success becomes co-opted by neoliberal values of individual achievement and aspiration. These girls are the bearers of what McRobbie, borrowing Gilles Deleuze's terminology, labels ' postfeminist luminosities': a kind of diffuse power which spreads rays of light across the bodies of young women. They are placed under a theatrical spotlight which highlights their visibility and movement, producing new 'technologies of the self': a self endowed with seemingly limitless capacity, but rendered visible/legible within the paradoxically narrow confines of a carefully delineated 'feminine citizenship'. Postfeminist luminosities are defined as 'clouds of light [...]

which give young women a shimmering presence' and that soften these disciplinary logics and their regulation of young women's lives.[37]

Mary Celeste Kearney enriches and extends McRobbie's concept of postfeminist luminosity and makes important conceptual links between her account of luminous girlhood, the celebrity culture discussed by Projansky, and girl media culture. While McRobbie is using luminosity as a metaphor to discuss the macro power structures that shape youthful femininity, Kearney argues that 'early twenty-first century American girls' media are *literally* luminous in their bedazzling, spectacular displays of girlhood.'[38] Kearney asserts that 'sparkle is so ubiquitous in mainstream girls' culture – and so absent in boys' – it vies with pink as the primary signifier of youthful femininity [...] girls' visual landscape [...] is now dominated by sparkly brilliance.'[39] She traces the ways in which sparkle has become this ubiquitous in girl culture, from fashion and cosmetics, often modelled by glamorous, dazzling celebrities, to glitter on previously ungendered objects such as plasters and pencil cases. The most significant site for sparkly glamour associated with celebrities and influencing girls' fashions and accessories, are the media industries. She goes onto comment that 'sparkle has increasingly saturated girl-influenced media, including animated movies, like *Frozen*, tweenpics, like *High School Musical*, TV dramas, like *Gossip Girl*, and even independent films featuring marginalized youth, like *Pariah*.'[40] Kearney thus undertakes what she calls a 'taxonomy of sparkle', arguing that sparkle is a particular feature of post girl-power texts and that sparkle's semiotic and discursive power is increasing. First, there is the association of sparkle with magic and the supernatural, that stretches back to earlier girl texts that are still in circulation globally, such as Dorothy's sparkling red shoes that can transport her from Oz to Kansas, or Cinderella's shimmering gown and gleaming glass slippers provided by a fairy godmother. The second form of sparkle is environmental, associated with stars, candles and lights, often used to invoke romance, but also possibly friendship (as in *Frozen*'s depiction of Anna and Elsa). The third form is adornment via sparkly make-up and costume: the above examples could all contribute to this third category, which also encompasses figures such as *The Hunger Games'* Katniss Everdeen, 'the girl on fire', or Disney's *Hannah Montana*.

It is not surprising then that in her consideration of girlhood as feeling, that when Monica Swindle lists a variety of signs, symbols and objects of girlhood, the first two items on her list are pink and glitter.[41] They form part of a distinct girls' culture that did not exist until girlhood came to be perceived as a period distinct from that of adulthood, with its own unique subjectivity of age and gender. Established in the eighteenth century, girlhood has burgeoned in the twentieth and twenty-first centuries and now circulates through objects and items that are designated by girls themselves and marketed at them by adult producers. As Swindle goes onto explain, the significance of these objects is frequently commented on through how they position girls as consumers, but objects are not merely commodities: they also have powers to inspire, console, revitalise or even transform their owners. The privileged objects of girlhood – trainers covered in pink glitter; sparkly dresses; hairbands and nail polish and stickers and *Frozen* wands, and so on – circulate girldom, modulating affect and provoking affective states. Swindle suggests that while many objects simply cir-culate without impacting on our understanding of girl, others become 'sticky' with affect and communicate a feeling of girlhood (even to bodies we may not associate with girlhood, such as boys and adults, so that a boy playing with Barbie is somehow transgressive, or an adult woman buys a Hello Kitty T-shirt in order to feel youthful). Girls are encouraged to believe that these objects and their associated aesthetics of shimmer, sparkle and pinkness will provide intense fun, joy and happiness, so that girlhood itself becomes constructed as a time of uncomplicated pleasures. Swindle goes onto comment that while indi-vidual girls will of course vary in their responses to these items, as will boys and adults, these differences are culturally and socially managed. Girls who fail to find pleasure in these 'happy objects' are 'affect aliens', out of line with the affec-tive community of girlhood. She also intriguingly suggests that while girlhood is culturally constructed as a time of freedom and joy, partially obtained at least through its proliferation of 'happy objects', female adolescence is a time when girls are encouraged to leave these behind and take up the objects of woman-hood, such as boyfriends, beauty, sex, career and family, which are meant to be pleasurable but all too often aren't, leaving women as affect aliens too.

Kearney pursues the question of happiness in girlishness at the conclusion of her article on sparkle. She argues sparkle should not be seen simply as a way of luring naïve girls into finding pleasure in the neoliberal disciplinary techniques that govern their lives, but also as a knowing performance of girlishness that self-consciously plays with its own codification. We can resist the moral panic associ-ated with girls' bodily displays, and interpret them instead as affective exploration and potential resistance. Dress-up games can be understood as a rich site of campy performance, navigating the gendered and social self, and girlhood's interest in sparkle links here to queer's love of glamour and light.

In Coppola's films, we can trace an investigation of girlhood which builds on the insights of the girlhood theorists discussed above. Coppola's cinema per-forms the kind of critical project that Kearney senses is possible. Rather than rejecting the aesthetics and tastes of femininity, all too often dismissed as vapid, shallow, or tasteless, Coppola embraces the prettiness of pink and the delights of shimmer and sparkle, revelling in a self-consciously pretty performance of girlhood (Coppola says that a friend's teenage daughter greeted the more deliberately strident colour scheme of *The Bling Ring* with disappointment as 'it doesn't look pretty like your other work').[42]

Coppola's girls are luminous in both McRobbie and Kearney's uses of the term. This creates a complex refraction of dominant ideas about girlhood in the culture and academic analysis of them, to the extent that we can see a philosophy of girlhood luminosities emerging in her films as they engage with light: light as spectacle and sparkle; light as cinematic quality; light as blinding. Through both the content and the form of her films, Coppola works through issues of girlhood as dazzling or luminous spectacle. She turns frequently to issues of girlhood and celebrity, demonstrating the match between the two that Projansky suggests undergirds much of contemporary media culture and providing us a way to think through some of the repercussions of Projansky's argument. Coppola's films offer us the spectacle of girlhood in all three ways Projansky identifies: she shows us iconic images of girls; she shows us girls being fabulous; she shows us girls in crisis.

Through the range of girls she shows us, Coppola rejects the binary constructions of girlhood that bedevil contemporary cultural texts. Anita Harris identifies the 'at-risk' girl and her equivalent 'the can-do' girl;[43] Gonick examines the competing narratives of girl-power and what she labels 'Reviving Ophelia' stories.[44] On the one hand, the 'girl-power' discourse positions girls as agents: assertive, dynamic, and unrestrained by traditional feminine expectations. On the other, 'Reviving Ophelia', named for a book written by US psychologist Mary Pipher, represents a 'new girl': vulnerable, voiceless, fragile. Gonick sets out to demonstrate that although these two narratives appear entirely contradictory, they are in fact mutually reinforcing and work together to help produce the discursive contours of contemporary neoliberal girlhood. Both discourses emphasise young female subjectivities as projects that can be shaped by individuals rather than as social collectivities, encouraging young women to work on themselves either through empowering statements of possibility and freedom, or through providing a series of remedies to their Ophelia crisis. Gonick thus concludes that 'girls are simultaneously recognised as the potential idealized autonomous neoliberal subject even as they are also always already at risk of failing to secure the position.'[45] Coppola's films mobilise both the 'girl-power' and the 'Reviving Ophelia' discourses, as she shows us girls as active, empowered subjects and as vulnerable and precarious victims. Rather than offering us girlhood as needing to fall on either side of this binary divide, however, Coppola offers us more nuanced portraits that, in accordance with Gonick's critical reading of girl culture, demonstrate the interdependence of spectacle and crisis, agency and victimhood, light and opacity, in the shaping of contemporary accounts of girlhood. She presents and merges the two anti-thetical poles of girlhood, offering more complex representations than those that dominate Western postfeminist cinematic cultures. She constructs and promotes an image of psychologically intricate young women with a sense of agency. They do not sacrifice their girlish femininity in order to acquire this agency; nor however, do the girlish pleasures they indulge necessarily fulfil all their desires. Consequently, Coppola's girls offer an unusual perspective on cinematic girlhood, unashamedly and unabashedly *feminine* girls who nevertheless strike a *feminist* position in their re-appropriation of girlhood iconography and its relation to aesthetics of light.

The Ambivalence of Girlhood Objects

Coppola's films showcase the aesthetics and objects of girlhood. She treads a fine line which operates along the sensitive issue of girl audiences. Is girl culture acquiescing to mass production or in rebellion against it? Coppola doesn't seem to come down on one side or the other of this divide, maintaining rather a position of cool ambivalence toward the desirable objects of girl culture.

Coppola's films frequently use shades of pastel and pink or glittering luminosity as part of their palette, allowing what Jacki Willson suggestively labels 'the potential for glitter to be flexible' (I discuss Willson's perspective on Coppola in more detail in Chapter 4 on fashion).[46] What Swindle's work on girlhood and Kearney's comments on sparkle demonstrate is that aesthetics are also emotions; that pink and glitter help to create the emotion of 'girl', circulating its paradoxical qualities of happiness, joy, and alienation. I am using the term objects here in the expansive way the concept is discussed by Swindle, where 'objects of girlhood' include both such items as plastic jewellery, stickers, and dolls, but also supposedly neutral objects coloured pink or that sparkle, and also the emotions that they are designed to evoke – make-believe, happiness, and giggles. Coppola's attentiveness to objects is of a piece with her interest in texture, mood, and tone. Objects, aesthetics and emotions are intertwined in Coppola's films, echoing Swindle's belief that they are also all bound together in girl culture. Where her films deviate from the dominant discourse concerning these objects and their roles in girls' lives is that Coppola demonstrates their ambivalence. She does not deny their appeal, and indeed makes commercials that play on their deep-rooted allure. At the same time, she suggests their inadequacies and short-comings in any kind of redressing of patriarchal injustices. This is what makes Coppola's films so intriguing and to my mind so useful. She does not criticise girls for being drawn to pink and glitter, rejecting the kind of moral panic that characterises some popular feminist writing about girlhood. Rather, she aligns herself more with the kind of analysis offered by Barbara Risman: 'much doing gender at the individual and interactional levels gives pleasure as well as reproduces inequality, and until we find other socially acceptable means to replace that pleasure, we can hardly advocate for its cessation.'[47] At the same time, she demonstrates the flaws in a system that holds girls responsible for their own happiness while only offering limited and somewhat facile opportunities for its articulation.

As girls and women are socialised to respond to their own failure to respond to what should make them happy with self-doubt rather than anger, they assume the lack comes from within and slump into apathy, anomie, or despair. Possibly one of the most poignant images of girlhood in Coppola's filmography and that summarises this line of argument is from *The Virgin Suicides*. Following Cecilia's return home from hospital after her suicide attempt, Mr Lisbon/James Woods persuades his wife to allow the girls to throw a party. While the other girls get ready for the party, brushing their hair and applying lipstick, oldest sister Therese/Leslie Hayman uses sellotape to strap brightly-coloured chunky plastic bangles and bracelets over the bandages on Cecilia's wrists (see Fig 2.5). 'There, is that ok?' she solicitously checks, before leaving the room to get dressed up herself. The contrast between

Fig. 2.5. Therese covers Cecilia's bandages with bracelets

the seriousness of Cecilia's depression and the banality of the bracelets is all too striking.

We can extend the reading of this image further if we turn to Anna Backman Rogers' discussion of *The Virgin Suicides* as a film that represses the 'messy' corporeality of adolescent femininity; specifically menstrual blood, the signifier of the passage toward womanhood, is visually denied or disavowed throughout the film.[48] With its carefully reconstructed 1970s period setting and strict bigoted religious mother, *The Virgin Suicides* evokes Brian de Palma's classic 1970s horror *Carrie*, as both Backman Rogers and Olivier Davenas point out.[49] In this film, menstrual blood signals Carrie/Sissy Spacek's burgeoning sexuality that is repressed by her mother, played as quasi-demonic by Piper Laurie. Carrie's period arriving while she is having a shower after PE confirms her failure to follow the rules of normal girlhood at her high school where periods are hidden and managed through the discreet use of tampons and sanitary towels, as urged by advertisements (where of course blood is also a light blue liquid). The bullying Carrie suffers as a result reaches its apogee at the high school prom, where she has a bucket of pig blood poured over her white dress.

Coppola's high school prom in contrast is an idealised ritual, at which Lux and Trip Fontaine/Josh Hartnett are crowned homecoming king and queen. The mise-en-scene evokes the kind of 'happy objects' of girlhood I discuss above: twinkling lights; stars painted with glitter; blue and white balloons; the silvery plastic tiara Lux wears when she is crowned homecoming queen. The prom culminates in the other Lisbon girls, Bonnie/Chelse Swain, Mary/A.J.Cook and Therese, dancing with their partners, twirling joyfully, discovering a hedonistic delight in bodily movement soon to be curtailed for ever, the immobility of their imprisonment anticipating the stillness of death. Meanwhile, Lux is persuaded by Trip to make her way to the football field. (In a really nicely observed insight into Trip's character and a possibly unheeded warning to Lux about his behaviour, he dodges having the crown placed on his head by the teacher, and never wears it, simply clasping it by his side: he is far too concerned with maintaining his air of cool to form the picture-perfect coupling Lux has already imagined – I doubt *she* noticed he doesn't wear the crown. The slight shift of his head from the teacher occurs in long shot, so that we too could easily miss it). Coppola drew inspiration from the photographic series *Suburbia* by Bill Owens. Owens, staff photographer on the *Livermore Independent* newspaper, attentively chronicled the daily lives of the inhabitants of a newly built housing estate in the Livermore Amadore Valley not far from Los Angeles. Coppola cites in particular a photograph of some kids at a high school dance surrounded by tinfoil stars as a look she wanted to replicate in her homecoming scene.[50] The narrative tension – that something might go hor-ribly wrong, as we will know from the implicit reference to *Carrie* – is displaced. Rather than having blood pouring down over her pretty white dress, Lux's vio-lation of correct feminine behaviour is her decision to accompany Trip to the football field and break her curfew. What exactly happens on the football field is never revealed. We cut from Lux and Trip walking under the fluorescent light to a close-up on a car dashboard clock showing the time as quarter to 11 and a boy's voice saying 'maybe they went home with your Dad'. We cut back from the car to a close-up on Trip lying on top of Lux, his breathing loud and heavy. The cam-era tracks up them, and they are lit up by a car headlight. Lux seems to struggle against Trip, pushing up against his body with her hands: Backman Rogers sug-gests the scene implies he raped her. We cut after only 11 seconds back to the car and Bonnie asking if anyone has any mints, a desperate attempt to hide the fact she drank peach schnapps at the prom but also perhaps a metaphor for her sud-den need to cover up what is happening to Lux and keep everything pretty, white and *fresh*.

The shot of Cecilia in a bathtub of bloody water is the only time that blood is visualised in the film, despite the presence of 5 adolescent girls (and Lux's loss of virginity/rape). The inevitability of their periods is signalled when Peter Sisten/ Chris Hale, invited for dinner as a reward for having helped Mr. Lisbon install a model of the solar system in his school classroom, goes to the upstairs bathroom in the Lisbon family home. He explores the girls' bathroom, fascinated by the accou-trements of adolescent girlhood and indulging in a sensory reverie as he sprays perfume or glides his finger over bottles of pink nail varnish, the otherworldly nature of his experience heightened by the extra-diegetic music playing. He opens a large cupboard and is confronted by stacked boxes of tampons; the camera stops its slow glide and we have a cropped close-up on them neatly arranged into rows. (see Fig 2.6). He returns to the sink and picks up a red lipstick, bringing it up to his nose and closing his eyes. The camera moves into close-up on his face and behind him the walls dissolve to allow a sunlit image of Lux to occupy the back-ground, as if this vision of luminous girlhood is conjured up from the smell of the lipstick. We then move to a close-up on this vision, Lux's face glowing golden against the sunset, her eyes half shut, her head tossed back as if in some kind of (sexual?) ecstasy. The redness of the lipstick subliminally suggests the red of the blood the tampons soak up, disavowed into a romanticised image of girlhood and light. The music and the image abruptly stop with a knock on the door, and we cut back to Peter in the bathroom rather bathetically holding the lipstick. 'I thought you died in there', says Lux. She walks past Peter to the cupboard containing the

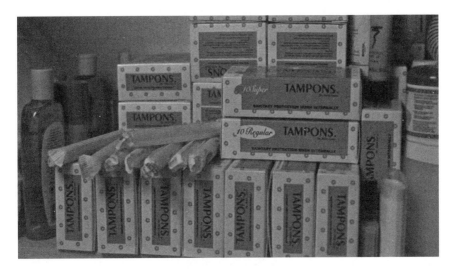

Fig. 2.6. The tampons in the Lisbon girls' bathroom cupboard

tampons. He still hovers. 'Do you mind?' she asks, reaching for the tampon. At this replacement of his vision of feminine sexuality compared to its (literally) bloody reality, Peter, overcome with embarrassment, runs away from the house. The only blood we see is the blood from Cecilia's veins, and the mere possibility that this may stain the white bandages is covered up by the sellotaped baubles and bracelets. The paraphernalia of girlhood thus both offers Cecilia compensation for, or even protection from, entering into womanhood – the baubles covering up the (disavowed) menstrual blood. At the same time, the inadequacy of 'happy objects' to the task of covering up the pains, injustices and restrictions of girlhood is made only too manifest.

Cecilia could be seen here as clinging onto girlhood, cleaving to its objects as a way of avoiding womanhood. It is in the 'putting away of girlish things' that girls become/are made women, but that given that these objects are associated with happiness, it is not surprising that chronologically adult women continue to wear pink, put glitter on their nails, and that when they gather together in homosocial groups, refer to themselves as 'girls together'. Girlhood is a place of fantasy, experimentation, evasion, and transcendence, standing not temporally before womanhood, but rather alongside it. In the case of *Lost in Translation*, we see Charlotte expose the performative element of these 'happy objects' as she tries them on, plays with them, but ultimately rejects them as an answer to her existential crisis. As Lucy Bolton explains, for the majority of the film, Charlotte breaks with a sexualised representation of femininity, dressing in neutral, non figure-hugging clothing, avoiding make-up and wearing her hair loose and natural.[51] This takes on a particular resonance within the context of the usual construction of cinematic femininity, especially that of the star image of Scarlett Johansson, who is known for her curvaceous form and who mimics the iconic sexy female star Marilyn Monroe. Indeed, Bolton reads the opening of *Lost in Translation* as a knowing reworking of the classic introduction of the sexy female star that helps the film destabilise stereotyped ideas about women. The initial sighting of Johansson's buttocks is reminiscent of many similar body-shots on screen, such as that which opens *Pretty Woman* (Marshall, 1990). We see an image in close-up of a young woman's back, bottom and legs. She is wearing see-through pink panties. She shifts her body slightly, drawing attention to her hips and legs. She is positioned as the object of our gaze, unaware of our presence and thus able to be indulged in as voyeuristic spectacle. However, two things interrupt the spectacle. First, the alluring pink pants are teamed up with a more prosaic and functional grey jumper, associating this young woman's state of undress more with ease and comfort in the privacy of a hotel room than a sexual image. Second, the image is overlaid with the title, 'Lost in Translation', signalling that 'the usual meanings of on-screen femininity may be effectively "lost" in their translation to a new filmic mode that foregrounds female subjectivity.' (see Fig 2.7). If the opening subtly undermines the meaning of Charlotte's pink pants, Coppola builds on this reworking through the film. The next highly girlish object we see Charlotte wear is a pink wig she dons in the karaoke box. Bolton reads this as an example of girlish masquerade, as

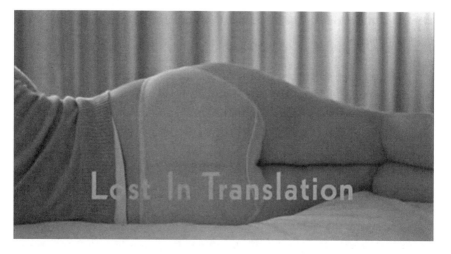

Fig. 2.7. *Lost in Translation* credit sequence

Charlotte self-consciously performs The Pretenders' 'Brass in Pocket'. In contrast to her usual self-contained and rather quiet demeanour, here she flirts, making lots of eye contact with Bob and entreating him to join in with her on the lines, 'I'm special, so special.' As Bolton explains, 'in a parody of showgirl performance [...] the artificiality of the scene is heightened not only by the unrealistic fancy-dress wig, but also by incongruity of the song's words and movements with respect to Charlotte's character and Johansson's previously understated performance.'[52] The pink pants and wig signal one set of meanings about objects and the girl. While they usually work to show us that she is sexy and fun, using the strategies of defamiliarisation and masquerade allows Coppola to rob these objects of any inherent natural associations with happiness. While they provide a momentary relief for Charlotte, they do not sustain any kind of solution to her feelings of 'stuckness'. Indeed, in the next scene, Coppola shows us Charlotte, still wearing the pink wig, silently smoking a cigarette outside the karaoke box, demonstrating the contrast of Charlotte's mannered and provocative performance against her more usual dour and reserved self-presentation and the limited ability of a pink wig to secure happiness.

The idea that girlhood 'happy objects' allow women access to respite has a strong appeal however, positing the position of girl itself as one of nostalgic appeal, a site of yearning and longing. However highly problematic it may be, as girl-culture trains female-identified subjects to associate powerlessness with relief and pleasure rather than anger and frustration, simply dismissing its pleasures avoids acknowledging and working through their strong affective pull and appeal, for many people, not just young female-identified children. Indeed, to my mind the most powerful evocation of girl culture as delightful escape in captured in the 'day off' Johnny spends with Cleo hanging out at the pool at Chateau Marmont in *Somewhere*. They dive together into the swimming pool in order to share an imaginary tea-party, and Johnny is the most animated and active we have seen him, his face breaking into a broad smile. He swaps his whisky, beer and cigarettes for lemonade drunk through a straw; he chats about the convoluted plot of *Twilight*; he plays table-tennis. The day stands out as special and fulfilling as Cleo lets Johnny feel the affective delight of girl culture and its happy objects. In this film, Projansky's alignment of girlhood and celebrity finds an intriguing crystallisation, as both Cleo and Johnny are buffeted by other people's plans and agendas. It is however Cleo who is able to carve out a sense of identity and self through her investment in the pleasures of privileged girlhood (ice-skating, petting puppies, ice-cream, imaginary tea-parties, *Twilight*): the strikingly parallel pleasures of privileged celebrity (pole dancing, one night-stands, beer, whisky, hotel room parties) in contrast seem to only reinforce Johnny's sense of emptiness, that he is somewhat less than a person.

The appeal of girlhood and its happy objects is particularly pertinent to the relationship between fashion designer Marc Jacobs and Coppola, whom he casts as his muse. Coppola is the fantasy figure of the eternal girl. Jacobs designs his clothes to look slightly geeky and awkward, with school uniform type colours and materials (pussy-bow blouses, navy gabardine, swathes of velvet, high neck dresses, shrunken cashmere jumpers) rather than the bombastic and highly sexualised look of much haute couture (still stunning of course to those 'in the know').[53] Coppola modelled for his 2001 perfume campaign photographed by Juergen Teller. Naked from the waist up and coyly draped over outsize perfume bottles, her topless pose makes her seem like a young prepubescent girl and the scale of the bottle recalls Alice in Wonderland. The association between Coppola and Jacobs continues. He recently (June 2015) 'leaked' an extraordinary photo of her modelling clothes from his 2015–16 Fall/Winter collection on his Instagram account. Taken as a profile shot, the pose accentuates her slightly crooked nose and strong features. Dressed in a swirling grey cloak, her dark hair slicked back, her eye-lids heavily coated in silver and black eye-shadow, and her hands resting on a black-and-white handbag, she looks more like Cruella de Vil than a naïve girl, a noticeable departure from the soft pinks, navy and whites she usually favours.[54]

She also directed the television advertising campaign for his 'Daisy' range in Spring 2014.[55] The final advertisements are clearly indebted to 1970s commercials, featuring bucolic images of adolescent girls in long white dresses, their hair long and loose, gambolling in meadows, grasses, rivers and fields. The 'Daisy' advert features a girl running through a meadow of grass and flowers before tumbling to the floor. The direct visual source for the image of a girl lying on the ground framed from overhead by the camera is a shot of Marcia Hare by William Eggleston from 1975; this was also a reference Coppola explored in *The Virgin Suicides* so now there is a reference to her own film work too.[56] The spot promoting all three variants on the perfume features four girls, all clothed in white, wearing daisy-chains in their hair, smelling bouquets of daisies, and plucking daisy petals from the centre of the flower. Overall, the collaboration with Marc Jacobs sidelines the more difficult and abject relations girls can have with their happy objects; while clearly there is a strong commercial imperative at work, the collaboration also allows Coppola to indulge in girlhood as a site of play, fantasy, dressing-up, and acting out. Indeed, we could argue that precisely the strong commercial factors at work, such as the incredible success of the 'Daisy' perfume range (according to the *Wall Street Journal*, sales of the 'Daisy' fragrance tripled sales in the Marc Jacobs fragrance business),[57] point to the power of the 'girl' consumer: that is to say, not just the under-18 year old female, but anyone who purchases something in order to 'feel like a girl'. Perfume is a product perfectly suited to expressing emotions of girlhood: ineffable, transient, a luxury rather than a necessity and thus a symbol also of consumerist excess.

Perfume's associations with the glamour of cinema and celebrity date back to the late 1950s and Audrey Hepburn's marketing of Givenchy's perfume range, building on their fashion designer-muse relation.[58] Perfume is part of a globalised commodity market place, responsible for the vast majority of the profits of couture brands (although a 'luxury' product, the perfume is a lot more affordable and accessible than the clothes). The female film stars and models are constructed as feminine ideals through their use of this commodity and simultaneously construct themselves as commodities, selling their image alongside the perfume. Yet this commodification is idealised and sold back to women as some kind of crystallisation of an ineffable femininity. Coppola's advert is typical here, as its evocation of a summer's day enjoying paddling in the river, lazing in a hammock, and making daisy chains evokes a set of ephemeral pleasures free of the taint of commodification. Coppola's ethereal advert and its linking of a relatively expensive perfume to the innocent and free pleasures of running through fields and making daisy chains may on one level seem disingenuous, and I wouldn't wish to argue totally against this perspective. However, it also pays serious attention to the joys of girlhood, and crystallises an abstract idea of freedom and happiness that is accessible through the activities that girls indulge in. While the intended viewer of the advertisement, and the probable purchaser of the perfume, is an adult, the girlish aesthetic circulates the positive and pleasurable affect, girl. The commercial is very slight – the 'Daisy' advert lasts just 22 seconds, and the 'Daisy Trio' advert just 31, and the only voiceover simply says 'Daisy: Marc Jacobs' – prompting the generally adoring Fashionista.com to rather caustically say it hopes the next advert has 'a bit more to it than the last one'.[59] This slightness however merges with a general trend in which marketing and media have become less about 'representation and the narrative construction of subject identities' than 'affecting bodies directly',[60] for after all, 'affect goes through bodies and not only through minds'.[61] The pleasure and other positive affects now associated with the figure of the girl as well as the attention it now gathers are used in an attempt to associate these feelings with Jacobs' perfume. It would be too much to argue that the deployment of an aesthetic that deliberately recalls and references *The Virgin Suicides* allows us to detect any critical edge in the advertisements themselves. However, it demonstrates the affective pull of girlhood, and the paradox of how Coppola's engaged and intricate work on girls is ready to be commercially exploited, given the powerful appeal of the girlhood aesthetic she has created.

In this exploration of the ambivalence of the object, Coppola's work across the differently-oriented sectors of American Indiewood films and perfume commercials nevertheless picks up on a major enduring theme of youth culture, which is its role as a site of tension between ideas of resistance and conformity. As Driscoll explains, the rise of mass culture in the twentieth century was accompanied by concerns that the singular taste of the cultured individual was being eroded, and furthermore, girls were routinely deployed as figures of late modern conformity, a deployment often evident in feminism and feminist cultural studies.[62] The high modernist version of this cultural criticism is associated especially with the Frankfurt School writers such as Theodor Adorno and Siegfried Kracauer. Adorno argued that mass-produced culture, such as popular cinema or music, no longer presented the highest possibilities for human improvement, but rather a *distraction* encouraging individuals to live compliantly within their social contexts. Kracauer's much-cited essay, 'The Cult of Distraction' positioned girls as the most ambivalent points of contact between the self and ideology through mass culture. Kracauer infamously narrated popular cinema through 'little shopgirls', identifying the audience for popular film as dangerously impressionable, immature and girlish. As Driscoll explains, 'this figuration does not rely on assessments of who bought tickets but theorises how a film audience works, within and outside film industries, describing processes of participation, capture and identification evident in theories of feminine adolescence at the same time.'[63] A conception of the audience as vulnerable was particularly pinned on impressionable girls, exemplary dupes of the culture industries, but this did not lead to an equal emphasis on girls in later studies of the resistance possible in relation to popular culture. Rather, anxiety about girl consumption, and a distinction between active (adult/ masculine) connoisseurship and (young/feminine) passive malleable consumers with poor taste persists.

Coppola complicates these questions of taste through exploring low-brow aspects of contemporary girl culture such as its love of trinkets and its obsession with celebrity in the relatively high-art form of the 'Indiewood' movie, whose production contexts I discussed in more detail in chapter 1. There is an aesthetic politics simply in airing these girlish pleasures in this form, and wanting to take teenage girls seriously. Indeed, Coppola mentions this as a motivation for her dogged pursuit of the rights for *The Virgin Suicides*, for as the now legendary tale goes, when Coppola first adapted the book into a screenplay after having become fascinated by it, the rights were unavailable and she undertook the task as an experiment. At a Q&A at the 2013 First Time Fest screening held in New York, Coppola explained that 'I felt that a lot of teen movies didn't really speak to me, that they always casted much older people and I just didn't feel like they were respectful of teenagers, so wanted to make something beautiful and sensitive (I hoped) for teenagers.'[64] This is a sentiment she expressed in an interview in 2000 with *Les Inrockuptibles*, explaining that:

> The distribution of the film is important to me. I want the film to be accessible to young people. I think that young people have got more sophisticated taste and are more intelligent than we're lead to believe. They deserve better than films like *American Pie*, like junk food. I even think that when you're young you ask loads of questions and you get lazy as you get older. The film was banned for under 18s in the US. In my country, youth suicide is a taboo whereas I think the fact we don't talk about it is part of the problem.[65]

That the film succeeds in offering teen girls the compliment of taking them seriously is supported by the considerable internet presence the film has some sixteen years after its release and its promotion on the Rookie website, aimed at teen girls. In an interview with the site, Coppola thanks them for helping encouraging an enduring teen audience for the film. She then explains her aesthetic choices for *The Bling Ring* in a similar way:

> You know, I loved John Hughes's movies, and I connected to those movies. But a lot of the movies that were made for teenagers were really, um, dorky and unsophisticated. And I feel like kids are more sophisticated and thoughtful than the [movie] studios give them credit for. I remember them worrying about *The Virgin Suicides*, like, girls are going to see it and they'll kill themselves. They didn't understand that teenagers are…it's a time when you're just focused on thinking about things, you're not distracted by your career, family, you know – it's a thoughtful time. There's a tradition that I love, movies like *Over the Edge* and *Foxes* – which I was thinking about when I made this movie – that had a real spirit and felt real and authentic to that age. Or *Rumble Fish*, my dad's movie that was like a teenage art film. I like that you can make a teen movie that has beautiful photography and try to approach it in an artful way. I feel like that's not that common.[66]

Part of the difficulty in interpreting whether Coppola's films approve or not of the objects of girl culture comes from their complex positioning in terms of taste politics. As Coppola's comments reveal, the idea of a girl teen audience being catered to within an art-house aesthetic is unusual. She wants her films to speak to an adolescent audience, but because she is positioned as an auteur her films are rarely read as teen films (as Driscoll notes, 'in teen film it is unusual to talk about the success or even the style of directing, and avant-gardism is consequently almost never an issue').[67] Furthermore, Coppola herself is associated with exquisite taste. The fashion press praise her for her 'understated chic' or 'elegant discretion';[68] such association of Coppola with lightness, elegance and delicacy even influences the range of wines that bear her name from her father's vineyard, with the first red in the Sofia collection deliberately designed to evoke a lighter drinking experience described as 'sophisticated' and 'demure' in contrast to the heavy Napa cabernets more usually associated with Californian wine.[69] Coppola's unassuming and low-key attitude is continued in her films and their minimalist approach to narrative and slow pace other than *The Bling Ring* which was deliberately loud. She explains in an interview with Richard Prince, 'the movie I did before *Bling Ring* was really slow and quiet, so I was just in the mood to do something obnoxious and faster, and something kind of in bad taste. Because I feel like that's not something I get to exercise in my life usually. [laughs]'[70] The idea that *The Bling Ring* is consciously in bad taste, with its bright, garish, fluorescent colours and loud music, places it as the film that most deliberately challenges the high culture equation of girl consumption and acquiescence.[71] Indeed, the film positions 'shopping' as a way of resisting authority and rebelling against the classic institutions of the teen movie – school and family.

The Bling Ring begins in media res, showing us a burglary taking place in its pre-credit sequence. The establishing shot mimics the style of CCTV footage as it is a high-angle static shot, observing a group of teens jumping over a fence. The film then cuts to handheld camera work and we mingle with the group as they make their way toward the house, establishing the film's careful navigation between detached outside observation of the group's activities and fascinated insider involvement. As the characters enter the house via an unlocked door, we follow them in, with (an as yet unnamed) Rebecca at the front. She turns around, stopping the camera (and us) in our tracks, smiles and says 'let's go shopping', triggering the credit sequence and its montage of close-ups and tracking shots over rows of shoes, handbags, underwear and jewellery to the strident guitar hooks and dissonant feedback of Sleigh Bell's 'Crown in the Ground'. Rebecca is identified as the most powerful figure in the gang in this opening sequence, and it is her subjectivity and desires which motivate the camera's delighted perusal of goods as we (both characters and spectators) 'go shopping'. Here Coppola smashes any associations with passivity and acquies-cence, building on shopping's ambivalent theorisation within feminist cultural studies.

Shopping is a way in which women can look and desire and take ownership of a gaze long presumed to be the provenance of men. This was particularly the case with the invention of the department store in the late nineteenth century which caused a moral panic not unlike the one we associate with girlhood today. As Jackie Stacey notes, ' department stores, using new glass technology and electricity to create a space characterised by openness, light and visibil-ity with large expanses of display windows, became the new palaces of con-sumption offering women the pleasures of escape from dull domesticity.'[72] The display of commodities as spectacles, offering the female shopper pleasure in looking, contemplation and the fantasy transformation of herself and her sur-roundings through consumption prefigured similar pleasures to be gained in the cinema. Charles Eckert argues that the cinema functions as a shop window for the female spectator.[73] In this case, the consumption is entirely imaginary and the process of looking itself has become commodified. Eckert argues that Hollywood cinema acted as a showcase for fashions, accessories, cosmetics, furnishings and other manufactured items. Women, as the chief consumers, were the subjects of this address. The pleasurable gaze for women then is addressed as if predicated on looking as the precursor to buying, and buying as the precursor to transformation of the self. This would seem to give women agency and control, calling them up as a subject. However, Mary Ann Doane argues, the position of subject is an illusion, for the women constructs her-self as an idealised object through this very act of consumption. Thus Doane concludes:

> the feminine position has come to exemplify the roles of consumer and spectator in the embodiment of a curiously passive desiring subjectivity [...] In her desire to bring the things of the screen closer, to approxi-mate the bodily image of the star and to possess the space in which she dwells, the female spectator experiences the intensity of the image as lure and exemplifies the perception proper to the consumer. The cin-ematic image for the woman is both shop window and mirror, the one simply a means of access to the other.[74]

The Bling Ring simply break through the screen/the window/the mirror. For Doane, proximity to the star could be acquired through the purchase of goods, a way of satiating the desire 'to possess the space in which she dwells'. Now, the Bling Ring takes this logic of possession and proximity to its logical conclusion by temporarily occupying the home of and then taking the actual goods owned by the star. This is not resistance to consumer capitalism, or rebellion against the norms governing femininity. In the postfeminist project of transformation of the self, frequently represented in film via the makeover, *The Bling Ring* simply enacts a superior version, reflecting back neoliberal values of an active feminine self constantly pursuing self-improvement through fashion and cosmetics. The question remains what we are to make of this re-inscribing of the female consumer, and it is useful here to compare and contrast Rebecca's shopping/shoplifting trips to that of an exemplary figure for this female address of looking/desiring/shopping without any actual monetary exchange.

The figure is that of Holly Golightly in *Breakfast at Tiffany's* (Edwards, 1961) played by Audrey Hepburn, herself a fashion icon of striking longevity and appeal that has considerable traction in postfeminist culture as exemplary of transformation and makeover narratives and enduring feminine style.[75] In contrast to the static camera, silent soundtrack and dimly lit night-for-night shooting that begins *The Bling Ring*, *Breakfast at Tiffany's* opens with the swelling chords of Henry Mancini's 'Moon River' and we see a yellow cab drop off a Givenchy-clad Hepburn in the deserted dawn-streets of Manhattan and she stops to indulge in some 5am window shopping. The mise-en-scène of the famous breakfast scene that opens *Breakfast at Tiffany's* communicates glamour beloved of fashion and cosmetic advertising. A series of whimsical oppositions between Hepburn's long evening gown and the hour of the day, her cheap Danish and the expensive goods she covets, accompanied by 'Moon River', a hymn to drifters 'off to see the world', gives a wistful, adventurous feel to the pursuit of goods. As Hepburn stares into Tiffany's window, so the larger shop window of the cinema frames her, a window through which female spectators can glimpse an illustration of the feminine ideal. The scene showcases a certain brand of feminine independence in the glamour of her early morning solitude, suggesting why Hepburn's image feels so contemporary and images of her as Golightly circulate so visibly and frequently in popular culture. She achieves a postfeminist vision reconciling femininity and independence, desire and girlishness, beauty and freedom, offering an idealised image of how girls should shop.

Of course, Holly is famously tamed in *Breakfast at Tiffany's*. By the end of the film, she has been identified as child bride Lula Mae Barnes and her enigma resolved. Her crazy plan to escape to Brazil fails and she falls sobbing into the arms of Paul/George Peppard, while cuddling her wild cat, symbolically rescued from the gutter. For all it may appear glamorous, *Breakfast at Tiffany's* positions Holly's feminine independence as kooky and out-of-step with social norms, and the charming Holly is simply too nice to really get the better of the rats and super rats she tries to exploit. The only shop lifting undertaken in the film is during a day when Holly and Paul decide to 'do something they've never done before', and steal grotesque children's face masks of a cat and a dog from Carters five and dime store. The sequence is light and playful, underscored by Henry Mancini's jazz score, ironically titled 'The Big Heist'. In other words, Holly steals for a thrill rather than for the goods themselves, and it is after this expedition that the film confirms the formation of a romantic coupling. As James Breen comments, 'the scene [...] is handled with such lyrical closeness, and the New York backgrounds are photographed so prettily and with such affection, that there can be no doubt the two have fallen in love.'[76]

In the end, this light-hearted shoplifting rebellion will be undone by heterosexual romance and containment within male determined family roles, as the seemingly playful masks make all too clear. Lying in bed with Holly, Paul looks up at the masks, now both being worn by the bizarre and ostentatious antique statue that has been placed into his apartment by his older middle-aged female *patronne* (who in fact describes herself to Holly as Paul's 'interior decorator'). As he looks up at the masks, Paul comes to understand that he must leave behind the material/maternal comfort of his relationship with an older woman that has allowed him to pursue a child-like innocent friendship with Holly (she even nicknames him Fred after her brother). As Chantal Cornut-Gentille D'Arcy explains:

> The dog and cat masks add a Dickensian touch as carnivalesque mirrors – more authentic than reality itself in their caricaturing of real beings [...] As an antique, the statue symbolizes the long-standing, immutable establishment. The indisputably male dog mask in the place of the head exemplifies how it is man's duty to guard and protect the established order while it is his potential for selfless love and faithfulness that will ultimately tame the wild, independent and lovable cat.[77]

Rebecca smashes these poetic and wistful associations of femininity and shopping outside of the exchange of money. Instead, she claims 'shopping' as an active, hedonistic, delinquent pursuit. She doesn't stand longingly outside glass windows, but climbs through them. As she enters the house, we hear the dissonant noise pop 'Crown on the Ground.' Furthermore, Rebecca's love of 'shopping' is never renounced in favour of a romantic/sexual relationship. While Marc hopes that his infatuation with Rebecca will lead to a closer relation, he does not realise his ambition of taming her, unlike Paul/Fred in the earlier film. Rebecca's rebellion then is not so much *against* anything as it is a way of *conforming* to the neoliberal ideology of pursuit of the perfection of the self at all costs, and it renders only too visible the paradox where this aspect of ideal feminine identity is incompatible with the more conservative postfeminist emphasis on 'family values' and the sacrifice of female independence for a heterosexual relationship based on traditional gender roles. Even when sitting in the courtroom next to Marc, Rebecca offers no explanation or justification, and the film finishes with her leaving town and taking Lindsay Lohan's neon pink suitcase with her. Here, the objects of girlhood have been re-fashioned as props to support the Bling Ring as a rebellious sub-culture. The extent to which we can read resistance and acquiescence/conformity is troubled, hence the rather strange and distanced tone that the film has. It is not so much that the association of pink, glitter and girlish consumption with conformity is challenged, as the very *meaning* of that conformity is questioned. The girl is a self-fashioning subject via commodity acquisition, so she is conforming to the neoliberal paradigm of the flexible improvement of the self. The fact is this action, far from enacting any change within the social matrix, simply reflects back (some of) its values. Conformity rather than rebellion has become the act of delinquent youth and perhaps what makes *The Bling Ring* seem to be demonstrating so threatening a social phenomenon is that this concentration on the self overpowers any interest in connecting to others. Holly Golightly's contemporary popularity illustrates the social and political conservatism that marks much postfeminist culture, where pursuit of the ideal feminine self is accompanied by domestic retreatism, support for 'family values' and women renouncing the idea they could 'have it all' (i.e., a successful career and a family).[78] *The Bling Ring* prizes apart postfeminist culture's uneasy compromise, demonstrating how its rampant consumerist individualism is ultimately incompatible with its politics of females 'choosing' to sacrifice their independence for the good of patriarchal systems.

Rather than resistance, it might be more valuable to introduce Emma Renold and Jessica Ringrose's concept of rupture to help us understand the ambivalent nature of Coppola's girls, their use of happy objects and how they shimmer in and out of regulatory norms. Renold and Ringrose outline the need for this concept of rupture in relation to a society in which a 'heteronormative grid of intelligible genders continues to govern the production, representation and lived lives of girls [...] within neoliberal and allegedly depoliticized postfeminist times. In this can-do culture, girls and young women are represented as unambiguous success stories of late capitalist societies, where discourses of choice, freedom and autonomy coexist in a schizoid fantasy alongside proliferation of highly restrictive and regulatory discourses of hypersexualised femininity.'[79] Drawing on the work of Deleuze and Guattari, they argue that in these schizoid conditions it is futile to 'to search for a "molar" or total theory of revolutionary resistance, or grand revolutionary change.' Instead, they propose that a more useful approach is attentiveness to tracking the 'molecular flows and disruptions which signal moments of deterritorialisations, becomings, and lines of flight.'[80] Coppola's girls deterritorialise the 'happy objects' of girlhood. Strategies include unusual juxtapositions, such as bangles on bandages; defamiliarisation and masquerade, such as Charlotte's pink wig; performances of excess and frivolity; sharing with those not normally in their orbit, such as Cleo and Johnny; and of course, in the case of *The Bling Ring*, simply stealing them. While Coppola's films do not posit a feminist position of resistance, they are nevertheless attentive to the micro, molecular movements that characterise girls' complex negotiation of girlhood norms.

Revisiting Iconographies of Femininity

In an interview with *Les Inrockuptibles*, Coppola is asked about her decision to film *Somewhere* using the lenses that her Dad used for *Rumblefish*. She explains that 'my brother Roman had kept them and got them repaired for *Somewhere*. My Dad has always teased me about my determination to shoot on film, he's so into digital. My fetish for celluloid touches him.'[81]

Coppola's opposition to digital film is well documented. Given the time it was made, the decision to film *The Virgin Suicides* on 35 mm was not particularly controversial, although Coppola explains that her decision to let the cameras just roll while the girls were in the bedroom caused some anxiety as they did not have that big a budget for film stock. She concludes the anecdote by remarking 'this doesn't apply anymore', as one of the advantages of digital over celluloid is that stock is not an issue.[82] The relatively low budget of *Lost in Translation* meant that Coppola had to defend her decision to use 35 mm film and resist pressure to use digital. Given its fairly widespread use of location and on-street shooting, digital may have seemed a more logical choice, but Coppola wanted the more romanticised and distanced impression given by 35 mm stock.[83] The only Coppola film to be shot on digital is *The Bling Ring*. She was persuaded to use digital by her cinematographer, Harris Savides, who she explains she trusted totally, and the film was shot on the Red camera. She explains that 'it made sense to shoot it digitally', given how the film incorporates surveillance style footage and internet images (Facebook pages,

Google Earth, fashion and celebrity blogs). Digital belongs to the film's tabloid world, even if Savides's artistry, such as his ability to light the nightclubs so they dazzle against the beige of the surburbs, manages to 'make a beautiful look out of this world which isn't so beautiful.'[84]

Coppola's careful attention to issues of film stock and lenses may seem an individual quirk, nostalgia for the past of cinema that will have to be lost. However, we can also understand attention to the sculpting of light in her films as a part of a resistant aesthetic that creates and deploys sparkle in ways that work against its dominant role in girl culture. To help us understand how much the contemporary expression of girlhood relies on digital culture, it is useful to turn to the work of Heather Warren-Crow.[85] She starts her discussion of media, mutability and girlhood by discussing the figure of Alice in Wonderland. Thanks to Lewis Carroll's stories, the name 'Alice' functions as an iconic sign for the transformative powers of female adolescence, one that was taken up by Gilles Deleuze and Felix Guattari as a sign of the potential of adolescent endeavours and the mutability of the body. Whether Carroll intended for Alice's journey to be read literally or metaphorically, she brings together girlhood and movement and his story lent itself to early cinema with its own dual fascination with the figure of the child and the ability to represent movement and change in new ways: Vicky Lebeau comments that the story of Alice was made into film no fewer than six times in the first decade of cinema.[86] Alice brings together girlhood and visual culture and how they function as exemplars of change, movement and possibility. Furthermore, she resonates with contemporary cultures' demands of the adolescent female, as her ability to move hastily from situation to situation as the needs of her mutating body dictate links her to the neoliberal subject as self-crafting success, always ready to move on at a moment's notice. Warren-Crow brilliantly mobilises the variability and scaleability of Alice's body to read her as 'a protodigital figure who emerges at the intersection of notions of girlish transformation and certain filmic practices.'[87] For Warren-Crow, it is not just that many digitally produced images invoke girlishness and cuteness, though many do (think of the popularity of kittens on the internet); there is something inherently digital in our current apprehension of girlishness. She goes onto comment that 'if the objectification and to-be-looked-at-ness of women drives much of classical Hollywood cinematography, then the manipulability and to-be-sharedness of girls drives much of postphotography.'[88] With their changing physiques, unstable body images and variable identities, generated and exploited by a culture awash with digitally produced visual images that value youth and transformation as key narrative devices and marketing tools, girls crystallise the complexities and ambivalences of our cultural moment. As Warren-Crow so powerfully and astutely comments:

> As Alice and her fellow plastics can attest, girlphilia in media discourse does not usually lead to improvements in the lives of girls, and the labile, mobile, transmutational subject has been co-opted by the Girl Talk of neoliberalism and globalisation. The plastic image is riven by such irreconcilable differences. Bearing the attributes of openness (or vulnerability), connectivity (or dependence), and flexibility (or weakness) it has come to stand for what digital media can or can't offer us and what forms of selfhood are, aren't, or should be available [...] The most pressing question isn't whether girlish images peddle nothingness or no-thing ness, whether they are really the empty faces of American cultural imperialism or figures of resistance to objectification. More fundamental is how nothingess and its corollaries, openness and potentiality, have become attached to girls and images in the first place.[89]

Warren-Crow's argument is crucial in that it links together ambiguous and contradictory discourses that circulate in the mass-media concerning girlhood, agency, victimisation and power, and demonstrates that they are intimately connected to shift to a digital culture: form as well as content matters.

Coppola resists the use of digital in her films, using a variety of celluloid stock and retro lenses to recall and reference earlier ways of visualising girlhood. She draws our attention to the very materiality of film itself, breaking the voyeuristic spectacle and resisting the invisible manipulation of girl imagery inherent to the digital format. *The Virgin Suicides*, given its period setting, borrows from a variety of 1970s filmmakers and photographers for its look. Edward Lachman, the director of photography, cites Terence Malik's *Badlands* (1975) as an influence.[90] Coppola deliberately draws upon advertising campaigns from the 1970s, with Cynthia Fuchs noting in particular the influence of 'the Breck shampoo commercial girl', the 'sunlight creating sheer, pale yellow halos from behind her'.[91] Backman Rogers namechecks photographers Eggleston and Sam Haskins, and Davenas argues that the diaphanous images recall those of David Hamilton.[92] All three evoke a sense of girlhood as a time of innocence, but crucially Hamilton straddles the awkward line between soft pornography and art, signalling a more general anxiety about the capturing of childhood by the camera. In her discussion of childhood on film, Lebeau intriguingly suggests that the cinema wants something of the child. She suggests that there is a certain longing, a yearning, for the child 'at once gnostic and erotic' as a body that is somehow without sex, that does not know sex as such.[93] Yet, Lebeau explains, while we may have a cherished notion of childhood as a time apart, it is nevertheless, as Freud demonstrates, a time of sexuality. She continues: 'as an institution devoted to stimulating, to pleasuring, the eye, cinema is deeply embroiled in Freud's rethinking of the concepts of sexuality and child-hood […] cinema […] is very conscious of the forms of sexual looking it invites.'[94] The concept of adolescence of a time and space apart, a rite of passage, depends partially on the modern idea of a fundamental difference between childhood and adulthood, in which regulation of sex and sexual knowledge is key. Lebeau explains that the image-making apparatus itself becomes suspect in such a configuration, as it becomes hard to disentangle our gaze through the camera from a sexualising process, one that thus makes any image of a child suspect. The child – the idea of the child, and actual children – is at risk, sexual risk, from the eroticised commodi-fication of the image through the visual media: photography, cinema and now the internet. Coppola's film cleverly references the risks to the Lisbon girls through the aesthetic she uses; she then allows them to resist this risk through absenting them-selves from the image.

The opening sequence of the film anticipates how this will work, partially by turning this aesthetic of light and girlhood against itself. The opening images of *The Virgin Suicides* are idyllic and provocative, nostalgic and troubling, using light to establish and then undercut idealised girlhood. Accompanied by the hypnotic, dreamy notes of Air's electronic soundtrack and the distant wail of a siren, we see a sun-drenched medium close-up of fourteen-year-old Lux standing in the road and polishing off a bright red lollypop before she drifts out of frame, and we segue into images of a man watering his garden and women walking a dog in the quiet sub-urban street. The camera pans up to capture an image of sunlight filtering down through the leaves of trees, bathing the whole scene in a golden glow. The image offers a reassuring containment of girlhood within the safe, heteronormative con-fines of suburbia, suggesting that while some progress may have been made in terms of feminine access to the world (notably the man is the one attending to the domestic while the woman walks the street), it can be carefully managed.

There is nevertheless an ambivalence to both sound and image here that belies this air of harmony and control. The distant wail of the siren is the sound of an ambulance, coming to take the youngest Lisbon sister, Cecilia, to hospital after her attempted suicide. It undercuts the reassuring, rhythmic pacing of the music with strident urgency, situating the girl as a figure who has the air of calm, but who is caught up in crisis, and who may even seem to bear the responsibility for this crisis. Equally, the image suggests something more troubling than a golden sunlit afternoon and the innocent consumption of a sweet by a girl, both about the girl herself and her appropriation as image by the camera. Lux's red lollypop recalls the stylised poster-art for Stanley Kubrick's *Lolita* which features Sue Lyon wearing heart-shaped red sunglasses and sucking on a red lolly. The image of a blonde teenage girl and a red lolly is iconic within Western cinematic culture, so notorious is the image created by Kubrick. This opening image thus also raises the spectre of precocious teen sexuality and resonates with contemporary concerns about the premature sexualisation of girls. The Lolita image has a far wider resonance beyond this individual film text, and allows Coppola to draw on a whole history of girlhood made into image, and what the implications of that might be, both for the girl-object and the viewer-audience. In the context of photographic images automatically always already assuming an adult (sexualised?) gaze at a child, Lebeau asserts that:

> The advertisement for Stanley Kubrick's film *Lolita*, released to considerable controversy in 1962, remains one of the most scandalous images in the history of cinema. [...] Appearing in various forms – the poster has long been cropped, re-framed and retouched for its various distribution of Kubrick's film since its first release – it is an image now synonymous with the commodification of adolescent sensuousness for the (older) male viewer.[95]

The film rejects this, both through Lux exiting the frame, and through cutting from the haze of golden sunlight and its evocation of that 1970s photographic aesthetic to an entirely different set of feminine iconographies. Coppola undercuts the reference to Lolita as in less than a minute of screen time we rapidly move to the harshly lit, blueish-grey image of Cecilia lying in a bathtub of bloody water, her attitude recalling John Everett Millais' 1851 portrait of Ophelia. Ophelia is the tragic heroine of Shakespeare's *Hamlet*, who killed herself after discovering that her lover had murdered her father. As with Kubrick's appropriation of Nabakov's Lolita, it is the visual image rather than the textual character that circulates as an icon of girlhood. Millais' painting shows Ophelia in a white dress, floating on her back, garlands of flowers around her. The Pre-Raphaelite model Elizabeth 'Lizzy' Siddal posed for Millais in a gruelling process. Millais used a bathtub to get the correct effect of a garment filled with water. The bathtub was heated with lamps underneath to keep the water warm; on one occasion, the lamps went out and Siddal caught a bad cold (her father threatened to sue Millais).[96] In later years, Siddal herself became associated with feminine despair, succumbing to laudanum addiction and possibly taking her own life. This painting, then, rather like the Lolita film poster, stands in for a whole set of ideas about girlhood, here invoking its relation to pain and morbidity. By quickly referencing such dense webs of feminine iconography as Lolita and Ophelia, sex and death, Coppola complicates any easy clichéd reading and the glow of the early evening sunset becomes mixed up with death and pain as much as sensual adolescence. She also suggests the complex reality behind the image-making process: the model who catches cold; the girl whose image is appropriated.

The Virgin Suicides offers a sustained reflection on the politics of form that enables us to understand its use as a feminist/resistant aesthetic choice that avoids the easy assimilation of girls to explanatory narrative. Through resisting decoding, the girls eschew the mainstream fate of cinematic femininity, with its masquerades finally undone by the all-seeing male detective. As Colin McCabe explains, women are constructed through a tripartite gaze: of the audience, of the male hero, of the camera.[97] In this schema, the narrative of the film consists in reconciling these three gazes and solving the 'problem' of the woman, usually by having her pinned down in close-up. In contrast, the Lisbon girls preserve their enigma, refusing to let the camera catch and interpret them.

The boys manage to get hold of Cecilia's diary, the first of the happy objects of the Lisbon girls they collect. The camera pans over detritus – ticket stubs; a scarf; lipstick; party invites – before settling on the green diary, its cover bearing a gleaming sticker depicting a rainbow arching between two clouds and Cecilia's name in a highly curlicued script, echoing the writing of girlhood undertaken in the credit sequence. 'Tim Weiner, the brain, decoded it' the voiceover informs us, as we see a boy holding it opening and reading from it. He diagnoses 'emotional instability' and links this to the *form*, rather than the content, of the diary. He performs graphology, arguing that the dots on the 'i's reveal Cecilia as a dreamer, someone who probably believed she could fly. However, the film then undercuts the supposed authority of his argument, as the boys read out entries touching and pathetic in their banality: 'Monday February 13th. Today we had frozen pizza'; 'Thursday: Mom made creamed corn for dinner; it's the worst.' Backman Rogers argues that 'the bathetic contrast' between Cecilia's tedious diary entries and the boys' need to read them as profoundly suggestive of her suicidal psyche 'serves to remind the viewer of just how elaborate the boys' fantasies are.'[98] This is clearly (and comically) the case; also, however, Coppola reminds us again of how girlhood is formatted through a specific aesthetic range which offers up the very condition of being a girl as open and transparent – the pleasures of glitter, pink, rainbows, clouds and curly handwriting are posited as dreamy and girlish; the act of suicide a foolish mistake rather than a forceful rejection. While this would seem to assert girlhood representation as obvious, the diary entry then precipitates another audacious and fascinating use of form where the transparency of girlhood is troubled.

Following the banal entries on the Lisbon diet, Cecilia's diary recounts a family trip: 'today we went out on the boat. It was pretty cold. We saw a couple of whales.' This entry triggers a sharp cut from the boy's bedroom to an over-exposed image of a hand moving through water, accompanied by a haunting, eerie high pitched sound. We cut to a high angle shot of Lux's blonde head almost translucent against the crystalline blue water. Lux turns and smiles excitedly up at the camera, and we see her lips moving as if she is chattering. The film cuts back to Cecilia's diary entry read by the boys and then another image of Lux, accompanied again by an electronic echo sound. Lux is clothed in blue, looking up at the camera and framed by the effulgent dazzle of sparkling diamonds of light on the sea. The image is a glorious, saturated image of blue and yellow, associating Lux with the colours of The Virgin Mary, and is filmed on 8 mm stock to mimic home movie footage, as if these images have been captured by Mr. Lisbon. The images are mute, as no sound recording would be available: the haunting music comes from some other imagined space entirely – the boys' fantasies perhaps. The status of these images as virtual or actual; recording, memory or fantasy, is impossible to determine. Backman Rogers reads them as fantasies triggered by Cecilia's diary, but these are fantasies formatted by a very particular type of film stock: a grainy, imperfect stock used by amateur filmmakers to capture family life, rather than professional 35mm film, designed deliberately to evoke the possibility that these images of Lux belong to Mr. Lisbon and could be part of the detritus of the Lisbon life later collected by the boys (they own photographs of the girls).

It is in the grainy nature of the image, its overexposure, its friability, that film itself as a perfect preserver of a truthful record is exposed as a fantasy. If the mere mention of the theme of a family day-trip on the sea immediately conjures up the most trite of clichés, its treatment here belongs to a wholly different imagery to that of tourism, advertisement, or commercial film and TV. The quality of these mute images imbues them with an oddly old-fashioned and intimate feel. Furthermore, the nostalgia and intimacy that attaches to these images isn't just because of their status in the film as a happy memory from a now shattered family, but because of the material and aesthetic qualities of the medium itself which endows these images with a specific corporeal and synaesthetic appeal. As Martine Beugnet explains in her discussion of Chantal Akerman's use of 8mm in *La Captive* (2000), 8mm film is characterised by an unrivalled sensitivity to changes in luminosity, making the images glow. The uneven, pulsating, grainy quality of the images gives us a haptic form of vision.

> The poignant effect that super-8mm film seems to yield comes from the specific quality of its projected images, fluttering as if they were

animated by an inner pulsation. The silent scenes and bodies that appear on screen, as well as the body of the film itself, thus convey a strange and affecting sense of vulnerability [...] the fragility of the super-8 film is always perceptible.[99]

Coppola and Akerman both emphasise the fragility and sensual richness of the world of the girls they film, drawing on the material qualities of super-8 film for its affective power. As Kodak closed its last 8mm factory in 2005, such images have now gained an extra layer of poignancy, as this film format is relegated to archival status.

Following this brief interlude, the diary reading then triggers a whole suite of images, mainly made up of stills and dissolves, of the girls associated with light and sparkle: an image of Lux in close-up, her golden hair back-lit by sunshine; a close-up of Cecilia in profile writing her diary over which is superimposed a sparkler; Mary playing with a sparkler superimposed over a shot of the summer sky; four short shots of Bonnie, Mary and Therese, all back-lit by sunshine. These images function in a similar way to the earlier graphology performed by the boys. On the one hand, they seem to decode girlhood, offering it up as a light-filled, transparent time. On the other hand, it is precisely as the girls glow from within, emanating light, that their motives and desires become more obscure and hidden. The girl repurposes light, her body reflecting back so strong a glow that it becomes blinding. The girl as spectacular reaches her apogee here. The paradox of spectacle as blinding brilliance is asserted.

If girls are cast as dazzling and effulgent, this very dazzle could well enable them to hide, to protect and maintain a level of privacy in a culture that deems girl-hood an overwhelmingly *public* concern. In the repeated association of girlhood and sunlight, Coppola is exploiting a long-standing association of the feminine with light, from Christian iconography of the Virgin Mary to the standardised use of Hollywood backlighting to makes the female lighter and brighter than the male from the 1910s onwards, as demonstrated by Richard Dyer.[100] In her recurrent use of bright sunlight, lens flare and blonde stars (Kirsten Dunst, Scarlett Johansson, Elle Fanning), Coppola creates a specifically racialised, white image of girlhood. Is ability to reflect back the light and dazzle the viewer the privilege of the white body? Coppola's films offer a radical vision of girlhood as they imagine differ-ent ways of thinking about the links between luminosity, agency and power, but they continue to depend on the association, long established in the media indus-tries, of white femininity with the appeal and soft power of 'glow'. In this way, her films confirm one of the problematics of postfeminist culture which is its default assumption of girlhood as a white condition. There is one intriguing exception to this rule – Rebecca in *The Bling Ring*, the luminous alpha girl of the group, is played by Katie Chang, of mixed-race (Korean, Irish and German) descent. *The Bling Ring* was accused on the internet of whitewashing the 'true story' of The Bling Ring group, especially in the fact that Coppola omits one of the members of The Bling Ring in her re-telling of the story. As was reported on the Jezebel website, the ColorLines website and mic.com, Coppola fails to include Diane Tamayo, an undocumented immigrant from Mexico.[101] Whereas in the film, Nicki's little sister Emily/Georgia Rock is recruited into the gang and uses her small frame to wriggle into buildings via catflaps, during the actual burglaries this role was taken by Tamayo. Upon her arrest, Tamayo was threatened with deportation if she failed to co-operate with police. She pleaded no contest and was sentenced to 180 days in jail. As all three websites discussing the whitewashing of the story explain, the race politics of Coppola's decision to remove Tamayo from the story are complex: how much desire is there for such a negative story about an undocumented immigrant to have more publicity? On the other hand, the film avoids offering a more complex and accurate picture both of the demographic make-up of Los Angeles, and the real lives of migrants, who may well commit crimes but still deserve to be treated before the law in the same way as anyone else (clearly not the case as Tamayo was threatened with deportation).

It is indeed only white kids that we see arrested and taken into custody, but nevertheless, *The Bling Ring* is a film about race in America, but the usually invisible privileges of whiteness. One of the arrest sequences does indeed comment on questions of deportation, ironically showing how invisible this threat has become to anyone other than those who fear it. This is in how Coppola stages the arrest of Chloe/ Claire Julian. Unlike the other arrests, which have been filmed dramatically with moving cameras, fast-paced music and police raids, this is filmed in a static tableau, with a locked-down camera, with no music on the soundtrack. The family are having breakfast in a well-appointed kitchen decorated in shades of beige, cream and white, as if to match the family's blonde hair and white skin. Chloe's mother is making beetroot juice at the counter at the back of the shot; it is the sound of the blender we hear at the start of the sequence. Just behind her the Mexican maid works at the sink washing the dishes. Chloe's father sits at a small table reading a newspaper, two small white dogs at his feet. The wail of a siren intrudes onto the soundtrack, getting louder, and the dogs start to bark. Chloe, who of course knows she has committed a crime, is the first person to react to the sirens coming her way, finding it more difficult to swallow her cereal. She is followed almost instantaneously by the maid, who pauses in her wiping of the dishes, and twice turns around anxiously, looking toward the door. Her distress is ignored, as Chloe's mother asks the dog, the aptly named Crystal, to stop barking. A moment later her father finally looks up from his newspaper. The people around Chloe become alert to the siren and its implications in ascending order of privilege.

Coppola's own background as Italian-American is intriguing to consider in the context of *The Bling Ring's* knowing negotiation of race privilege and girlhood. Coppola distances herself from the teens' fascination with celebrity culture and excess, commenting that 'I'm not part of that world.'[102] She avoids social media, using neither Twitter nor Facebook, and has a deliberately understated look (the schoolgirl chic of American Marc Jacobs rather than the 'unabashed sexiness' and 'vulgarity' of Italian Versace).[103] Her demeanour is quiet and thoughtful rather than loud and demonstrative like her father (a personality trait she claims to have inherited from her mother).[104] All this means that despite her appearances in her father's *The Godfather* trilogy, Coppola's image of femininity is thus not marked as ethnically white, and her fashion image and authorial persona are much closer to an idealised, classic, WASPish white femininity, for as Stephen Gundle explains, Italian culture is stereotypically read as glamorous precisely because it is excessive: 'always more than average: more showy, more visible, more beautiful, more sexy, more rich.'[105] Coppola and her character Rebecca share then the possibility of being read as exotically other, but demonstrate how powerful alpha girlhood depends too much on the characteristics associated with whiteness of calm and control. It is not that a non-white girl can't perform powerful girlhood, but she must perform the qualities associated with white identity, one that will be all the more difficult for her to appropriate and that demonstrates the enduring appeal of whiteness and its association with (naturalised) positions of power. It is useful here to consider Raka Shome's comments on Michelle Obama, the first non-white First Lady. As Shome comments, Obama's presence has indeed made a powerful black woman more visible in the nation's media. But her acceptability came at the price of taming her image. Branded at first as an angry black woman, who was unpatriotic and wrote an angry thesis on race while in graduate school, as her husband became a serious contender for the White House, Obama's image became more disciplined:

> Her image as a fashion icon and a mother committed to her children (without calling attention to the specific challenges of black motherhood) is dominant on screens and is comforting because it reflects

scripts of nationalized femininity *that have already been naturalized by white femininity.* Her beautiful fashion style makes her even more palatable [...] Further, her attention to the problem of (child) obesity and her campaigns promoting healthy eating [...] suggests an 'in-control' – disciplined – black female body. Although the script of white femininity through which Michelle is articulated sometimes ruptures – as in the images of Michelle doing pushups or dancing – [...] for the most part Michelle's example illustrates how the norms of white femininity are what she has to negotiate to be acceptable.[106]

Coppola's decision to avoid incorporating Tamayo into her version of the Bling Ring affair demonstrates how, for her film to have something 'universal' to say about girlhood and celebrity culture, she had to avoid addressing the specific racialised challenges certain girls face. Furthermore, just as Michelle Obama's blackness is used to offer an image of a postracial society in which cultural difference is celebrated but issues of systemic racial tensions are suppressed, so Coppola too offers an image of powerful girlhood that can be performed by girls of any colour, so long as they still operate within naturalised white norms (and in practice, these girls are far more likely to be white, and not ethnically marked). Thus her films illuminate, without necessarily agreeing with, a postracial logic in which all girls are understood in terms of meritocracy instead of as human beings caught up in wider systems of structural inequality.

What is particularly striking here is how both Lux and Rebecca's performance of alpha girlhood is linked to luminosity and whiteness. Consider the similarity of the way that Coppola presents her image of girlhood in *The Bling Ring* and *The Virgin Suicides*, despite the differences in source material, genre and tone between the films. Just as *The Virgin Suicides* associates the feminine enigma with a hazy, soft lit glow around a close-up on Lux's face, so *The Bling Ring* produces a similar image of Rebecca. As Marc arrives at school one morning, he sees Rebecca leaning against a fence. She is wearing a white dress with a slim pink belt. He approaches her, carrying an oversized drinking cup with a straw, and hands her a drink. 'I love your shirt' she says, and the two walk toward school together. At this moment, the camera frames the two of them against a heavily sunlit background, and light bouncing off Rebecca's hair and lens flare at the front of the image gives the feeling of being saturated in light. Lens flare in particular draws our attention to the prevalence of light, and its paradoxical resistance to being made into image: the flare occurs when light bounces back off the lens and fails to be recorded correctly, causing images of reflections and scattered beams rather than any actual object. Against the generally realist flow of the film, Coppola fades down the diegetic soundtrack, and introduces soft music and birdsong over it. She also uses slow motion, so that Rebecca's walk and swinging arms become more deliberate and pronounced. The camera moves alongside Rebecca, framing her head, shoulders and upper body, and she turns (toward Marc/the camera/ the viewer) and smiles. Marc says in voiceover 'I loved her, I really did. She was the first person I felt was my best friend.' This is the only non-diegetic voiceover in the film. As Marc explains his feelings for Rebecca at this idealising moment, she walks out of the frame, and we cut to a more satirical, comic mode as we see Nicki and Sam being homeschooled by their mother. By the end of the film, the focus has shifted from Rebecca to Nicki, who is more than happy to justify herself (even against the advice of her lawyers). She has (literally) the last word, speaking direct to camera in close up and telling us to check out Nickimooreforever.com for more information on her life. Rebecca remains ethereal and out-of-frame, refusing to engage with the media and her motives are less clearly delineated. Rebecca shimmers, moving in and out of light at will, and subverting notions of feminine perfection. She creates the perfect look through breaking the rules rather than conforming to them. She shares with Lux the ability to retain agency within the appearance of girlish femininity, reconciling the spectacle of bright light and the construction of the girl self away from facile appropriations and simplified decodings.

Conclusion: Luminosity, Whiteness, Disembodiment

The association of Coppola's top girls, Lux and Rebecca, with both light and white renders them impossibly inspiring and beautiful for the boys who admire them: the neighbourhood boys and Marc respectively. It is not so much that the girl herself needs to be white, as she needs to be associated with the idealised/ idealising qualities of lightness, brightness and whiteness, and frequently this will pertain more closely to a white body. Richard Dyer reminds us however that nobody is as white as the ideal demands, for 'whiteness, really white whiteness, is unattainable. Its ideal forms are impossible.'[107]

Coppola reconciles this paradox through disembodying whiteness. Her girls reach the condition of perfect whiteness through becoming 'no body', whereas ironically the fear of becoming nobody animates a lot of these girls activities to begin with (committing suicide in *The Virgin Suicides*; stealing from celebrity homes in *The Bling Ring*). Whiteness becomes a quality belonging to her films themselves, in their repeated deployment of bright light, sun, back lighting and lens flare. The girls themselves escape, enacting 'a line of flight' that sees them vanish from the screen. It's useful to briefly mention Ridley Scott's now iconic *Thelma and Louise* (1991), which offered a feminist twist on the buddy road-movie genre by making its two chief protagonists the eponymous Thelma/Geena Davis and Louise/Susan Sarandon. The film starts with the two friends planning a weekend getaway, a break from the humdrum domesticity that circumscribes their lives. When a man she meets at a bar attempts to rape Thelma, Louise shoots her assailant. The two women then go on the run from the law and attempt to flee to Mexico. The film finishes with them at the Grand Canyon, the police having finally caught up with them. The two women, having shared adventures together, have to decide whether to give themselves up, or commit suicide by driving the car over the edge and into the canyon. Thelma tells Louise to keep driving, and we see Louise's car soaring above the canyon before a freeze frame stops its motion and the screen fades to white. The reason this is a valuable film for us to consider is that Lux and Rebecca, Coppola's most luminous girls, bring out different aspects of how Thelma and Louise also challenge regimes of representation, albeit from within a very different generic and generational context.

Rebecca is an outlaw, escaping the punishment awaiting her by leaving the State. Lux commits suicide, using a car to do so (she asphyxiates herself in the garage, highlighting the naivety of the boys' fantasy of a road-trip rescue mission). Like Thelma and Louise, they find a way out of the film and out of the frame, but the question remains at what cost? Both girls choose a kind of death. In Lux's case, the death is literal, as her suicide becomes an agentic action in the face of oppressive constraints. For Masafumi Monden, the film articulates an argument similar to that of Elizabeth Bronfen, for whom the choice of death within a fictional frame is a 'feminine strategy within which writing with the body is a way of getting rid of the oppression connected with the body [...] feminine suicide can serve as a trope, self-defeating as this seems, for a feminine writing strategy within the constraints of patriarchal culture.'[108] By bringing death to herself, a woman is able to destroy a socially-constructed passive image, and bring about an autonomous self-image. In Rebecca's case, the death is more metaphorical, in that the social group she has constructed falls apart. Lux and Rebecca feminise and girlify the rebellious actions associated with Thelma and Louise, who both become more stereotypically masculine in appearance and behaviour through the film. In contrast, Lux and Rebecca remain associated with lightness and whiteness, associating a sense of empowerment to girls and the aesthetic imagination of girlish femininity. On the other hand, this very whiteness demands an absence from the body and a loss of corporeal selfhood.

Post-Oedipal understandings of desire recognise desire as self-expansion, embracing plenitude and abundance and not only feelings of lack and melancholy. For Emma Renold and Gabrielle Ivinson in their ethnographic survey of girlhood, it is through their bodies in active motion that girls come to understand desire as aspiration and hope, a forward movement. They conclude that 'if girls do not move they also do not explore, take risks, experiment and therefore miss out on ways of being and becoming that may open up new imaginative worlds including worlds in which they build houses, work abroad and, dare we say it, desire.'[109] The world of the Coppola girl may well be attractive, playful, transcendent and fun, but it is hampered in its embrace of desire beyond the happy objects that preserve a girlish, youthful, asexual persona. For all that they show a delightful and patient attendance to the micro movements, fleeting emotions, and shifting rhythms that disrupt hegemonic accounts of girlhood through an emphasis on the ambivalence of objects and the reconfiguring of girlhood iconography, Coppola's films do not show us these girls sustaining the lines of flight their ruptures may have initiated. In this context it is noticeable that Coppola's two most hopeful films in terms of their ending and in their representation of a girl continuing to move, in that the girls do not end up dead/ in prison, *Lost in Translation* and *Somewhere*, nevertheless contrast a man in literal flight (leaving for the airport/getting into his helicopter) to a girl on the ground. These are girls who refuse to grow up: coming-of-age films that avoid maturation. Girlhood remains idyllic and agentic at the price of remaining ethereal, sparkling, bloodless, disembodied, rather than temporal, historical and located in the changing body. Coppola's films demonstrate/enact a severe restriction on girls' power, which is dependent on a markedly asexual account of girlhood empowerment. In contrast to the postfeminist masquerade which demands hypersexualised femininities, Coppola's films empower their girls through rendering them outside of, or severely repressing, the sexual. Indeed, her films go so far as to intimate that it is by avoiding the sexual that girls can sustain their power. Any growth into sexual desire requires loss of free will. Coppola's films empower their girls on the condition they leave the body behind, unable to imagine a femininity that is both powerful and sexual without being threatening.

In this discussion of the impossibility of embodied desire for Coppola's girls we come back to the figure of Alice from *Alice in Wonderland* and *Through the Looking-Glass*. Alice circulates within contemporary visual culture as an icon of girlhood, whose image seems to me to articulate the paradox of a body that is simultaneously powerful and contained, mobile and stilled, curious and muted.

As such, she offers a powerful corollary of Coppola's girls whose experiences of girlhood are strikingly similar. Both Alice and the Coppola girls experience the girl body as site of possibility, movement and power: a place from which to express curiosity about the world – desire in its most expansive sense of interest. Yet these girls are also halted in their growth. Alice discovers this world is just a dream. Furthermore, this dream could possibly not even belong to her: her presence in Looking-Glass world could in fact be because the King is dreaming that she is there. Here, Alice is thoroughly disembodied, being made into a mere figment of the King's imagination, and it is in this condition of disembodiment that girlhood desire and curiosity can be managed. In other words, girls can be empowered as long as it is within the confines of a dream: the hazy glow of the flower-filled meadows with unicorns of the boys' fantasies of the Lisbon girls; the jet-lagged otherworldliness of Tokyo; partying until dawn at Versailles; fantasy underwater tea parties at the Chateau Marmont; the reckless stealing binges in celebrity homes.

It is perhaps not surprising that Alice emerges in the late nineteenth century, as she can be seen as part of a broader cultural engagement with childhood, growth and change, also expressed in the development of psychoanalysis and its interest in the formation of subjectivity from infancy onward. Indeed, our understanding of girlhood as time of mutability, experimentation and elasticity, so perfectly crystallised by Alice, can also be seen as an extension of attitudes forged in the late nineteenth and early twentieth centuries, when adolescence itself emerged as a psycho-sociological category (usually associated above all with the work of G. Stanley Hall, an American psychologist who published two volumes on adolescence. Although he tended to concentrate on boys as default 'youths', he did also write on the particularity of girlhood adolescence, labelling it a 'baffling problem' and then dedicating an entire chapter to the adaptability of girls, seeing it as both a feminine pathology and as the purest expression of humanity).[110] Robert Latham argues that contemporary American ideas of youth are indebted to the 1920s and the 1930s, when Taylorization prioritised the 'energetic pliability' of youth in its radical restructuring of industrial practices.[111] The rather nebulous quality of 'youthful energy' is promoted as a desirable quality for all workers, regardless of their chronological age (but perhaps a more difficult quality to display if middle-aged apathy and exhaustion have taken their toll). As Warren-Crow goes onto explain, such an energetic pliability has a specific girlish quality when it comes to the corollary of production: that of consumption. The 'modern girl' is an expert consumer, fashioning her image through cosmetics and fashion, themselves indexes of her ability to shift, even if in a usually less dramatic way than Alice herself. Anita Harris notes the similarity between fin-de-siècle youth and twenty-first-century girlhood: both are charged with embodying flexible subjectivity and transformative energy.[112] Alice then comes to work as a paradigm of girlishness: 'from her earliest manifestation as one of Lewis Carroll's photographic models to her recent appearance as Tim Burton's *Alice in Wonderland* (2010), she embodies the elastic, metamorphic and transmedia qualities of the plastic image.'[113]

As Helen Pilinovsky reminds us, Alice has passed from being a specific character to being a near archetype.[114] Partly because of the very malleability inscribed into her from Carroll's narrative, partly because the charming and appealing novels are out of copyright, partly because she works as an intermedial figure who mobilises some cultural notions of girlhood as flexible and pliable, Alice functions as a trope, available to us across literature, photography, animation and live-action film. The very particular image of Alice that most clearly illustrates her potential illumination and enrichment of Coppola's filmic take on girlhood is one shot by photographer Annie Leibovitz for a *Vogue* 'Alice in Wonderland' fashion shoot featured in American *Vogue* December 2003. The shoot recreates various scenes from the book, including the one where Alice visits the White Rabbit's house. She enters the house as a tiny creature, but while she is there comes across a bottle from which she drinks in the hope it will make her large again. To quote Carroll: 'it did so indeed, and much sooner than she had expected: before she had drunk half the bottle, she found her head pressing against the ceiling, and had to stoop to save her neck from being broken [...] still she went on growing, and, as a last resource, she put one arm out of the window, and one foot up the chimney.'[115] The sentence chosen to illustrate the *Vogue* photograph, reproduced in white type in its left-hand corner, comes just a few lines after this, and demonstrates in some ways the paradoxes also contained in the image. On the one hand, we have a strong sense of Alice's unhappiness with her vertiginous changes and her sense this excursion is disempowering rather than fantastical. On the other, Alice acknowledges it as the basis for curiosity – the beginnings of desire and growth. ' "It was much pleasanter at home", thought poor Alice, "when one wasn't always growing larger and smaller, and being ordered about by mice and rabbits [...] and yet – and yet – it's rather curious you know, this sort of life!" '[116]

Leibovitz's photograph places her 'Alice', model Natalia Vodianova, into a house in which her head bumps up against the ceiling, her arm is crooked against a window and she arches her leg up. Her foot, clad in a beautiful black shoe with a ribbon tied around her ankle, nestles into the fireplace. Rather as Carroll accentuated the littleness of his child models in his photographs through having them wear baggy clothes or be near large furniture, here Alice's excessive size is demonstrated through her placement against a miniaturised table laid with a tiny tea-set. It is as if Alice has wondered into a doll's house, ironically underlining her girlishness even as her huge size is made evident. As suits the photograph's provenance, however, this Alice is beautifully dressed, in a bright blue Helmut Lang organza dress. The image marries together playful girlishness and desirable clothing and accessories but the body of the girl is nevertheless subject to aggressive constraint. In its circulation of an image of a girl's body as simultaneously metamorphic, beautiful, flexible, powerful, and trapped, squashed, contained and vulnerable, the photograph condenses the paradoxes of Coppola's girlhood. If she were to grow any more, Alice would smash through the walls of the house that contains her, gesturing toward the subject of my next chapter: the recurrent theme of exploded homes in Coppola's films.

3

'There's No Place Like Home!' The Exploded Home as Postfeminist Chronotope

'A definite and absolute concrete locality serves as the starting point for the creative imagination. But this is not an abstract landscape […] No, this is a piece of human history, historical time condensed in space.'[1]

'It's so cool to be in the real places. There's something that just gets you into the mood. They let us shoot in places people weren't allowed to normally, like Marie Antoinette's private theater. They were like, "This is your home."'[2]

Filming on Location

For theorist Mikhail Bahktin, place brings together time and space and renders two abstract concepts concrete, an idea pursued by Coppola in her assertion cited above that 'something' about shooting in real places is key to her films' narrative, style and themes. The importance that Coppola accords to the influence of place is obvious when considering her films and their often spectacular use of location. The Tokyo Park Hyatt, the Chateau Marmont, the Presidential Suite of the Savoy hotel in Milan, the Chateau of Versailles and Paris Hilton's mansion, have all featured in her films. This is enabled by Coppola's power, influence and reputation, so that the very material grounds of her films – the locations in which they are shot – speak to her particularly privileged position. For example, the manager of the Chateau Marmont, Philip Pavel, explains that the hotel receives many requests to shoot on location there, most of which are refused. However, Coppola has a longstanding personal connection to the hotel – one of Pavel's first duties as general manager when he joined the hotel was organising a birthday party for her. As Pavel continues, the decision to grant permission for *Somewhere* to be filmed at the Chateau 'was specific to Sofia's relationship with the hotel. She's been a member of the Chateau family as long as I've been here. When she approached André Balazs, the owner, there was an innate sense of trust that her

project would have integrity and reflect the true nature of the hotel.'[3] We can find similar narratives of influence, personal connection, and a sense of integrity to location
inflecting other discussions of Coppola being given permission to film in particular
settings. Her ability to film *Marie Antoinette* on location at Versailles was similarly
imputed to her personal family connections and the sense that she is an artistically
serious and credible director. She was given 'unprecedented access' to the Chateau,
filming there for 12 weeks in Spring 2005, a decision that the *New York Times* imagines
as partly thanks to the fact that 'Coppola is something of a cult figure in France [...]
The French admire her talent. She won a best foreign film César, the French Academy
Award, in 2005 for her last film *Lost in Translation*.'[4] The newspaper continues, however, that 'they also esteem her much photographed, tastefully chic personal style. And
her status as Hollywood royalty doesn't hurt: her father [...] is a demi-god in France.'[5]

If such rhetoric is held to sway the notoriously bureaucratic hearts of the
French administrative classes, it is striking that we get a very similar explanation
of personal connections and artistic status from Hollywood 'A' list celebrity Paris
Hilton when she explains why she allowed Coppola access to her mansion when
filming *The Bling Ring*. In an interview included as an extra on the DVD, Hilton
explains that

> I had my birthday party here last year at my house and Sofia came with
> some friends and approached me and told me she was doing a film *The
> Bling Ring*. She really loved the house and it would be impossible to rec-
> reate for the film so it would really mean a lot to her if she could shoot
> the film here. The only reason I said yes is because it's her and I have so
> much respect for her [...] she is such an amazing director. Every film
> she does is always so beautifully shot. Every time you see one of her
> films you know it's a Sofia Coppola film.[6]

Perhaps rather disingenuously, given that she approached Hilton at her birthday
party, Coppola claims in an interview with Lee Radziwill, the New York socialite
and younger sister of Jackie Onassis, that she was 'surprised' by Hilton's decision
to allow her to film in her house, commenting that 'she wasn't there, but she let us
into her closets and we were in her bathroom. I think it was also this idea of no
privacy – no privacy, or mystery, or anything.'[7] Radziwill replies that 'it seems like
nothing is private anymore. That must particularly fascinate you, because you have
such a sense of mystery about you [...] And I think that's one of the things that has
attracted so much curiosity about you.'[8]

The interview itself adds to the complex entanglement of personal friendships
and professional activities that also is evidenced by Coppola's access to location and

the imprint this leaves on her films, as the two women carry onto discuss how their friendship is formed partly through this joint suspicion of celebrity culture (a culture that nevertheless both are intimately connected with and has ironically become part of the very star image of privacy and mystique that Coppola projects). This discussion between Coppola and Radziwill illustrates in a microcosm the broader contention of this chapter: that Coppola's recurrent choice of locations – hotels, celebrity homes, chateaux – stage meetings between public and private, spectacle and intimacy, notoriety/celebrity and anonymity. Coppola's ability to film in these locations speaks to the way her auteur persona straddles the boundaries of personal and professional, with her privileged access attributed both to her intimate connections (birthday parties, admiration for her father and so on), and her skill and ability as filmmaker. The very material stuff of which Coppola's films are made – the places that she records – depends on a savvy negotiation of the intimate and the public, the familial and the professional, that is thematised within the locations themselves. Furthermore, Coppola's access to Paris Hilton's home draws a sharp distinction between her celebrity, achieved through her films as well as attributed to her via her family connections, and what Chris Rojek labels 'celetoids': those who achieve fleeting notoriety, such as *The Bling Ring* teens.[9] The teens themselves fail in their performance of cool celebrity when they are overwhelmed by their proximity to Kirsten Dunst in a nightclub: Dunst's cameo once again, of course, is due to Coppola's connections and also her status as a successful director.

The locations navigate between the private and the public, the intimate and the external. As such, although her films all take place within what we could broadly define as domestic milieu, and have some generic affiliations with such typically 'female' genres as the teen-pic, the costume drama, the melodrama and the romantic comedy, Coppola explodes rather than explores the typically 'female' space of the home, the privileged location of these female film genres. She consistently questions what exactly a home is (is a hotel a home? Is a palace a home?); private retreats are reinvented as sites of public anxiety, spectacle and display; the semi-public arenas of hotel lobbies, karaoke bars and swimming pools become places of private affection and bonding. I thus label Coppola's locations 'exploded home chronotopes.'

Chronotopes in Film: A Brief Account

The notion of the chronotope in relation to narrative was first developed by the Russian literary theorist Mikhail Bakhtin. The term, derived from physics, is meant to emphasise the absolute interdependence of time and space in the constitution of narrative and its significance, but also the human relativity of their ratio. Michael Holmquist, glossing Bakhtin, explains that the chronotope is

> a unit of analysis for studying texts according to the ratio and nature of the temporal and spatial categories represented. The distinctiveness of this concept as opposed to most other categories of time and space in literary analysis lies in the fact that neither category is privileged; they are utterly independent. The chronotope is an optic for reading texts as x-rays of the forces at work in the culture system from which they spring.[10]

Clear in Holmquist's discussion here is the power of the chronotope as a spatio-temporal structure that links the actual world as source of representation and the world represented in the work. While Bahktin's discussion is directed at analysis of the development of the novel and literary realism, this demonstrates the force of his analysis for cinema, which other than in computer generated and animated films, navigates in its very form between an actual world and a represented world. Cinema is an art of both time and space, knitting together these categories in its very moment of recording before we even layer on issues of character or plot. Out of the actual chronotopes of our lived world emerge the orders of verisimilitude which enable certain narratives to be plausible within certain locations. As Vivian Sobchack explains, the power of the chronotope is that it

> references real-life situations with everyday associations for audiences, helping to create a sense of shared place. Through long-standing artis-tic usage, chronotopes also become associated with 'fixed expressions' and metaphorical patterns of thinking [...] text and context, the repre-sented and the real world, are 'indissolubly tied up with each other and find themselves in constant mutual interaction in a continual process of uninterrupted exchange.'[11]

Certain stories belong to certain chronotopes, so that, for example, the road as chronotope configures events as journeys or passages through time and space. Its essential transience renders possible encounters and experiences that could not occur for example in the fixed and stable chronotope of the home, which generates other narratives. Sobchack neatly summarises for us that

> chronotopes serve as the spatiotemporal currency between two dif-ferent orders of existence and discourse, between the historicity of the lived world and the literary world (here, the world of cinema) [...] For Bakhtin, then, chronotopes are much more than topological patterns.

> Never merely the spatiotemporal backdrop for narrative events, they provide the literal and concrete ground from which narrative and character emerge as the temporalization of human action, significant in its diacritical marking of both time and space.[12]

She continues that the power of the chronotope is thus not so much as a tool for synthetic analysis, but a manner of 'comprehending historically the phenomenological relation between text and context in a way richer than that afforded by traditional generic analyses.'[13] A return to the chronotope of the road illustrates this point, showing the inter-relation of the hermetically sealed environment of the story world, and broader historical shifts. For example, in the case of the film discussed at the end of the last chapter, *Thelma and Louise* (Scott, 1991), it is not so much the case that the film itself reflects social change, but rather that the chronotope it uses, that of the road, now accommodates female as well as male travellers, so that the chronotope itself shifts in the encounters it fosters. Given that the chronotope is highly gendered, the encounters that Thelma and Louise have are marked by sexual violence and sexual liberation in a way that does not occur with male travellers. As Lee Wallace argues, 'the social (and sexual) encounters that emerge in these particular narrative spaces – the spontaneous liaisons or sexual adventures of the road […] the slow-burning romances or emotional crises that are resolved within the unvarying confines of the marital home – are settled in advance of the interventions of plot or genre affiliation.'[14] This is useful for us to bear in mind when understanding why a chronotopic approach is so useful for illuminating Coppola's attention to location. It highlights how her recurrent chronotope of the exploded home cuts across what could seem to be significant genre divides – from costume drama to romantic comedy, from contemporary literature adaptation to minimalist personal portraiture. Just as with Michael V. Montgomery's sustained analysis of the shopping mall chronotope of 1980s Hollywood film, 'the advantages of cultivating genre distinctions are slight';[15] what is revealed through attention to the formal features and recurrent motifs of the exploded home chronotope is how Coppola's reference to the 'real' social space of the home, and the subsequent deformations and metamorphosis it undergoes across her body of her work, speaks to the complex metonym and metaphor that the home provides for feminist investigation of the contemporary cultural formation. By referencing a real, dynamic social space, the exploded home setting functions as a chronotope, and as a result, a commentary on the culture is developed. Through her exploded home chronotope, Coppola offers us a stylised, hyperbolic take on the fraught politics of domesticity in the contemporary postfeminist landscape.

Home and/as the Gilded Cage

We should not ignore the fact that Coppola's locations are frequently glamorous and luxurious: palaces, hotels, mansions. They speak to us of wealth, a spatio-temporal articulation both of the élite position her characters frequently occupy, and, as I explain above, a material trace of Coppola's own affluence and influence. The recurrent and ubiquitous spaces of her films foreground them as commenting on contemporary culture from a position of privilege. It is hardly surprising that the notion of the 'gilded cage' enters into both popular and academic discussions about Coppola's film locations, as for example in Jonathan Shia's comment (à propos of *Somewhere*'s Johnny Marco) that 'Hollywood, per Coppola, is a gilded cage, much as Versailles was for Marie Antoinette.'[16] In her discussion of Coppola's locations, Sharon Lay Tin argues that the hotel, the palace and the girls' bedroom all form gilded cages that cloister women. She argues that the characters in *The Virgin Suicides* and *Marie Antoinette*

> remain in their cages and march respectively towards their tragic ends [...] and thereby revise Virginia Woolf's reflections on the need for a room of one's own. While space for thought and creativity is imperative, one needs to emerge for air, society and engagement. [...] Therefore, Coppola's oeuvre may be seen to be critiquing the implicit lack of female participation outside of these rooms.[17]

The metaphor of the gilded cage is clearly a pertinent and useful one, summing up as it does the uneasy combination of luxury and oppression that characterises Coppola's portraits of emotional emptiness and miscommunication in middle-class suburbia, celebrity private lives and royal courts, and also conjuring up the emphasis on light and dazzle in her films that I discuss in chapter 2. The image of the cage also speaks to the peculiar tension between permeability to the outside and entrapment we see in Coppola's spaces. The cage is made up of thin, golden bars, that permit air to enter and the small bird to see out; yet the door is barred and the bird unable to fly. The female protagonists do indeed lack the solution to their cloistered existences that Tay promotes of 'air, society and engagement': Lux complains she can't breathe; Charlotte is lost in a foreign country, unable to connect to its society; Marie Antoinette is protected even from mud on her hens' eggs at Versailles. Yet I sense something rather different in Coppola's chronotope than a gilded cage, hence my decision to label it an exploded home. While Tay places Coppola's politics into an implicit criticism of Woolf's high modernism, I see her rather as in a postfeminist moment of debating the complex politics of the home and its talismanic status within second wave feminist politics. As Rebecca Munford and Melanie Waters explain, 'the housewife has enjoyed renewed visibility in the twenty-first century in texts which have sought to excavate the complexities of domestic femininities.'[18] They cite a range of recent television franchises such as *Six Feet Under* and *Desperate Housewives*, and reality shows such as Bravos' *The Real Wives Of …* franchise. They argue that the early twenty-first century has been marked by domestic revivalism, a claim echoed by Diane Negra and Joanne Hollows.[19] For Munford and Waters, the housewife, 'whether happy or desperate, glamorous or dowdy, sexy or saintly […] is a prevailingly powerful symbolic presence whose increased cultural visibility allows us to reflect on the current state of feminist debates regarding women and the work they do within and beyond the home.'[20] Coppola also addresses the complex status of the home for women, but she does not do this through the figure of the housewife associated with the range of television shows cited above. Rather, housewifery is notably absent in her films, populated as they are by rebellious teen girls, hotel-dwellers, queens, party girls, celebrities: the position of housewife is avoided, whether through wealth or death.

The term 'exploded home' helps articulate the unusual stance Coppola's films occupy within postfeminist cultural production. The exploded home chronotope enables Coppola to explore the significance of the domestic space to feminine identity, but she rejects doing this through the familiar binary tropes open to the housewife enumerated by Munford and Waters cited above and displacing them onto the home itself, simultaneously open and closed, cosy and threatening, enabling and oppressive, glamorous and tarnished. I also favour the phrase 'exploded home' because it suggests the powerful, indeed possibly violent, impact of feminist consciousness-raising on the shape of these girls' lives.

They may be surrounded, indeed cocooned, by wealth and privilege. Often, however, their demeanour is similar to that of someone suffering from post-traumatic shock: numb, unresponsive, supine, in torpor. It is as if there has been an actual explosion, and the domestic space is still feeling its force. I interpret this impact as the feminist insight that domesticity weighs heavily on women's shoulders, and the apathy of her protagonists as a postfeminist melancholia that effecting escape has not been as easy as may be hoped. This is where it is useful to recall Nathan Lee's observation that 'no-one throws girls onto pillows like Sofia Coppola.'[21] Lee traces the multiple appearances of listless, fed-up girls across Coppola's trilogy: 'the Lisbon girls sprawled in a languorous tangle of limbs'; 'the panty-clad appetizer to *Lost in Translation*, that luscious morsel of pastel booty'; '[Marie Antoinette] wakes up late, cozies in carriages, rolls in meadows, passes out on the couch, tumbles into cushions, and droops on damask whenever possible.'[22]

Her girls may thus in some ways seem to echo the pattern of domestic retreat that Munford and Waters, Hollows and Negra see as intrinsic to postfeminist culture, as they are shown in comfortable or luxurious interiors. But they also offer us a rather different view of that retreat. Rather than providing them with a base from which to reclaim traditional feminine pursuits as an empowering choice, the home threatens to suffocate, imprison, or engulf its girls. Nor is it as if the 'social earthquake' of feminist consciousness-raising hasn't happened. We're now aware the domestic space can have this oppressive impact on girls (this is a key way in which Coppola's domestic spaces can be differentiated from the postfeminist houses of the popular culture texts outlined by Munford and Waters), even as it is also a place of immense privilege. The 'explosion' within the exploded home chronotope speaks to the impact of feminism on representations of girls in the home. While feminism itself is no longer present, it has left behind its traces. The domestic space as idyll is simply not available to Coppola's characters, although they also seem unable to access the vocabulary and methodology of feminism to articulate dissent, but simply physically experience the home as alternately asphyxiating, dislocating, or engulfing.

The Temporality of the 'Exploded Home' Chronotope

Clearly, this discussion of the explosive catalyst as feminism is where we come to account for the temporality invoked by Coppola's use of the exploded home chronotope. The chapter's overall emphasis on location shooting and the significance of Coppola's ability to film in real-world dynamic locations may seem to privilege the spatial over the temporal, but notions of dynamic explosion followed by numbing shock and torpor interpolate also questions of time. Indeed, we should not forget that the chronotope is the device Bakhtin uses to explain the interpenetration of time and space in the concrete historicity of the lived moment. The chronotope is, as Lynn Porter explains, a metaphor to explain the inseparability of time and space, or rather, time as the fourth dimension of space. She goes onto cite Bakhtin: 'In the literary artistic chronotope [...] time, as it were, thickens, takes on flesh, becomes artistically visible; likewise, space becomes charged and responsive to the movements of time, plot, and history.'[23] In the exploded home chronotope, Coppola uses two complementary strategies to give time flesh: on the one hand, there is an emphasis on repetition, circularity and mechanistic rituals; on the other, this monotony is broken up by an attention to fleeting, transitory moments that give expression to the various components that make up any cinematic image: light, movement, texture, colour, sound.

Time becomes visible as heavy and wearisome by being spatialised as a circular loop that reifies the repetition temporality of the exploded home. This motif is made most obvious for us in Coppola's minimalist study of boredom, *Somewhere*, which opens with Johnny driving his powerful black Ferrari in circles around a race track; shows him distractedly watching blonde twins spinning around poles in his hotel bedroom; and lingers on Cleo's delicate ice-skating routine of looping jumps and curving arcs (see Fig 3.1 and 3.2). Indeed, perhaps one of the reasons we should interpret this film's ambiguous ending positively is because it finishes with Johnny walking in a straight line to somewhere, as if he has finally managed to escape these circles. In chapter 1, I discussed how the film repays sustained comparison to *La Dolce Vita*. In her reading of this film, P. Adams Sitney in turn compares it to Dante's Divine Comedy, tracing a Dantean web of allusions, from the opening of Christ turned to stone to the end where Marcello fails to recognise the call of Matelda's innocence toward Eden.[24] Although these connections may by this point seem to be stretching the long arm of intertextuality to the point of dislocation, it is nevertheless suggestive to bear in mind the alignment of Coppola's circles with this portrait of hell, hinting at the despair that lies beneath her gilded worlds. We may also wish to speculate on a growing sense of claustrophobia and despair, as activities become increasingly futile and meaningless even when at first they were exciting, such as the all night parties in Versailles, or the continual breaking into celebrity homes in *The Bling Ring*.

Fig. 3.1. Cleo's ice-skating routine

Fig. 3.2. The twins' pole dancing routine

Considerable attention is paid in her films to inconsequentiality, with an emphasis on atmosphere and emotion over plot development. These are films marked by
everyday events (cooking, eating, reading, hanging out, sleeping, walking, driving,
listening to music), ellipsis, dedramatisation and stillness. The overall tenor of her
films is one of great attention to small things, so that we are kept to the insignifi-
cant and the everyday. In *Marie Antoinette*, we spend time with Marie Antoinette
and her friends and daughter at her hamlet, Le Petit Trianon; Coppola privileges
lingering close-ups, showing us a blonde toddler gingerly reaching out toward
a bee, and a skirt swishing against meadow flowers, concentrating on capturing
transient moments of pleasure within the everyday round. Similarly, Charlotte in
Lost in Translation has a trip to hospital while staying in Japan, but only because
she has stubbed her toe while climbing down from her bed (and the hospital visit
occurs some time after the initial incident, which is also downplayed; Charlotte
stumbles and exclaims, but we have no close-up on the foot, and may even miss
the event on first viewing). The film spends time with her simply exploring her
surroundings: getting the *shinkansen* to Kyoto, travelling on the Tokyo under-
ground, walking the rainy streets. One of the considerable charms of *Somewhere*
is in the careful attention it pays to the activities of pre-adolescent girlhood, as we
spend three minutes watching Cleo perform her ice-skating routine, with a touch-
ingly intense focus and concentration; or we may notice her at the back of the shot
as she pulls a Sudoku book out of her bag and quietly does puzzles while her Dad
is talking to his hosts at the Italian hotel. Coppola's films concentrate on isolated

moments that crystallise a mood, a feeling. In such a world, when events do occur they come cataclysmically and seemingly without warning: multiple suicides, the French Revolution; Cleo's heartbreak at the mother's abandonment of her.

With this tendency to make time visible through boredom, waiting, monotony and circularity, commentators on Coppola's work have drawn attention to its interest in the possibilities of repetition. For Belinda Smaill, it is Coppola's emphasis on predictability and recurrence within the female experience of the everyday that allows us to see her films as 'more entrenched in a feminist sensibility than is immediately apparent.'[25] She turns to the work of Patrice Petro to support this idea. Petro argues that ennui, boredom and repetition have been central to women's lives and culture. Moreover, Petro notes, much feminist work over the past decades has involved 'an aesthetics as well as a phenomenology of boredom: a temporality of duration, relentless in its repetition, and a stance of active waiting, which, at least in their feminist formulations, allow for redefinition, resistance, and change.'[26] Following Smaill's logic, it is in the expansion and dilation of time, its looping repetitions within the exploded home, that we can insert Coppola's work into a feminist continuum, where ennui comes both from the drudgery of life in the home (as compared to the rewards for labour performed in the public sphere) and the falteringly slow pace of political change.

Perhaps the most well-known piece of feminist counter-cinema to exploit devices of repetition within the everyday is Chantal Akerman's *Jeanne Dielman, 23 Quai du commerce 1080 Bruxelles* (1975) (specifically cited by cinematographer Harris Savides as inspiration for Cleo's cooking scenes in *Somewhere*).[27] The film, which lasts three hours and twenty-one minutes, is described by Ivone Margulies as 'a mesmerising study of stasis and containment, time and domestic anxiety.'[28] Jeanne performs a predictable schedule of cooking, bathing, eating and shopping, recorded in long stark takes. Margulies continues: 'each gesture and sound becomes imprinted on our mind, as we are lulled by familiar rhythms and expected behaviour [...] the perfect parity between Jeanne's predictable schedule and Akerman's minimalist precision deflects our attention from the fleeting signs of Jeanne's afternoon prostitution.'[29] The film finishes with Jeanne dressing, tucking her shirt into her skirt and stabbing her client with a pair of scissors. The final seven minutes show Jeanne sitting at the dinner table with a striated neon light playing over her face. Margulies argues that the feminist power of the film is in its insistence on duration and the materiality of female existence and its figuring of the impact of time on the (female) body. For Smaill, Coppola and Akerman share an interest in slow narrative pacing, dedramatisation, stillness, alienation and the texture of time passing. However, it is worth considering a fundamental difference between Coppola and Akerman which to my mind undermines our ability to read Coppola's repetitions as feminist in the same way as Akerman's but rather places them into a knowingly postfeminist world. Lee argues that it would be easier for us to sense a 'hardcore' feminist impulse behind Coppola's supine girls if only she would finish her films with an outbreak of brutal violence. He cites Akerman and also Catherine Breillat, whose film *A Ma Soeur* (2001) carefully and painfully documents a girl's loss of virginity in real time, only to finish with a deliberately gratuitous double murder and rape, as examples of the kind of film-making that uses violence to express the pressures and tensions building behind the only too-smooth surface repetitions.[30] While I concur with Lee that a fundamental difference between Akerman and Coppola's use of time is that Coppola does not finish with an outbreak of violence, I would suggest that nevertheless, there is an aggression in her work captured in my term 'exploded homes.' However, the violence has occurred before the films begin. They have a postfeminist temporality, meaning that they come after (post) the feminist counter-cinema of Akerman and her understanding of the oppressive nature of domesticity and the heaviness of time on female bodies. The postfeminist world that these girls live in has already shattered their homes, questioning their nature and purpose and opening them up to the gaze, even as it also holds them within its walls. In other words, the repetition has continued beyond the feminist revolution, throwing into doubt its potency to effect radical change even as we still feel its effects.

For Anna Backman Rogers, repetition in Coppola's films is closely tied to the more culturally sanctioned acts of ritual. If for feminist art, repetition is associated with sheer drudgery and the daily grind associated specifically with women's labour, ritual speaks to more official and formal reifications of the repetitions involved in all human existence. Backman Rogers argues that *The Virgin Suicides* and *Lost in Translation* both offer 'sensitive portraits of the female rite of passage' and that *Marie Antoinette* intensifies this focus on 'the female adolescent body and the way in which it is re-fashioned and controlled through various rituals.'[31] In a series of persuasive and beautiful close readings of sequences from the film, Backman Rogers demonstrates how 'the ritual process through which Marie becomes a queen serves to control and re-fashion her identity and body; as such she becomes absorbed in the mechanistic procedures that maintain Versailles as an institution.'[32] Most useful for our purposes is how everyday activities such as eating, waking and dressing become subject to a series of baroque and cumbersome rituals. The ritual becomes a means in and of itself, a way to signal the unchanging nature of the world and its power hierarchies. The viewer infers that one day is exactly like the next. This impression is underscored both by the extra-diegetic

Baroque music, which has a strict, repetitive rhythm, and the repetition, no fewer than three times, to comic effect, of a sequence which shows Marie Antoinette rising, dressing, attending mass and taking lunch with her husband. Against these mechanical institutions, it is hardly surprising that the film finds such pleasure in the movement and unpredictability of fountains spurting, fireworks exploding, champagne cascading and elephant trunks flailing (of course, we can hardly ignore the phallic connotations of this, and they signal of course also the terrible personal pain and political problem caused by Louis XVI's impotence). As the camera plays impressionistically and intimately over the dresses, fans, jewels, shoes, sweets and the bodies of Marie Antoinette and her girlfriends, part of the pleasure of the infamous 'I Want Candy' montage sequence is that it shows clothing being re-appropriated by Marie Antoinette from the ritual of the lever for the expression of personal desire and to help forge intimate female friendship.

The film invites us to laugh at the sheer stupidity of such banal activities as getting up in the morning being treated with such high ceremony, as Marie Antoinette shivers, naked, while ladies-in-waiting bicker over who has the right to handle her clothes. The ossification of the processes of living into complex, baroque rituals are denounced by the lively young princess as ridiculous, only for her to be chastised by the curt rejoinder that 'this is Versailles!', the very location demanding and justifying the grotesque parody of domestic bliss. Although the term 'ridiculous', and Kirsten Dunst's distinctly LA Valley girl inflected delivery of the line, give this complaint the tone of a contemporary comment on the outrageously extravagant and absurd nature of Versailles life, all too out-of-touch with the impending winds of political change, it is in fact directly inspired by biographer Antonia Fraser's account of a 'notorious occasion' when Marie Antoinette was left cold and naked while various courtiers of greater rank arrived and handed over dressing duties. 'She tried to cover her impatience by laughing, but not before muttering audibly: "This is maddening! This is ridiculous!"'[33] It is only fitting to agree with Backman Rogers that Coppola's film produces a feminist discourse here as she shows how the female body is controlled and appropriated through ritual.

We can usefully compare this to a sequence early in *Lost in Translation* where Charlotte visits a Buddhist shrine in Tokyo, which offers a more optimistic reading of the potential ritual offers for a transformation rather than stultification of the self. Marie Antoinette and Charlotte share the fact they are foreign to the rituals being performed. As Backman Rogers explains, in Marie Antoinette's case, her foreignness is wiped from her when she is transported from Austria to Schüttern, a neutral area between Austria and France, where she is handed over to the French court. The ceremony takes place in a forested area, reminiscent of fairy-tales such as *Sleeping Beauty* or *Little Red Riding Hood*, intimating the quasi-magical nature of the transformation Marie Antoinette will undergo, from youngest daughter at the Austrian court to dauphine at the most prestigious court in the world at Versailles.[34] Marie Antoinette is divested of all her property, including a beloved pug dog, and all of her clothes: a cold female voiceover tells us 'this is an etiquette always observed on such an occasion.' The removal of her clothes is shown in a flurry of close-ups that fragments her body before we cut to a long shot where we see her final undergarments being removed by two maids. Marie Antoinette is filmed in long shot, from behind. The slenderness and delicacy of her naked adolescent frame is emphasised as she is framed between the thick dark curtains of the ceremonial tent in the foreground of the image and a huge chandelier balances over her head. Beyond her the bright light of the forest can be seen, as she is poised between two worlds: the innocence and naturalness of her childhood, and the vast machinery of the court and its trappings. In this image, the precarious vulnerability of her situation as foreigner is made all too visible, as she is dependent on others for her clothes, and by extension her new identity. The stifling and difficult nature of her new life is made clear as the first French garment we see her being clothed in is a bright blue cage-like crinoline (clothing and identity are discussed in more detail in chapter 4).

Charlotte also has her identity placed under erasure in *Lost in Translation*. She comments that she doesn't know who she married, or what she's supposed to become. In contrast to Marie Antoinette, no-one is there to force her to take up a new identity, and she struggles to find one for herself. She attempts to gain some kind of spiritual insight through attending a ritual ceremony at a Buddhist shrine. The brief sequence (it lasts less than a minute) begins with Charlotte consulting a metro map on the wall at a station. She then confidently makes her way through the system, captured by Lance Acord's 'guerrilla' camera as part of the ebb and flow of Tokyo city life.[35] She is intrigued by aspects of her journey, noticing for example the manga magazine of a fellow traveller, and the editing allows us easily to follow her journey through the station and out via escalator, as each cut shows us Charlotte in a new location (looking at map; waiting for train; in the train; leaving the train; on the escalator; near the top of the escalator; in the new station). This contrasts to the style in which Marie Antoinette's journey to Schüttern is filmed, where Coppola also uses sharp cuts and ellipses, but here to emphasise lack of change of the scenery, so that her journey appears interminable. Here, in just 7 fairly rapid shots that take 15 seconds of screen time, Charlotte has arrived at her destination, the Buddhist temple.

She is shown to the left of the frame in mid-shot, and the camera moves with her as she makes her way through the courtyard grounds to the temple (see Fig 3.3). Acord uses 35 mm film stock of higher than usual speed (Kodak's Vision 500T 5263) which enhances the soft and slightly desaturated look of the images, and emphasises the pastel tones of the grey stones and green trees in the rainy temple courtyard, giving an otherworldly and ethereal feel, suggesting a move to a different plane. Soft ambient extra-diegetic music, a minute long track by Brian Reitzell called 'On the Subway' that Coppola labels 'Tokyo dream pop', has been playing throughout the sequence; now it comes up slightly higher in the sound mix.[36] The deep resonant chime of a bell plays rhythmically through it, to the extent that it is difficult at first to tell if the bell is part of the music or not: in fact we first heard this bell when Charlotte was on the escalator, blending into the hubbub of voices, disembodied announcements and general sounds of city life, but again it was difficult for us to distinguish.

The camera follows Charlotte through the courtyard, but we cut before she arrives at the temple. The next shot is from inside the temple, so that we get to see her entrance from inside. We have now subtly shifted the perspective from which we see Charlotte's encounter with Buddhist ritual: while we were alongside her through her train journey, seeing what she saw, now we are watching her, emphasising her outsider status. We cut to a shot from Charlotte's point of view as she creeps round the door frame, half of it obscuring her view of the room. We then see six shots that alternate medium close-ups on Charlotte watching with images of kneeling, chanting monks in saffron robes performing a ceremony involving

Fig. 3.3. Charlotte visits a temple

striking a bell and burning incense.[37] We then cut back to the image of skyscrapers that Charlotte can see from her hotel bedroom window, gleaming pink in the late afternoon light; the rhythmic chanting of the monks and the chiming bell recalled now by the staccato wailing of a siren and the pulsing beeps of a ring tone. The phone is picked up, and a women says 'hello?'. We cut to a medium close-up of Charlotte, filmed from the side and slightly behind, giving this scene a feeling of intrusion, as if we are covert witness to her moment of crisis, as her voice shaky with tears, she answers 'Lauren?'

Her tears are provoked we learn because she 'didn't feel anything' at the ceremony she has just witnessed. Lauren is busy and distracted, not really listening to Charlotte, nor picking up on her distress. But the ritual has ironically unlocked something for Charlotte as she senses her terrible lostness and confusion. She has the beginning of a self-knowledge that will lead her toward the empathetic friendship she shares with Bob and possibly ultimately be the way out of her unhappy marriage. As Homay King explains in her beautiful reading of the film, Charlotte as 'lost girl' is an important corrective to the masculine insistence on mastery of the world[38] (one implied in the rituals of *Marie Antoinette*, which attempt to corral the messiness of human existence – sex, eating, ablutions – to the intransigence of absolute order). Lucy Bolton's comment that while her wonderings in Tokyo are aimless, they have an investigative quality to them which means they are not random, demonstrates usefully the difference between the activity of the male detective in a (district of the) city coded as 'the exotic East' and Charlotte.[39] The male detective, such as Jake in *Chinatown* (Polanski, 1972) or Deckard in *Blade Runner* (Scott, 1982) investigates a crime he thinks took place 'out there' in the world, only belatedly realising that he has been duped, blinded by his own sense of superiority; in contrast, Charlotte understands the necessity to know herself and desires to explore Tokyo rather than decode it. For all that 'one might wish that the lost girl would stop soul searching for a moment and see something other than her own alienation reflected in the windows and television screens around her', a reading that is attentive to gender allows for the film's more positive encounters with alterity to emerge.[40] We witness Charlotte as a lone female wanderer who attempts to translate her own experience into the terms of Japanese ritual. According to King, Bob remains a hopeless fish out of water (although even here we might want to note his comment to his wife that he wants to start eating more healthy Japanese food at home, suggesting he too is open to change and a closer relation to the other). However, while Bob remains baffled by Japan, Charlotte remains open to the possibility of a meaningful encounter with Japanese culture. When Charlotte is upset that she wasn't affected by the Buddhist ceremony, we glimpse a longing for a transformative encounter that the ritual promises to provide. King argues there is a naivety to Charlotte's quest and that her looking to Japan to provide answers about herself participates in a potentially Orientalist fantasy of the exotic East, and it is only when safely tucked under Bob's protective wing she can truly risk engaging with Tokyo as a ludic and playful space. Yet, as Bolton points out, it is Charlotte who facilitates Bob's encounter with Tokyo nightlife, via her friend Charlie Brown/ himself [Fumihiro Hayashi], and generally the film establishes a relationship of reciprocity between them, so that, for example, Charlotte introduces Bob to an aspect of Tokyo he otherwise would not have seen; he then carries her up to her hotel room and tucks her into bed after she has fallen asleep.[41] Furthermore, Charlotte's trip to the temple, her witnessing of the ritual, and her disappointment when it fails to move her testify also to a desire to be open to that which is new and unknown, to foster ritual as a tool of self-knowledge and advancement. The ritual can be refashioned for a feminist purpose when it is framed as a means to change, rather than an attempt at (impossible) stasis. Charlotte's tears of frustration and disappointment testify perhaps to the rather Utopian aspect of this reading of ritual, caught as she is in a chronotope that privileges repetition over revolution, but also at least demonstrate that she senses the need for change.

Taking together Smaill, Backman Roger and King's attentiveness to various aspects of repetition, rite and ritual in Coppola's work, and using them in a chronotopic analysis where we understand this temporality as inherently linked to the quasi-domestic space of the exploded home, allows us to come to a more complete view of Coppola's project and its relation to the postfeminist cultural formation. Unlike the prefeminist site of hidden female labour, or the mainstream postfeminist site of (often ironic) domestic revivalism and retro-chic, Coppola's exploded home chronotope offers us a view of a place shattered (and thus opened to the outside) by feminist insight but unable to find new forms or expressions, and doomed to repetitions rather than revolutions.

Public Femininity: Postfeminism, the Girl, and the Exploded Home

The exploded home chronotope offers an attractive metaphor for, but also a concrete realisation of, a key aspect of contemporary culture: the flourishing of what Lauren Berlant terms an 'intimate public'. As its name implies, the intimate public blurs the boundaries between the private and the public spheres, in a way that is reified in Coppola's glass houses, celebrity mansions and swanky hotels.

The intimate public enables 'a reframing of intimacy [...] to engage and disable a prevalent U.S. discourse on the proper relation between public and private, spaces traditionally associated with the gendered division of labor.'[42] If this seems an opportunity for a reimagining of how life might be organised, the intimate public still fosters an attachment to this division, especially in its normative definition of what it means to 'have a life': 'the couple form and its spinoffs [...]effectively siphon off critical thought about the personal and the political: to refuse the maturational narrative of "a life" would require a confrontation with another idea, that social forces and problems of living that seem not about you are, nonetheless, central to the shape of your story.'[43]

In terms of cultural production, Berlant defines the intimate public as operating 'when a market opens up a bloc of consumers, claiming to circulate texts and things that express these people's particular core interests and desires [...] participants in the intimate public *feel* as though it expresses what is common amongst them.'[44] Women's culture was the first intimate public of significant scale in the United States, and flourishes in the largely female and frequently girl-focused address of postfeminist cultural production as

> a market domain where a set of problems associated with managing femininity is expressed and worked through incessantly [...] In all cases, it [femininity] flourishes by circulating as an already felt need, a sense of emotional continuity among women who identify with the expectation that, as women, they will manage personal life and lubricate emotional worlds.[45]

Samiha Matin's gloss on this is that this explains femininity's resonance as 'a structure of emotional expectation and identity-making that imaginatively binds together women *who may have nothing else in common*.'[46] This chimes with Benedict Anderson's famous definition of the nation itself as an imagined community.[47] For Anderson, the dawning of print culture, and especially its widespread dissemination and consumption in the bourgeois nineteenth century, was key to the creation of a community bonded by a written national language united above the oral dialect vernacular but below the transnational sacred Latin. The baker reading the same French-language morning newspaper in Strasbourg as a banker in Marseille would feel a more intimate connection to him than to a fellow baker reading a German-language paper just over the border in Karlsruhe, creating a sense of cohesion and identity through belonging to a nation-state that trumps affinities of profession or class. Furthermore, it seals the importance of the connection between language and national identity, for as Anderson explains, it is possible to have intimate relations without sharing a means of common communication, as long as one is in the same room; but for communication to occur across distance, the mediation of language is necessary. It is not irrelevant to understanding the shift in the status of the dynastic royal family, as their supranational constituency, once a sign of prestige and power, became a handicap that needed to be hidden in the modern age (hence the invention of the Windsors). Marie Antoinette, a Habsburg, and thus from a family whose power was sealed through sexual politics, to the extent that its motto was 'Bella gerant alli, tu felix Austria nube' [let others wage war; you, happy Austria, marry], falls foul in some ways of this increasing sense of national sovereignty and identity.[48]

Most significant is the unlikelihood that our two newspaper-reading French men will ever meet. Their shared consumption of the paper (enabled of course by the growth of literacy) gives them a sense they belong to the same community, a connection that exists only on an imagined plane. Indeed, a nation is of necessity an imagined community, as it is impossible for all its constituent members to meet and know one another. Important for my purposes here is the connection Matin implies between Berlant's imagined community of women identifying with femininity, and Anderson's imagined community of people identifying with the nation. Clearly in Anderson's case, the place where these imagined identities circulate is that of the territorially defined and bordered nation-state. In Berlant's case, the territories in which the intimate public of femininity can be located are both more specific and more diverse, cutting across the borders of nation, but embedded also in a very particular language and powerful feeling.

Coppola's films offer us a particularly acute set of locations that give material form to this contradictory and paradoxical management of femininity, concentrating in particular on the 'intimate public' of girl culture, and the transnational connections of feeling it enables. Girlhood is a private knowledge but also a public concern, a blurring of borders enabled by the exploded home. Through their emphasis on youthful femininity shaped by these spaces, Coppola's films offer us the potential to think through these 'exploded homes' as the ideal chronotope of the postfeminist condition, its notion of girlhood as 'spectacular', in Sarah Projansky's sense of the term, and its reliance on an intimate public sphere.[49] They provide the material grounds for an imagined community of girlhood in a way that is analogous to Anderson's imagined community of the nation. Of course, just as Anderson's imagined community depends in fact on the repression/exclusion of difference (in the example of the baker and the banker I gave above, that of class), postfeminist culture's intimate public of girlhood also denies difference in its celebration and circulation of young feminine identities. Coppola gives a particular shape and form to this femininity through this exploded home chronotope, which depends on the privileged access previously discussed. The paradox of the intimate public as a space that offers girls emotional connections, values the subjective experience of femininity, but brutally denies the impacts of gender, class and race difference, is both sign and symptom in her films.

Coppola's exploded home chronotope can be divided into two highly gendered variants. In her films that concentrate on girl protagonists, and use various devices to marginalise male experience, the exploded home is one in which private experiences become made public, in which the homes' fractured and friable borders let the outside in: the invasive prurient television cameras of gossipy local news in *The Virgin Suicides*; the rioting mob in *Marie Antoinette*; the celebrity-obsessed teens in *The Bling Ring*. In contrast, the films which place a male mid-life crisis into dialogue with the identity crisis of a young(er) girl, *Lost in Translation* and *Somewhere*, suggest more the search for a home to return to, the desire to take public places and try to restore to them a sense of privacy. In both these films, girls turn the anonymous spaces of hotel rooms into more individualised, cosy and welcoming spaces; Charlotte decorates her room in the Park Hyatt in Tokyo with artificial pink cherry blossoms, imitating the *sakura* for which Japan is famous, in *Lost in Translation*; Cleo turns her father's suite of rooms in Chateau Marmont into a sanctuary, cooking him eggs benedict (with perfect hollandaise) after ordering up ingredients from room service, and snuggling up with him on a sofa in the lobby. Both these films offer a more optimistic view, where public or semi-public places become quasi-private spaces of intimacy and understanding between the two characters, such as in the karaoke booth where Charlotte and Bob surreptitiously flirt with each other through the lyrics of the songs they perform, or the day Johnny and Cleo spend in the grounds of the Chateau Marmont hanging out together. The sequence communicates a tender, unhurried enjoyment of spending time together, with its slow paced camera-work, inconsequential activities (playing table-tennis, goofing about in the pool, sunbathing), and laid-back, mellow demo-track by the Strokes (I'll Try Anything Once). The achievement of a private understanding within the semi-public spaces of the hotel is especially communicated by the slow zoom out of Johnny and Cleo sunbathing and drinking lemonade. We begin the sequence in a relatively tight frame that shows Cleo and Johnny on sunbeds with greenery behind them. As the camera slowly zooms out (the shot lasts for 90 seconds), more information is added, so that we see Cleo and Johnny are by a hotel pool, and are accompanied by fellow guests. We have moved from what we could imagine to be a private garden to a more public arena, and the sense that privacy is fleeting for the celebrity is communicated by the sense this is a day snatched from a rather meaningless and random schedule of interviews, publicity stunts and parties.

Privacy then is a fleeting sensation, and of course, we should notice that even here, the hotel can take on some of the aspects of a prison or a cemetery: Bob first bonds with Charlotte in the Park Hyatt's hotel when he suggests they organise a prison-break. Johnny Marco drives his black Ferrari 360 Modena past a smashed-up car crashed into the wall of the Chateau (a reference to fashion photographer Helmut Newton, who died in 2004, when his car sped out of control leaving the Chateau Marmont and crashed into a wall: he was 83 and it is assumed he had a heart attack at the wheel. Coppola had met him in the hotel that very morning).[50]

As Julianne Pidduck comments, Berlant's account of intimacy's presence within contemporary culture can be seen as an extension of Jürgen Habermas's description of the bourgeois intimate sphere of the family: 'an idealised site that facilitated the emancipation … of an inner realm, following its own laws, from extrinsic purposes of any sort.'[51] Pidduck goes onto explain that, for Habermas, the intimate sphere fosters the masculine citizen-subject, a certain Western model of subjectivity that corresponds with the transition from the objective, social and public orientations of the classical world to the subjective, individualist and private orientation of life and its associated artistic expressions (such as the literary forms of the letter and the novel). Pidduck further explains that 'the conditions of possibility of the modern subject arise symbolically from a mythology of home, an interior and anterior (gendered and classed) place to be overcome and returned to.'[52] In this description we see echoes of Coppola's gendered exploded home chronotope. When the film concentrates on the young girl, the home is figured as a prison, a tomb, or both: a place to be overcome. When, conversely, the film moves towards male melodrama, the home is here a Utopian space that is not figured into the film but is strongly implied as a site of welcome retreat following the revivifying impact of youthful femininity: a place men wish to return to?

Clearly, the contemporary period described by Berlant differs enormously from that defined by Habermas, not least in the admission of women as citizen-subjects into the political/economic realm. However, these connections outlined by Pidduck demonstrate the inter-relation of a certain political sense of the individual self, modes of expression and the home. As my use of the term 'exploded homes' suggests, Coppola's chronotope operates as a device that shatters selves as much as offers them grounds for expression, the very possibility of constructing a stable sense of self placed under erasure by the blurring of private and public. The grounds of this girl-focused postfeminist intimate public would seem then fundamentally insecure, echoing Diane Negra's claim that for all postfeminist culture celebrates female visibility and success in the public sphere, it remains a period that feels 'punishing and anxious' for many.[53] The girl-focused films begin frequently showcasing often glamorous and ostentatious homes, but for all they offer the backdrop for an enchanting/iconic/aspirational performance of youthful femininity, they finish with the homes abandoned, destroyed, invaded, vulnerable. This beautiful but precarious home poised always on the brink of its own unravelling thus comes to symbolise the insecure sense of self that forms the lining of what may on the surface seem to be an attractive and grounded subjectivity. For Gaston Bachelard, the home is a site of very particular sort of topophilia: 'before he is "cast into the world", as claimed by certain hazy metaphysics, man is laid in the cradle of the house.'[54] The image of the house puts us 'in possession of a veritable principle of psychological integration' and provides us a 'topography of Intimate Being.'[55] He explains that 'our soul is an abode. And by remembering "houses" and "rooms" we learn to "abide" within ourselves. Now everything becomes clear, the house images move in both directions: they are in us as much as we are in them.'[56] Bachelard's insight offers us a guiding principle as to why postfeminist culture returns with such relish to a retroactive fantasy of the home: it suggests also the possibility of reclaiming a solid sense of self in a culture where choice is promoted to such an extent that identity itself becomes a dizzying array of possibilities. In contrast, Coppola too builds on Bachelard's understanding that homes and bodies have a reciprocal relation, mapping out a beautiful, ornate, ostentatious but vulnerable home for her girls to inhabit, demonstrating the perilous position of the beautiful successful girl in the postfeminist moment.

Shattered Selves and Uncanny Ghosts

This notion of a shattered self is most concretely demonstrated in the final shot of *Marie Antoinette*. Following some unspecified time after the royal couple's departure from the chateau, it displaces the violence of their deaths onto the image of a wrecked bedroom. In a static image lasting 15 seconds, with sounds of bird song and what at one point seems to be the sounds of a bird's wings fluttering in some off-screen space, we see a room opened to the elements: sunlight pouring in through smashed windows, an ornate door hanging off its hinges. Dominating the image, and therefore signalling its metaphorical status, is an enormous glass chandelier that has fallen or been ripped from the ceiling, lying prone on the floor, its glass shattered across the room. The proliferation of glass at Versailles (particularly mirrors) that symbolised Marie Antoinette's continual public performance of a private self is smashed, the very tenuous existence of Versailles as home finally over.

We find a similar logic in *The Bling Ring*, in which the performance of celebrity selfhood via the internet (in particular, tweeting one's absence from home in order to attend parties) allows teenagers to break into the homes, so that actual and virtual spaces of celebrity become enmeshed and boundaries are trangressed. In a virtuoso single shot lasting 1 minute 45 seconds, the camera slowly zooms towards a house made almost entirely of glass, so slowly that the movement is barely perceptible.[57] The high-angle mimics that of CCTV surveillance cameras and thus recalls the surveillance footage we have seen earlier in the film (see Fig 3.4). The house is perched on a hill high above the backdrop of the city: as we slowly move toward the house, the trees and the cityscape fade from view so the house and its swimming pool fill the frame. Throughout the sequence, we see Rebecca and Marc as small figures running in and out of rooms, and lights turning on and off as they dart through the house. The soundtrack blends together manufactured and natural sounds of night time Los Angeles, as we hear helicopters, sirens, and the screeches, howls and coos of wild life (mainly coyotes).[58] This sequence underlines the breaching of borders, between interior and exterior, city and country, urban and rural, in the idealised contemporary celebrity lifestyle where fame leads ironically to a retreat into 'the hills' above Los Angeles. Coppola's image of the glass house and the two small dark figures running through it illustrates the incommensurate nature of the simultaneous desire for fame and privacy, and the untenable contradiction of constructing a self based wholly on the ability to appeal to the gaze of others, and then rejecting

Fig. 3.4. Audrina Patridge's glass house

that gaze. It is perhaps unsurprising that this home belongs to Audrina Patridge, a reality TV star, and thus absolutely paradigmatic of this blurring between personal and public life, as the TV series she starred in, *The Hills*, purported to show her 'real' life, particularly her tempestuous love life. Coppola references this by showing us footage of Audrina in front of a hoarding advertising the show at a red carpet promotional event, being interviewed about what venues she enjoys frequenting when she goes out, and whether or not she has stopped partying so hard now she is a relationship. We cut to an image of Marc and Rebecca sitting on a bed, both with laptops, scrolling through information about Audrina, and thus implicitly having just watched the footage. 'Oh my God, I literally love Audrina's style,' exclaims Rebecca, as they click through dozens of images of Audrina. 'Can you see where she lives?' In the next image, the two of them are running through Audrina's home, the blurring of boundaries between the private home life of the star and what is readily available for public consumption now complete. Later in the film, we see a similar image of Marc and Rebecca in Patridge's glass house on a television set in Marc's bedroom: Patridge has released footage from her private security cameras that she has trained on her house to the media in an attempt to discover who has burglarized her house. The unexpected intrusion of his own image, made visible and public, into the privacy of his bedroom (underlined by his hostile and panicked reaction to his father knocking on the door) makes Marc uneasy and nervous, another illustration of the uncertain borders between private and public, invisible and notorious.

The mapping of the death/destruction of the self onto the shattered environment is echoed in the suburban setting of *The Virgin Suicides*. The 1970s, the period in which the film is set, was an era characterised by an awareness of and anxiety over environmental degradation. The ecology movement flourished, with the setting up of the Conservation Society, Friends of the Earth, Greenpeace and later the Socialist Environment and Resources Association. *The Virgin Suicides* shows us a suburban landscape dotted with trees marked for removal on account of Dutch elm disease. At the end of the film, the atmosphere is overcome with a swamp smell rising from a spill at a processing plant that has increased phosphates in the lake. Cecilia mourns the fact that another animal has been added to the endangered species list and the four eldest Lisbon sisters protest the removal of a tree from their front yard. 'This sense of environmental decay acts metaphorically for the narrative's account of the short lives and suicide of the five adolescent Lisbon sisters.'[59]

At the same time as Coppola's exploded home chronotope renders concrete and material the notion of an 'intimate public', making the domestic space itself an arena of spectacle and display, a peculiar theatre of the gaze where femininity is relentlessly performed, she equally presents us the home as a site of trauma and breakdown in terms that cannot help but recall Sigmund Freud's notion of the uncanny. In its original German term, *unheimlich*, literally meaning unhomely, etymology reveals to us the term's ability to express the ambivalence of the home. Indeed, etymology is key to Freud's careful explication of what exactly this term connotes. For him, the term is redolent with meaning. The word heimlich is not unambiguous, but

> belongs to two sets of ideas, which, without being contradictory, are yet very different: on the one hand it means what is familiar and agreeable, and on the other, what is concealed and kept out of sight. 'Unheimlich' is customarily used [...] as the contrary only of the first signification of heimlich, and not of the second. [...] thus heimlich is a word the meaning of which develops in the direction of ambivalence, until it finally coincides with its opposite unheimlich. Unheimlich is in some way or other a sub species of heimlich.[60]

Unheimlich thus picks up several shades of meaning. It means that which is unfamiliar, strange, or spooky, from contradicting the first meaning of heimlich. However, it is used interchangeably with the second meaning of heimlich, to mean that which is hidden, concealed, secret, unknown. At the very heart of the definition of the word there is a kind of discursive unease which is carried over into its application. Freud places the emotions of fear, uncertainty, unfamiliarity and strangeness into the heart of the private sphere, the home (heim). Its emotions are inchoate, the result of a trauma of strangeness taking place in that which should be the most familiar, the most known, the most safe. 'Uncanniness' (the widely agreed translation for the German term unheimlich) is not thus simply unfamiliarity: it expresses rather the trauma of the unfamiliar irrupting into that which is thought to be known and safe.

Consider for example the type of language used by Paris Hilton as she discusses the experience of watching CCTV footage recorded on her personal security cameras of teenagers breaking into home and enjoying her nightclub room and riffling through her jewellery closet.

> The first time I saw the surveillance videos from my security tapes I was so freaked out. It just really weirded me out to see these people walking into my house with their hooded sweatshirts on, running up and down the stairs [...]It was just very creepy to me that people could actually do that.[61]

Hilton's vocabulary – weird, freaky, creepy – names in so many words the uncanny experience she had and that Coppola's film re-enacts. She both recognised and did not recognise her home: she both knew and did not know where the teens were going.

In Freudian theory, the uncanny moment is the moment when the boy child sees his mother's genitals and believes her to have been castrated. This is repressed through fetish substitution i.e. through the operation of the fetish, the child can believe that his mother has a phallus, whilst simultaneously knowing that she has also 'given it up', sacrificed it. The fetish, unlike other perversions, works not just through repression, but active disavowal. The fetish can then become revered. The trauma is thus masked through the reverence of fetish objects (typically items that obliquely reference the genitals such as shoes or fur), which both substitute for the lost phallus and smooth over the very story of that loss. As Louise J. Kaplan comments, 'a fetish is designed to keep the lies hidden, to divert attention from the whole story by focussing attention on the detail.'[62] Robert Stoller also picks up on the narrative quality of the fetish object by commenting that it is 'a story masquerading as an object.'[63] The object or the detail can be revered and mask the whole story of loss.

Given the uncanny nature of the Coppola home, it is not surprising that objects come to take significant roles, called upon to overcome significant lacks and conjure up proximity. Beginning with the procurement of Cecilia's dairy, the boys in *The Virgin Suicides*, 'collect everything we could of the theirs [the Lisbon sisters]', and the film visually catalogues various and sundry items such as year book photographs, invitations, eye-lash curlers, lipstick, records, hair brushes and nail polish, as if the material objects could stand in for the lack of physical proximity to the girls the boys have. *Marie Antoinette* has its infamous 'I Want Candy' montage, where to the soundtrack of Bow Wow Wow's punk song of the same name, Coppola shows us a series of images of shoes, pastries, champagne, raw silk and ostentatious jewels to depict a decadent and frivolous world of conspicuous consumption. The placing of a pair of lavender Converse trainers in Marie Antoinette's shoe closet (a joke from her brother, Roman, whose second unit filmed the montage sequence, and that Coppola enjoyed so much she kept in the final film), along with the punk soundtrack, draws our attention to the gap between the time period depicted and the time of the film, as if here objects will be able to compensate for lack of historical proximity (see Fig 3.5).[64] In *Lost in Translation*, objects from the banal American domestic space seem to take a on a strange life of their own in the Tokyo hotel rooms: a series of near identical red carpet samples arrive by Fed-Ex and spills to the floor; a fax churns out

Fig. 3.5. Marie Antoinette's shoe closet

templates for shelving in the middle of the night. Bob's apathy and bewilderment at his wife's attempts to engage him in the project of redecorating his study speak to the lack of emotional proximity between them that these objects represent a futile attempt to fill. Finally, the obsessive interest in and knowledge of designer fashion in *The Bling Ring* culminates in the physical theft of objects that have come to stand in for the celebrity themselves, as a way of reaching out towards them and being closer to them. The film showcases the teens' instant recognition of designer labels, as they exclaim over Paris's Louboutin shoes, Alexander McQueen sunglasses and a Balmain dress, or recognise the dress Rachel Bilson wore to the Cosmopolitan awards. This is a world in which all experience is increasingly mediated and abstracted, as the girls recognise objects they have never seen before from images of them, and then go on to upload images of themselves with the objects to Facebook. In all the films, the lived relation of the body to the phenomenological world is replaced by an interaction with objects that somehow come to stand in for it. 'Authentic' experience becomes elusive and allusive, placed beyond the horizon of the everyday and pushed into a series of fictive fantasy lands of the exotic, the pastoral, the élite – the travel catalogues ordered by the Lisbon sisters; the aesthetically stimulating nightlife of Tokyo; the carefully cultivated idyll of the Trianon; the celebrity mansions of Los Angeles.

As such, Coppola's exploded homes chronotope captures perfectly the strange fusion of the homely and the traumatised captured in Freud's term. It offers a vision of a home made strange by feminism, as the domestic idyll was fiercely criticised by second wave feminists such as Germaine Greer, Kate Millet and Shulamith Firestone, and suggests feminism itself as a traumatic unsettling of the home that will not go away but continues to render it uncanny even if its effects are disavowed or repressed through the use of the fetish. In this way, Coppola's exploded home chronotope can be placed into a continuum of postfeminist cultural production that debates feminist politics and influence through such tropes of the supernatural as ghosts, hauntings, vampires and telepathy which Munford and Waters summarise by using the term 'postfeminist gothic.' They argue that the Gothic and feminism share an interest 'in what goes on behind closed doors' (a suitably spatial metaphor) and that 'seeking to intervene in the legislation of women's choices and experiences, feminism necessarily trespasses on the "dark" Gothic territories of power, sex and violence [...] In light of such critiques, the Gothic suggests itself as a *heimlich* venue for "ghost feminism".'[65]

Munford and Waters use their apposite and brilliant pun of ghost feminism to refer to a tendency within popular and academic scholarship to Gothicise feminism and feminists, casting feminism itself as a kind of ghost that haunts the contemporary postfeminist moment. To flesh out this idea, Munford and Waters invoke Jacques Derrida's attempts to theorise the post-communist era's spectres of Marx via the concept of 'hauntology', suggesting that this concept could also illuminate some of feminism's spectral dimensions. They go onto explain that

> deliberately evocative of 'ontology', with all its implications of being and presence, hauntology refutes such certainties by invoking the ghost as a figure of undecideability that productively unsettles received categories of identity. More crucially, though, Derrida uses hauntology as a tool for excavating the strange temporality of the haunting [...] in which the ghost functions as a sign of a slippage between the past, present and future in order to reveal the radical contingency of the 'now'.[66]

The ghost is both legacy and prophecy – a spectre from the past that may return (and keep on returning). For Munford and Waters:

> hauntology appears to encompass many of the issues that have beset debates in the late twentieth and early twenty-first centuries about feminism's relationship to the past and its potential to intervene in women's futures [...] if feminism is an ontology, a way of being, then it is also a hauntology in the Derridean sense – a way of being that is shaped by anxieties about the past, concern for the future and an overarching

uncertainty about its own status and ability to effect change in a world where its own necessity is constantly thrown into doubt.[67]

While none of Coppola's films could be deemed supernatural as such, some of them do have elements of the gothic imagination and her spaces often seem spooky, uncanny, potentially traumatic. Bree Hoskin labels *The Virgin Suicides* 'suburban Gothic', commenting that its thematic concern of the destruction of childhood is 'as much about anxiety as it is about longing, thus sharing similarities with a Gothic filmic and literary tradition in which fear and desire are often inextricably linked.'[68] Similarly, Wendy Haslem argues that 'the presence of the Gothic casts a shadow over the promise of romance for Bob and Charlotte.'[69] It is in Coppola's refusal of the romantic comedy convention that would bring Bob and Charlotte together as sexual and romantic partners that Haslem locates the Gothic impulse of the film. She argues that

> Coppola's primary characters seem to be caught between convention and indeterminacy, a distinctly Gothic trap. According to Vijay Mishra, Gothic characters are 'shadowed by others and their individuality, their radical difference or uniqueness, dismantled through a technique of duplication or uncanny repetition' (p. 54). Coppola gives her primary characters a Gothic twist replacing the older, brooding, tired masculine figure and the young, naive heroine with a feminine adventurer who provides the masculine figure with the motivation and opportunity to journey into the unfamiliar landscape. Charlotte offers Bob an invitation to explore the unimaginable and unknowable in Tokyo, ultimately a sublime experience that defamiliarises and renews his perspective.[70]

Once they escape the Gothic castle, Bob reverses his T-shirt and Charlotte dons a pink wig, and it is in disguise, as their energised superhero doubles, that they can explore Tokyo as a playground and fantasy-land before finally succumbing to elusive sleep.

I am tempted, following the adjectival examples provided by Hoskin and Haslem, to label *The Bling Ring* 'Bling Gothic'. As Paris Hilton offers us a tour of her home, she explains that the jewellery closet was completely emptied by the teens, but the closet we *actually* see is full of jewels: absence and presence co-joined, one actually speaking to the other. On the one hand, this recalls Freud's fetish and its play of substituting absence via presence (and vice versa); on the other, it speaks to a deep seated anxiety about the impermanency of things. Underlying the spectacular performances of femininity that occur in these homes is a fear of emptiness; hollowed-out rooms that speak of loss: a loss of objects that prefigures a loss of self, given that objects come to stand in for the self. This loss of self occurs through imprisonment, or death, or both. Desire is slippery and ungraspable, as Coppola's films are filled with girls who variously can't get what they want (Lux Lisbon); don't know what they want (Charlotte); only want what they want because celebrities want it (the Bling Ring). There is a paradox here in which the home seems either too open – too vulnerable to pillage, attack, theft; or else too closed – a site of containment, oppression, suffocation. Although Coppola's films tend toward a dreamy, feminine, light-infused aesthetic and tone, under the glossy repeating surfaces lie gothic consequences: homes as tombs; homes as prisons; homes as empty, hollowed out shells vulnerable to attack.

Homes as Spectacles

Coppola's recurrent exploding home chronotope erases the boundaries between private and public, intimate and notorious. The private space of the home is opened to public inspection, censure and fascination, as the girl and her home become intertwined and read as one in *The Virgin Suicides*, *Marie Antoinette* and *The Bling Ring*. Coppola theatricalises the domestic setting, so that private homes become spectacles designed for the gaze. In particular, the girl in the home becomes an object of fascination, and the home becomes a kind of theatrical site for the performance of girlhood both within and outside of the diegesis – it is notable that the creation of the domestic spectacle is for an on-screen as well as an off-screen audience (courtiers, celebrity-obsessed teens, news programme viewers). At Versailles, intimate and/or everyday activities such as sexual intercourse, childbirth, dressing and eating, are performed for a crowd of gawping courtiers in the rituals discussed above. Marie Antoinette acknowledges her status as eroticised spectacle and historical curiosity for the contemporary viewer in the film's credit sequence when, dressed in white underwear with grandiose feather plumes in her hair, she turns to the camera, and breaking the fourth wall, smiles and winks at the audience.[71] The film cleverly draws our attention to how a contemporary media audience demands spectacle of its celebrities in a way that could be seen as analogous to the demands for private life to be made public in the court of Versailles. In the film's penultimate scene, Louis XVI and Marie Antoinette sit at an enormous table, with an ornate dinner of jellied vegetables and fish in front of them, exquisitely displayed. Louis is served wine by his servant, as has always been the case, and the scene is shown frontally, emphasising its status as theatrical presentation. Now, this presentation is only for the off-screen spectator, for the once-fawning courtiers have fled. The soundtrack is dominated by the noise of the shouting, rioting, starving mob

125

outside, whose presence fails to impinge on the utterly stultifying ritual, in which no food is actually consumed. Spectacle has replaced nourishment, the public performance of eating more significant than the ingestion of food.

Paris Hilton's mansion functions to showcase Paris as spectacle, from the repeated display of her image in framed magazine covers on the walls to the notorious 'Paris pillows' (cushions featuring a close-up image of her face) that draw delighted and shocked recognition from the teens who break into her home (see Fig 3.6). The girls comment on the amount of mirrors in her closet and her nightclub room features two enormous soft-porn style photographs of Hilton: one a close-up head-and-shoulders profile shot, her head thrown back as if in ecstasy, her hair billowing; the other a full-length nude portrait with her entwined in rope. The moments where Marie Antoinette melts into the décor of her surroundings, such as when she is wearing a dress identical to the wall-paper, or when a zoom out reduces her to a tiny figure dwarfed by the sheer scale of Versailles, are here hyperbolised. Paris's home has taken up Paris's image and reflects it back to her, so that the mirror-function itself has become dispersed and diffuse. The body of the girl and that of the home are at these times indistinguishable, the home exploded in a different way here. On the one hand, it loses its function as domestic inhabitation, and becomes a device for the showcasing of the celebrity body. On the other, it also becomes more powerful, able to overwhelm the individual so that she becomes nothing but her appearance, a surface rather than an agentic subject. In this case, the 'explosion' of the home also enables an amorphous expansion.

Fig. 3.6. Paris Hilton's staircase

While Versailles and Paris's mansion, marked as they are either by historical significance, or the trappings of contemporary celebrity culture, are arguably
unusual homes, we find the same trope of home as site of spectacle and absorption
of the girl body in the 'ordinary' suburban home of the Lisbon sisters. Arguably,
it is all the more significant that this suburban home of ordinary girls is just as
vulnerable to the paradoxical logics of postfeminist domesticity as the more obviously iconic houses of Marie Antoinette and Paris Hilton, and it is therefore to
this home that I dedicate the rest of this section. It is staged as spectacle several
times within the film's diegesis. It becomes spectacle for the group of boys over
the street, one of whom (as a middle-aged man) narrates the film. The boys spy
on the house using both a telescope they cluster around and a pair of binoculars,
the use of two vision aids here underlining their desperation to catch even a mere
glimpse of Lux Lisbon making out on the roof. As they watch, they eat popcorn, a
subtle indication of their position as members of an audience not unlike the one
watching the film. This is of course part of their doomed exercise to see beyond
the effulgent dazzle of girlhood I discuss in chapter 2, but it nevertheless signals
the boys' desire to gaze at the home, and the alignment of the domestic space
with the girl herself. Coppola demonstrates how the use of audio and visual technologies constantly undermines the borders of the home: telescopes, binoculars,
television cameras, record players, telephones. While *Marie Antoinette* and *The
Bling Ring* show us homes placed under explosive pressure by the public nature of
their inhabitants and the perceived glossy visibility of their iconic performances
of girlhood (as princess, as celebrity), *The Virgin Suicides* in contrast places itself
into the mundane everyday world of suburbia. Hoskin powerfully demonstrates
the importance of this suburban setting to the film, as it draws on the suburbs'
complex mediation of nature and technology. She quotes Susan Stewart's meditation on the suburbs:

> Let me begin with the invisibility and blindness of the suburbs [...]
> The suburbs present us with a negation of the present, a landscape con-
> sumed by its past and future. Hence the two foci of the suburbs: the
> nostalgic and the technological.[72]

It is through the technological that the Lisbon family home is exploded, its intimate
moments rendered public. The sequence that demonstrates the power of television
to break through the seemingly hermetically sealed home, and open up its private
griefs to public prurience, begins with a ground-level shot of a pair of feet walking
over a tarmac drive through what seem abandoned newspapers, before moving
to a close-up of a hand knocking on a front door, and then a medium-close up

profile shot of a woman, notebook in hand, standing at the door. The door opens a crack, and an awkward conversation begins about Cecilia, who has just committed suicide, between the woman, who introduces herself as Lydia Perl/Suki Kaiser, and Bonnie and Mary, who stand in the doorway. In the shot-reverse shot pattern of the sequence, the sense that the journalist will not succeed in her aim to cross the threshold of the home and enter into its private parts is emphasised by the fact the dark door takes up over half the image of Bonnie and Mary. Bonnie's face is partially obscured by the door and although Mary speaks, her arm placed defensively against her hip and the angle of her body block our view into the home. As they answer Lydia's questions, which rapidly move from facile to intrusive ('did she have any special interests or hobbies?' 'Did she ever talk about ending her life?'), Mrs. Lisbon comes to the door, asks what's happening, and firmly shuts the door in Lydia's face. However, Coppola's edit cleverly shows how the shutting of the door will not prevent the Lisbon home being made into image, discursive object and fascinating spectacle, as we cut to a close-up of a television set screening a news programme from Channel 8. We see the dark wood of the TV set framing Lydia in shown in full frontal close-up, microphone in hand as she talks directly to camera, the Lisbon home behind her. This close-up is subtly different from the one where she spoke to the Lisbon girls: whereas there, she was filmed at a slight low angle, indicating that she was being looked at by the Lisbon girls, here the camera looks directly at her. Partly, of course, this is an accurate reconstruction of TV news presentation style, but it also speaks to the presumed neutrality of the news journalist who is speaking to a generic homogenous television audience (and, by implication here, cinema spectators). Lydia claims that 'the suicide of an East side teenager last summer has increased the awareness of a national crisis. I now stand in front of the home where Cecilia Lisbon, a 13-year-old who liked to paint and write poetry tragically put an end to her life.' As Lydia explains where she is standing, the film cuts from the television set to a shot of a family (father, mother, two children) sitting on a sofa, their gazes directed toward an off-camera TV set, and Lydia's voiceover continues. As she mentions Cecilia, we cut back to a close-up on a television whose screen is displaying a black-and-photograph of Cecilia, but this is a different television set to the one we were shown before – metallic and grey as opposed to dark wood (see Fig 3.7). As Lydia continues to discuss the fraught nature of adolescence, we cut to two further lounges, the mise-en-scene a collection of settees and fussy décor which suggests the stifling repetitions of suburban interiors, themselves penetrated by the televisions we see the characters avidly watching, confirming 'the erosion of boundaries between private and public spaces signalled by television's relentless projections of the outside world within

Fig. 3.7. Cecilia Lisbon featured on television

the supposedly secure walls of the home.'[73] Coppola fragments Lydia Perl's news reports across different spaces, as the Lisbon's private tragedy becomes recycled as a matter of public debate. As we cut to an image of the Lisbon family home in darkness, the camera, outside of the house, slowly zooms towards the kitchen window through which we can see Mrs. Lisbon drying the dishes, and we hear two anonymous female voices talking on the telephone. 'It's the mother I feel sorry for. You'll always wonder if you could have done something', one opines, and we see how Cecilia's suicide has made the Lisbon home itself an object of curiosity and gossip, based on gazing at, and judgement of, girls and women.

The use of technology to render porous and open the seemingly sealed boundaries of the Lisbon family home is made more poignant and more intimate when the neighbourhood boys communicate with the girls through two further technological devices, the telephone and the record. The film has already intimated to us the significance of her records to Lux for her sense of self, when her mother forces her to burn them as punishment for breaking curfew. Sobbing, she begs her mother to relent, clasping the box of records to her chest, but Mrs. Lisbon, as the voiceover recounts, 'arriving home from a spirited Church sermon', insists on the ritual purge. She forces Lux to throw a black vinyl disc onto the living room fire, and noxious fumes pour out. A girl's plaintive voice can be heard from off-screen asking 'what's that smell?' as Mrs. Lisbon and Lux both cough and choke, a typically wry observation by Coppola on the practicalities of demanding your teen daughter burn her records. As Mrs. Lisbon leaves the house, still coughing, she is surrounded by increasing clouds of smoke that pick up an orange-red glow from the hallway and porch lights so that she looks positively demonic, as if the mise-en-scene has taken up Lux's resentment of her mother's actions. For Lux, it is (perhaps) not so much the music that matters to her, as the way that the record collection enables her expression of identity, the building blocks of her sense of self.

As Robynn Stilwell explains, the role of the records in the film enables the exploration of what she argues is a gendered dynamic when it comes to record collecting. The record collector is usually seen as a masculine stereotype, reiterated in films such as *High Fidelity* (Frears, 2000) and *Ghost World* (Zwigoff, 2000), in which the 'record collector' is shorthand for a type of behaviour that equates the accumulation of records with hunting skills and displays of arcane knowledge and superior taste. She concludes that femininity is barely even acknowledged in these depictions: masculinity is the norm, even if that norm is a little peculiar. However, if record collecting can be seen as (and is frequently represented in film as) reinforcing stereotypical masculine behaviours such as competitiveness, aggression and mastery, it also depends on a set of behaviour more stereotypically regarded as feminine in western culture: creativity, nurturing, preservation. So, rather than being the domain of one gender or another, collecting benefits from both masculine and feminine behavioural traits. For Stilwell, the unusual depiction of a female record collector, Lux, allows *The Virgin Suicides* to examine a different relationship to the record object than that depicted in *High Fidelity* or *Ghost World*. For Lux, unlike the stereotypical male collector, each record is unique and worth fighting for, rather than finding its value as an element in a collection. 'Not Kiss, not Aerosmith', she pleads, defending each record as precious. Stilwell's research into (the very limited) empirical accounts of female record collecting leads her to conclude that 'the record is an artefact or object, but one that is inscribed with something more; as the testimonials, direct or oblique suggest, its grooves trace not just sound, and not even just memory, but the building blocks of the self.'[74] She goes on to explain that 'this intimate relationship of girls and music, mediated by records, is often central to the cinematic articulation of girl's self-discovery.'[75]

The neighbourhood boys are searching for a way to communicate with the Lisbon girls, now imprisoned by their mother 'in maximum security isolation', trying at first to interpret obscure clues (such as saints' prayer cards left in the spokes of a bicycle wheel) or making inept attempts at deciphering light signals via Morse code until they hit upon a solution 'so simple it took us a week to come up with it': they telephone the house. Rather than speaking directly to the girls, they play them a Todd Rundgren record with the lyrics 'hello it's me /I thought about us/ for a long long time.' We see the record placed on the player, the needle drop into the groove, and the boys hold the telephone up to the speaker. The girls respond by telephoning back and playing Gilbert O'Sullivan's 'To Think that Only Yesterday.' Again, we see the needle drop onto the player, and the four girls on the bed clustered around the telephone. We cut back to the boys' bedroom, but this time the action of telephoning is cut out, so that we cut directly from O'Sullivan to The Bee Gees 'Run to Me.' The thick wall of sound comes up in the soundtrack, and the image divides into a horizontal split screen, with a close-up of Lux's face in the top segment and a shot of all four boys in the lower half. The music has now completely crossed the divide between the boys' and the girls' rooms, drawing them together in the frame in the lush orchestration and yearning vocals of rescue and release. A series of differing images fill the split screen which cut at different moments, sometimes focusing on a close-up of a face lost in musical reverie, sometimes panning over the white plastic telephone. A smooth gliding panning shot over the receiver in the bottom half of the screen is roughly matched by an image of the clunky handset held in Therese's hands in the top half, the technology enabling the communication between rooms made manifest and even beautiful. We then cut to close-ups on beatific faces before leaving the split screen and coming back to a close-up on a black whirling vinyl disc, unable to identify in which room this record might be playing as the boundaries between homes are erased in this double mediation of telephone and record player.

This Utopian moment of boundaries overcome and harmonious exchange of song lyrics is brought to a shuddering halt. The music fades and we cut to an image of Mr. Lisbon standing on the first floor landing of the Lisbon family home, his head bowed. He is caught in a position more usually associated with the female protagonist of melodrama, framed within two sets of doorways (the one in front of him and the one behind him). The claustrophobia of the hallway is underlined by the mirror on the opposite wall which reflects back the wall opposite, including a small oil painting of a road and trees, as if to emphasise the lack of escape routes available here. Carole King's sweet voice singing of a lover 'far away' is replaced by an off-screen conversation between Lux and her mother. Mrs. Lisbon says, 'Lux, you're safe here', and Lux replies in one of the film's most important lines, 'I can't breathe here', anticipating her death by asphyxiation. The boys try again to telephone the girls, but this time there is no answer, and the soundtrack is dominated by the sound of a chainsaw, indicating the chopping down of the dying elm tree

that Cecilia had loved (and in whose branches she hovers as a ghost) and anticipating the girls' last grasp at self-determination in the act of suicide.

Conclusion: There's no Place Like Home

For girls, the home is a suffocating, oppressive space, which they seek to escape.
In the films where we have identified the home as an object of public interest
and spectacle, the home is frequently figured as similar to a prison or a tomb,
anticipating the narrative fate of characters who finish the films either dead or in
prison (this is true of the Lisbon sisters, Marie Antoinette and several members of
the Bling Ring). In this way, 14-year-old Lux Lisbon's cry to her mother that she's
suffocating in the house would seem paradigmatic, and the neighbourhood boys
seek to rescue the girls from the house their mother has forbidden them to leave.
For the teens of the Bling Ring, the houses of celebrities are desirable because they
present excessive contrast to the everyday homes they live in.

The home is constructed as restrictive, oppressive, boring, a space to escape
from into a world of sensuous excess. These escapes takes various forms: the fren-
zied (possibly fantasised?) sexual trysts Lux has on the Lisbon roof, and the exotic
locations represented in the travel magazines the Lisbon girls order; the wild parties, carousing until dawn, at Versailles, or conversely wallowing in the bucolic
idyll of the Petit Trianon and its hamlet (we see the hen's eggs carefully cleaned by
servants, their faces cropped from the frame in a way that evokes the invisibility
of the labour that manicured this 'natural' environment); the luxurious celebrity
homes filled with designer goods, there for the taking, as the teens not so much
rebel against as complacently ignore the constraints of the law.

Of course, the question remains in all of Coppola's films to what extent this
excess provides any sort of solution to the frustrations of the domestic, and
what exactly the girls are escaping to. The desire to escape the home here does
not map easily onto the desire to leave behind childhood and grow, as other
than in the case of Lux (whose promiscuous behaviour could anyway be read
as male adolescent fantasy rather than one belonging to the girl) the desire
to leave home seems disconnected from any kind of desire to move through
puberty and into being an active (sexual) subject, and the sexual incontinence
evidenced once by Bob in *Lost in Translation* and more frequently by Johnny
in *Somewhere* meets disdain and disapproval from Charlotte and Cleo respectively. Perhaps the desire is for excess for its own sake: certainly this reading
works for *The Bling Ring*, where as Coppola says, 'It was about the stuff – and

dressing sexy and getting attention in clubs, and maybe being discovered. It was never about sex. It was about being sexy to get where they wanted to go.'[76]

If the figure of Alice in Wonderland provides a useful figure for us to consider some of the paradoxes of girlhood in its empowerment through disembodied disinterest discussed in chapter 2, Coppola's sustained investigation of homes also finds a significant resonance with another late Victorian fictional girl character, Dorothy, as this chapter's title suggests. As Ina Rae Hark explains, the figure of Dorothy indulges spectators in a fantasy of home-leaving: indeed, such a fantasy animates many archetypal plots in myths and fairy-tales. However, as she further argues:

> the transformation of L. Frank Baum's *The Wonderful Wizard of Oz* into the MGM musical fantasy *The Wizard of Oz* (1939) reveals how, when processed through the studio system, even a tale about a child's quest to return home underwent substantial revisions aimed at establishing the incontrovertibility of the proposition 'There's no place like home!' and severely censuring even a passing wish to find a better life somewhere over the rainbow.[77]

One of the most significant changes made in adapting the book to the screen was the decision to have Dorothy/Judy Garland dream her entire experience in Oz, rather than the natural occurrence of the tornado *really* sweeping away her home from the plains of Kansas. By positing Baum's really, truly live Oz as nothing more than a dream, the film makes sure there's no place like home by denying Dorothy any other place to go. However, before Dorothy can return to Kansas, either in her dream or in the fantastical otherworld contiguous to ours she finds in the book, she has to strike out on a quest, first to find the Wizard, and then to kill the Wicked Witch of the West at his behest. 'By compelling her to travel further away from Kansas in order to return there, Dorothy's odyssey indulges the home-leaving fantasy she denies harbouring.'[78]

For several critics, Dorothy takes the boy's realm of adventure, exploring and heroic pursuits, and makes them into a girl's adventures too: the search for Aunt Em as is as central a childhood tale to American culture as Huck Finn's escape from Aunt Sally. Yet, Hark comments, Dorothy's gender intervenes, and she has to revert to dependent child-like status at the end. While Huck and his equivalents leave home in order to save the world, Dorothy is compelled to relinquish the world and return home, having learned a harsh lesson of rebuke. (In the interpolated frame story in Kansas where Dorothy runs away to save Toto, she returns repentant but is still punished by being shut out of the shelter during the storm and hit on the head by a flying window frame. In the dream world of Oz, her trials and tribulations are various). Dorothy is compelled to forget her home leaving fantasy, and equate home precisely with the fulfilment of all feminine desire – but a fulfilment via renunciation. When Glinda, the Good Witch of the North/Billie Burke turns up in Emerald City as a pink ball of light, she tells Dorothy that she has always had the means to return home, but she needed to learn the lesson for herself. Dorothy, in close-up so we can see the tears glistening in her eyes and her touching sincerity, earnestly tells Glinda that, 'it wasn't enough just to want to see Uncle Henry and Auntie Em. And it's that if I ever go looking for my heart's desire again I won't look any further than my own backyard because if it isn't there I never really lost it to begin with? Is that right?' It is at this point the ruby slippers, their colour changed from silver in the book for the sake of Technicolor but suggestive perhaps also of the menarche and thus adolescent femininity, take Dorothy back to Kansas while repeating the film's iconic closing sentiment that there's no place like home.

As Hark argues, the convoluted sentence of Dorothy's lesson foregrounds the ideology: Dorothy doesn't learn that one's own backyard will satisfy all (feminine) desire: rather, she must learn to renounce any desire that can't be fulfilled within the parameters of the home. However, as Hark goes on to comment, the film has many cracks and fissures in its ideology. While some of them are inevitable given its strained production history of four directors and ten script writers, it also speaks to a wider contradiction within American mass culture at the time: that the film itself had to persuade spectators to leave their homes in order to come and see it. Accordingly, publicity materials featured only Oz, and vaunted the wonders of the Technicolor technology used to produce it (when my sister and I, as children, watched the film on VHS in the 1980s, we fast-forwarded through the 'boring' monochrome bits in our eagerness to get to Oz). In other words, the 'explosion' of the tornado that whips Dorothy's home to Oz, resonates with some of the ambiguities of Coppola's later exploration of a similar chronotope. For all that Dorothy tells us there's no place like home, she makes valuable new friendships in Oz, and cries as she leaves behind the Tin Man, the Lion, and above all, the Scarecrow. It is also through her journey in Oz that Dorothy comes to new understanding of herself. The film can't help but show us the explosion of the home as an opportunity for growth, connection and opportunity.

The exploded home chronotope perfectly expresses the contradictions and pressures of the postfeminist moment in ways that map relatively neatly onto a historical periodization. Coppola's 'prefeminist' films, in terms of time frame (eighteenth-century France; 1970s Michigan), show us girls whose houses kill them. Her 'postfeminist' films, in terms of time frame (contemporary Tokyo and Los Angeles) show us girls who can escape the home, but who still find existence bound up in repetitive loops and alienating rituals and are unable/unwilling to move into the adult position of an active desiring subject but like Dorothy seem to renounce desire, even if they do not return home. Coppola's films suggest that the feminist movement's explosion of the domestic idyll and its containment of women leaves us in a fraught situation. The exploded home offers more light and air – room to breathe – than the enclosing oppressive space deconstructed by the second wave, and this has to be welcomed. Yet the explosion has left behind rubble these girls are picking their way through, still attempting to find a way out of the maze.

4

Dressing Up and Playing About: Costume and Fashion

'Women of fashion become the "speaking" subjects of a symbolic system which inseparably entangles signs of oppression and liberation within the fashionable feminine body.'[1]

'I enjoy the whole visual aspect of films, and the costumes was [sic] a strong part of this movie, so I was glad people in fashion responded to it. But otherwise I think it's sort of a novelty because most director guys dress pretty nerdy, so it's just a novelty [laughs].'[2]

The Intermediality of Fashion

Commentators on Coppola's films never fail to notice how fabulous the costumes are, even if they criticise other elements of her production. As Coppola explains in the quote above, her interest in and knowledge of fashion is unusual for a director. Of course, most other directors are 'nerdy guys' rather than celebrity women. The identification of women with fashion has a complex and thorny history in feminist theory and fashion, for as Leslie Rabine explains, fashionable women are symbols of both oppression and liberation.

Fashion is key to the management of Sofia Coppola's auteur identity. Her films; her music videos; her participation as a model in advertisements for Louis Vuitton and Marc Jacobs; her internship at Chanel as a teenager, obtained through a friend of her parents, and regularly referenced in interviews; her direction of advertisements for a variety of fashion designers, from Sonic Youth singer Kim Gordon's X-Girl clothing range in 1992 to Christian Dior's Miss Dior Cherie perfume in 2008; her own range of clothes under the Milk-Fed label and her shoe and bag designs for Louis Vuitton, as worn by celebrities such as Kate Moss and Sienna Miller; guest editing positions at *Vogue Paris* (Dec 2014) and *W* fashion magazine (April 2014); all have one common thread: they are all marked by fashion, both in the sense of a deep interest in and passion for clothes and clothing, and in the sense of capturing the fashionable zeitgeist.[3] Partly as chapter 1 explains, her interest in fashion, as model, muse and designer, helps shape Coppola's branded auteur image and makes her a celebrity: certainly it increases her visibility and the chances that her face will be recognised. For example, she has been on the cover of fashion and lifestyle magazines such as *Vogue*, *Stylist*, and *Red* and she is cited as a muse by Louis Vuitton and Marc Jacobs (she was even featured as one of six 'timeless' Vuitton muses at an exhibition held at the luxury hotel Tokyo Station in Tokyo in August 2013).[4] More usually, we would expect to see (super) models and female movie stars in this position, and it is this visibility that allows Caitlin Yuneun-Lewis to analyse Coppola as a star with great conviction.[5]

Pam Cook persuasively suggests that this celebrity auteur identity is carefully curated by Coppola: her work spans the popular cultural arenas of music, film, fashion and photography, and it is her own sense of style and proclamation of creative autonomy that gives it coherence. Partially, Cook suggests, the fact that it is through fashion that Coppola achieves this coherence works to feminise her auteur image, for after all, women are usually associated with interest in clothes and fashion. Far from constraining her, fashion works for Coppola as the ideal vehicle through which to create a credible, cool auteur persona across the media zones of magazines, films and television, but it does so in a girlish register. In particular, Cook draws attention to how this auteur persona marks Coppola as different from her father, Francis Ford Coppola, and his embodiment of the role. First, fashion takes Coppola's auteur identity beyond the film text, giving her the kind of transmedia visibility more usually associated with the stars of films rather than their directors and making her all the more valuable in a globalised commodity-driven market in which 'different' films have to find their own ways to generate audience appeal. Coppola's image informs her films both as a point of brand appeal and by creating a smooth homogeneity between the worlds they evoke and the world in which Coppola is perceived to operate, one in which high fashion is of significance *and* accessibility. Second, Francis Ford is a 'monumental figure' whose film-making is above all associated with the counter-cultural New Hollywood of the 1970s; in contrast, Sofia Coppola does not reject popular or commodity culture, but is much more obviously enmeshed within it. Rather than portraying the auteur film as somehow outside of commerce and industry as 'art', Sofia Coppola's auteur persona acknowledges how art itself is a commodity product that must make its accommodations with the society from which it is produced.[6]

Fashion blurs the line between private and public, leisure and work: Coppola designs clothes and films adverts with a network of friends, such as Stephanie

Hayman, Zoe Cassevetes and Marc Jacobs; and the couture houses she is associated with for work are also intimately involved in her personal life (for example, she directs adverts for Dior and it was their principal designer, John Galliano, who designed the wedding dress for her marriage to Spike Jonze). Through fashion, the contradictions of Coppola's image caught between the public arenas of success, commerce and work, and the private intimacies of friendships, art and family, are not merely smoothed over, they are made attractive, glamorous and cool. Yuneun-Lewis defines coolness as a 'passive resistance to the work ethic through personal style' and as 'always conceptualised as at odds with the status quo, though this is often one of the very things it upholds'; furthermore, 'coolness's basic credo is nihilism.'[7] Although this nihilism is often associated with masculinity and a rejection of the maternal, Coppola demonstrates a 'cool femininity'. She takes up looks and ideas that were counter-cultural, such as punk, and promotes a femininity that is at once bourgeois and bohemian.[8] Her films both illustrate the sense of lack and nothingness that characterises girls' lives in postfeminist culture and its struggle to balance power with femininity, and commodify this very despair into part of a 'lifestyle' package where solutions are to be found in consumption. Fashion makes sense of the Coppola auteur image, its visibility, and its position within what Maureen Orth calls 'the celebrity industrial complex', a phrase that gestures towards the intricacies of celebrity culture and its extension into many areas of public life (not just art and sport, but also politics and business) with concomitant economic, cultural and political impact.[9]

Coppola has directed two films that this chapter demonstrates offer self-consciously reflexive variants of the fashion film genre: *Marie Antoinette* and *The Bling Ring*. When Coppola makes films that are in some ways about fashion, then we can read these as metaphorical comments on her own authorial persona: its complex accommodation with the worlds of cool celebrity, commodity forms and girlish frivolities. It is through fashion that Coppola expresses most clearly and competently the paradox of her auteur persona. It is through fashion that Coppola retools the idea(l)s of image dominating script and flourishes of personal style that dominate classical auteur theory, giving them a feminine makeover. And she does so through a device that has earned opprobrium from both mainstream cultural critics and feminist campaigners. Her interest in fashion marks Coppola films, pushing them for some critics into a feminine sphere marked as trivial and/or self-absorbed (a charge that particularly affected *Marie Antoinette*) and for others into the problematic postfeminist myth of feminine beauty as empowering and agentic. Through adopting fashion as the key to unlocking her auteur persona, Coppola ironically and self-consciously makes that persona simultaneously all the more ambivalent. On the one hand, fashion draws Coppola into the world of celebrity and consumerism, and positions her as an object of the gaze as she features in advertisements and on magazine covers. On the other hand, fashion is how Coppola asserts the difference and the significance of her female auteur agency, marking out her films as concerned with feminine experience and attending to its contradictions rather than merely dismissing it as superficial and trivial. Indeed, Coppola defends her interest in the allegedly frivolous area of fashion, pointing out in an interview with *Vanity Fair* that 'you're considered superficial and silly if you are interested in fashion, but I think you can be substantial and still be interested in frivolity.'[10] Could we perhaps go further and suggest her films show us that the distinction between the superficial and the deep, the frivolous and the substantial is a subjective matter of taste rather than an absolute? Indeed, the matters of look and style – the very stuff of fashion – inform the basis of the 'masculine' auteur theory and its insistence that film is a form that communicates to us through the techniques of shot composition (movement, angles, framing, depth). Style is key to the philosophy of film elaborated by André Bazin, and his fellow traveller Eric Rohmer explained that his early 1980s Comedy and Proverbs series of films were deliberately 'superficial'. They are interested in the dilemmas of young women trying to find love; and also surely not incidentally infused with contemporary design and fashion, from Pascale Ogier's bright yellow or blue scarves in *Les Nuits de la pleine lune/Full Moon in Paris* (1984) to Marion Dombasle's shimmering silver swimming costume in *Pauline à la plage/Pauline at the Beach* (1983). This is partly because Rohmer believes in the 'profundity of the superficial'. Rather than searching for one absolute truth, attention to the frivolities of style turns our mind to contingencies, transformations and the ever-changing reality that shifts according to our perceptions. There is no contradiction between an emphasis on the fleeting shades and caprices of moods and emotion and an attention to the 'bigger picture' of history and politics; rather, it is the realisation we can only access history and politics from the point of our own personal perception and to pretend otherwise is an act of intellectual arrogance (what Rohmer describes as superficial profundity).[11]

> There is no formula for truth; it isn't in assertions. But I mean to stay superficial with these films. I don't want to make profound films. Bazin used to say that there was a profundity of the superficial in American film, but I also think that there is superficiality to profundity.[12]

The Politics of Fashion: Indexes and Icons

Historical, philosophical and film feminist scholarship on women and clothing indeed suggests that fashion can indeed be a rich site for the exploration of feminine identity and complicate notions of both superficiality and agency. Tania Modleski explains that the dismissal of fashion as trivial functions as a double bind for women and a contemptuous attitude toward fashion is itself worthy of unpicking. In her assessment of Hitchcock's *Rear Window* (1954), Modleski explains that Lisa/Grace Kelly's involvement with the world of fashion is valuable to consider. The film's main character, Jeff/James Stewart, is a sports journalist who has broken his leg; his girlfriend Lisa is a socialite and model. In her analysis of the film, Laura Mulvey argues that Lisa constructs herself as an object of Jeff's gaze, trying to get him to notice her rather than the neighbours. However, Modleski points out, it is important to note that fashion is key to Lisa's professional and personal identity, making her a subject as well as Jeff's object. We are introduced to her in a dreamy full close-up as a drowsy Jeff awakens to find Lisa bending down to give him a kiss. When the camera pulls back, we are presented with a stunning outfit: a dress 'fresh from the Paris plane' with a fitted black bodice, deep V neckline and cap sleeves, and a white mid-calf full tulle skirt gathered at the waist. Jeff asks 'Is this the Lisa Freemont who never wears the same outfit twice?' to which she responds 'only because it's expected of her.' Jeff insists on the necessity of access to excitement and adventure for his sense of self, but fails to see that fashion is as significant and important for Lisa: new outfits (paradoxically) help define who she is and her place in the world (what's expected of her). Fashion, far from representing women's total assimilation into the patriarchal system, acts as a signifier of feminine desire and female sexual difference.

Jeff's attitude towards Lisa's outfits chimes of course with a wider cultural attitude toward fashion. As Modleski points out, if on the one hand, concern with appearance quite obviously serves patriarchal interests, this very concern is also often denigrated and ridiculed (as Lisa's is by Jeff, despite the fact that it is his interest in race cars that caused his broken leg: he stepped out in front of an upcoming car to get a spectacular photograph). This situation puts women into a familiar double-bind in which 'they are first assigned a restricted place in patriarchy and then condemned for occupying it. For feminist critics to ignore the full complexity of woman's contradictory situation is to risk acquiescing in male contempt for female activities.'[13]

As Juliet Ash and Elizabeth Wilson explain, this contempt for fashion is longstanding. 'Fashion has always faced the difficulty of not being taken seriously [...]

it has rarely been afforded the serious contemplation reserved for the arts of literature, painting, sculpture, music and theatre.'[14] They trace the delegitimation of fashion in mainstream cultural discourse to three forms in particular. First, fashion is condemned on economic grounds. The work of nineteenth-century critic Thorstein Veblen is influential here, as he objects to the 'conspicuous consumption' of fashion – and of nineteenth-century bourgeois culture in general. He argued that female dress was an important feature of female subordination, with fashionable dress used to declare the status and significance of the husband of the bourgeois wife; meanwhile, workers, mostly women, worked in dangerous, exploitative conditions to produce these clothes. The second line of attack is psychological. Associated with the classic study by J.C. Flugel, this interprets all clothing as a neurological symptom, expressing messages of which the wearer is unconscious. In this scenario, any attempt to send a conscious message through clothing – such as the rebellious sub-cultures of goth and punk may attempt – is held up to ridicule as the demented chattering of an angry baby. Third, and linked back to Veblen's discourse again, fashion is associated with snobbery, status value and politics of class.

In this light, Coppola's investment in fashion as a significant and important material and discursive practice (both an object which she designs, models, advertises and also subjects to regimes of representation) can be seen as a feminist intervention. She insists on how clothing is vital to girls' negotiation of their identity in a world still marked by sexual difference. Far from trivial and narcissistic, clothing is political, negotiating the fraught border between the girl and the world. While all clothing performs this role to some extent for all humans (no one goes out into society naked), it is of particular moment for girls' identity precisely because fashion is marked as an area of their interest and desire and allows for a self-conscious exploration of subjectivity.

Clothing is necessarily political in that works across the double borders of body/object, self/world. The work of Alexandra Warwick and Dani Cavallaro in *Fashioning the Frame* is a highly theoretical meditation on dress as a kind of boundary project, one that seems to constitute boundaries between body and world, self and others, but also simultaneously questions the making of these boundaries. Warwick and Cavallaro locate the significance of dress in the way it '*represents* the body as a fundamentally liminal phenomenon by stressing its precarious location on the threshold between the physical and the abstract, the literal and the metaphorical.'[15] They suggest that dress constantly introduces into the psyche reminders of an archaic and intractable entanglement with materiality. The subject, according to Warwick and Cavallaro, is formed in part by dress;

dress is an Other that nevertheless lends itself to the making of identity. Unable to divorce herself from this very material Other, the subject is in part forged by it. Warwick and Cavallaro's clothed subject is, then, always already a social subject, since dressing is a project that incorporates multiple Others (perceivers, as well as the otherness of the clothing itself) and the social logic of becoming intelligible.

After all, at the most basic level, to go out into the world, the girl must be clothed, and the notion of clothing as a material manifestation of the social/ political body is acted out most clearly in the 'handover' scene in *Marie Antoinette* when Marie Antoinette's fitness to be dauphine (and for her womb to bear the future King of France) is dependent on the correct clothes. She is stripped of her simple travel suit of pale cream and simple undergarments and completely re-outfitted in in a much more elaborate, fitted and adorned suit of a light French blue. The blue bow tied at her neck highlights the sense that she is an object, a gift from Austria to France (see Fig 4.1).[16] Furthermore, the blue of the suit is the exact same shade as the blue of the furniture in her private apartments at Versailles. We follow her curious exploration of this suite of rooms a few moments later in the film: she is like a doll dressed up ready to blend into her new environment with any individuality erased.

Clothes' function in expressing one's relation to the world is taken up by Marie Antoinette herself as she learns the sartorial codes, and a commentator on Coppola's film draws parallels to Diana, Princess of Wales, another ill-starred royal blonde who used a developing confidence in her personal style to challenge

Fig. 4.1. The blue ribbon at Marie Antoinette's neck wraps her up like a gift

the oppressive court machinery.[17] Clothing as a form of expression takes on a particular significant role as Marie Antoinette has access to the money and power to create herself as spectacle but has little voice. In this world, costumes, hair and make-up take on a particularly important function. Coppola shows us how important minor details of costume become for Marie Antoinette in a scene where the Austrian Ambassador, Mercy/Steve Coogan, tries to discuss an impending diplomatic crisis with her, in which France and Austria find themselves on opposite sides in a power grab involving Poland. Initially, Marie Antoinette plays the silly girl, telling Mercy she hasn't read the brief and asking him if he prefers the sleeve of her dress with or without ruffles. However, when he reiterates the seriousness of the situation, she responds, 'where will I be if there is a rupture between our two families? Am I to be Austrian or the Dauphine of France?' Taken aback by her only too acute understanding of the impossibility of her situation, Mercy can only offer, 'you must be both.' In this context, her sartorial dilemma, that cuffs can be either ruffled or plain but cannot be both comes to stand for the difficult decision she must face between loyalty to the Habsburg or the Bourbon court, and her wider lack of agency in deciding her own political identity, as she is exchanged between Austria and France.

As Christina Lane and Nicole Richter explain, the film insists on the way in which Marie Antoinette's voice is limited while her ability to look is emphasised.

> For example, as Marie scans her new quarters in Versailles, she actively searches out the contours of the room and then, upon finding a box of treasures, pulls out a fan and pauses to glance at her gaze in the mirror. She places the fan over her mouth and eyes her own reflection while striking various poses [...]Marie's voice is limited, but her eyes remain wide open.[18]

Diana Diamond's sensitive appreciation of the film's costuming enumerates the various accessories and styles that Marie Antoinette uses to communicate her paradoxical desire to be simultaneously powerful and free, adored and feminine. On the one hand, her clothing becomes increasingly ornate – gold encrusted gowns, elaborate jewels – signalling her role and power as queen. On the other hand, the full scope of her sexuality, femininity and creativity is only fully realised in the 'alternative world' of Le Petit Trianon, where she 'adopts free-flowing, uncorseted muslin, silk, or linen chemises worn with lightly powdered, uncoiffed hair [...] the homespun white chemises and simple straw hats [...] signify resistance to the constricting fashions and behavioural rules of Versailles.'[19] Her hair style of a 'towering pouf' marries the oxymoronic position into one fantastical and over-the-top statement: 'the tower of powdered hair represent[s] a compromise between the queen's desire to be both the phallic subject and the desired object.'[20]

The Bling Ring offers a different perspective on the relation between clothing and identity. If for Marie Antoinette, clothing can be used an index of power, whether that gained within the structures of the court or her personal ability to resist those very structures, clothing seems to take on an iconic role in *The Bling Ring*. By this I mean that the importance of the clothing is not what it can point to, or demonstrate, but simply that it once belonged to a celebrity, and therefore is worthy of fetishisation. Anyone could own/steal a Marc Jacobs handbag, given the right circumstances: what makes the Bling Ring's behaviour extraordinary is the desire to own the Marc Jacobs handbag that belonged to Paris Hilton. One wears clothing not to perform one's own identity, but to suggest how close one's identity can be to that of a celebrity. While Coppola's film gives us some fairly conventional material to meditate upon why the teens become delinquent burglars – a closeted gay boy desperate to fit in, three girls home-schooled by a wacky New Age spiritual mother, a girl left to her own devices as her mother works and her father has left the family home – it remains silent on what exactly the celebrity themselves gets out of their acquisition of so many items of clothing that they fail to notice when some of it goes missing. It leaves tantalisingly open the idea that their enjoyment of these goods is exactly the same as that of the teens: it comes from the very fact they are owned by them. The objects confirm their celebrity status (so Paris thinks delightedly 'I own a handbag that belongs to Paris Hilton!'), rather than the celebrity status giving one the money to buy such goods.

Clothes are material and discursive objects that are embedded into other power structures, and it is in the moment of the clothing being seen on another body (such as in this case, a celebrity body), or being worn on one's own body, that these power structures leave their own personal marks. Ilya Parkins insists on how the

> ephemeral appearances of clothing […] can be seen as power-saturated phenomena, triangulating consuming subject, the fashion industry and its material-ideological interests, and the garments themselves [… We need to] be attentive to the marks left on bodies; this is the ground of the real, the 'objective.' Those marks are material, and they issue from power-saturated discursive and material fields. In the case of fashion, they might be understood as the ways in which a garment shapes a body, both materially and visually: the marks left by bra straps, the way a body is thrust forward on high heels. They must also be seen, though, in the realm of production, in the traces of the production process on

workers, for example, and in the transnational flow of garments in the global marketplace. These phenomena are real, they are mutable, and they are also systemic. If we can hold these elements of a system in view, and remember that material consequences issue from the movements of the fashion industry, we are, I argue, best able to navigate the ambiguous reality of fashion, its way of simultaneously invoking and foreclosing agency.[21]

Parkins's insistence on the objectivity and political materiality of her discussion of fashion is made in the context of its frequent dismissal as worthy of attention. While attacks on fashion by nineteenth-century critics as economically exploitative, riddled with class politics and capable only of symptomatic expressions have considerable traction, fashion has also come under sustained attack from feminist critics. Indeed, Veblen himself was influenced by dress reform movements of the period, and in her account of feminism's conflicted relationship to beauty and fashion, Linda M. Scott argues that in America there is a received wisdom in which 'an enlightened cadre of feminists' formed dress reform movements. Headed up by Susan B. Anthony and Elizabeth Cady Stanton, these women refused to conform to fashion, and rose up to save their sisters from the plight of constricting corsets, swathes of fabrics and miniscule slippers. For Scott, to represent these women as representing a universal feminist cause is to deny a history of competing sectarian interest groups. She argues that 'the feminists led by Anthony and Stanton belonged to the most aggressive and powerful cultural subgroup in industrialising America: the Yankee Protestant descendants of the pre-Revolutionary aristocracy.'[22] Dress reform, continues Scott, was one of several social initiatives aimed at enforcing dominant cultural norms. While prevailing orthodoxy may hold the 'industrial revolution' as mainly concerned with heavy industry, Scott argues that 'in truth, America's first industry [...] was fashion. Textile mills, followed rapidly by factories producing shoes, hats, jewellery and notions, produced an explosion of prosperity [...]The fashion economy forever changed class relations among women.'[23] Working, independent women dressed differently from their aristocratic counterparts, and their brand of feminism was much more interested in cultivating appearance as an act of self-fashioning.

Further disagreements can also be traced to generational conflicts between different groups of women. Once again, Scott traces this back to the 'dress reformers' of the nineteenth century, explaining that when Stanton and Anthony were deposed by a younger generation, they deeply resented the way their new leader asked them to dress like ladies, seeing the younger women's attention to dress as a mark of complacency in the face of battles they had won on their behalf. This generational conflict resonates throughout the twentieth century, from moralists' reactions to the flappers of the Jazz Age, who linked freedom of dress to freedom from the sexual double standard, to contemporary debates about what girls should wear. 'The echo down the decades is deafening. Through these arguments, made in many venues, a continuing maternalism gives "women of education and refinement" license to tell "the less intelligent girls" how they can dress.'[24] Scott's tract forcefully demonstrates her belief that feminism can be reconciled with fashion, but it also perhaps unwittingly reveals the matrophobic impulses that propel girls to certain clothing choices over others. In the case of Coppola's films, clothing as an act of resistance to maternal injunctions is clear. In *Marie Antoinette*, Marie Antoinette indulges in her most hedonistic fashion spree following her breakdown after she receives a letter from her mother warning that her failure to conceive is a threat to the security of the Austrian-Franco alliance; in *The Bling Ring*, Nicki Moore's stealing flies in the face of her mother's pseudo-spiritual education and when interviewed by a journalist, Nicki won't let her mother get a word in edgeways.

Clothing may well be used as a way to assert agency, identity and authority: but the rebellious anger seems mostly directed at the mother, rather than any overarching patriarchal structures that may make such statements necessary. Yet the very point of *fashion* (as opposed to clothing) is its ephemerality: its ability to demonstrate the mutability of feminine identity. As Parkins explains:

> fashionable clothing's constant, cyclical 'disappearance' produces a potential ambivalence about the status of its wearers, who are also its primary imaginative costumers. The evanescence of fashion can be seen to issue a material challenge to conceptions of feminine *being*, and as such to counter the essentialist discourses that continually write femininity as static and invariable.[25]

In Coppola's films, such an affirmative view of fashion seems available to girls, where it contributes to a logic of shifting and changing identities. All Coppola's girls enjoy dressing up, indulging in the delight of different looks, from Charlotte's pink wig in *Lost in Translation*, to Cleo's smart evening dress in *Somewhere* before we even come to the more obvious and outrageous fashion fantasies of *Marie Antoinette* and *The Bling Ring*. Mothers however do not seem to have the same access to either fashionability or the attendant possibilities of difference and change.[26] Coppola presents us with the daughter's eye view of fashion as expressive and empowering, ignoring how it also produces chillingly static portrayals of

feminine roles, through, for example, its insistence on the significance of generational difference and appropriateness (through concepts such as 'mutton dressed
as lamb' or 'cougars'), gender difference (the alignment of gender with specific
items and colours of clothing) and class (the sheer cost of making one's self so
fabulous). Fashion as expressive, anarchic and fun works if one is pretty, young
and rich enough to be able to make use of it.

In her study of fashion, Pamela Church Gibson concludes that a feminist
engagement with fashion entails 'celebration and repudiation – or [...] the
oscillation between them.'[27] Fashion underlines the possibility and desirability of change, which gives it a particular charge for feminists. As Parkins
explains, 'feminism is a change-oriented philosophy, one concerned with
re-imaginings and reconfigurations of the world.'[28] She explains that fashion
shows us how change can adhere in the material as well as the social and
cultural realm, and that indeed it also confirms that 'the separation between
these realms is not as great as it might seem.'[29] She concludes that fashion
provides a model for thinking beyond stable identities. However she also
insists that we must remain attentive to 'marks on bodies', the irresistible
pull of identity logic that organises gendered lives and the restrictions and
punishments fashion can also mete out. Coppola's films act out a variant on
this contradictory approach. Within the defined and limited context of cosseted privileged worlds of royalty and celebrity, Coppola's films demonstrate
fashion's ability to renegotiate identity. Both films however also show more
awareness than they are generally credited with at what might be at stake for
those bodies in publically making use of fashion as a means of transformative
power, for they also underscore the vulnerability of an identity that can be so
manipulated. These fashionable bodies' power is tenuous, as Coppola shows
us royalty and celebrity as precarious, shifting on the whims of the people, as
opposed to absolute and static.

The Fashion Film: Anachronism and Anarchy

As Hilary Radner explains, while the connection between fashion and film is long-
standing, dating back to the classical Hollywood studios, the fashion film is a relatively recent genre.[30] In the classical era, the tendency was to eschew haute couture
with the aim of producing more accessible versions of French designs. Shifts in
the post WW2 fashion industry resulted in the reformulation of the major fashion
houses such as Chanel and Christian Dior as advertising vehicles for ready-to-
wear, mass manufactured lines, which became the core business.

Given his voracious appetite for analysing the rapid changes in the relation between elite and popular culture at this time, it is no surprise that the sociologist Edgar Morin turned his attention to fashion. His analysis is worth quoting at some length, as the changes Morin identified still resonate through the fashion industry and its relation to film:

> There's a perpetual desire for the new [...] which answers two needs: to stimulate the economy, and to affirm the individual. That's why fashion has entered into the mass culture life cycle. Fashion has descended from the peak of haute couture to wrap itself up in seductive attributes [...] Fashion has descended from the elite to the feminine masses [...] and mass culture, through fashion, reveals its true nature: it gives us access to the great gods of seduction and individuality. It allows for us to identify with celebrities through mimesis. At the same time, it creates an abiding obsession with consumerism whose importance as an economic stimulant is increasing in Western societies.[31]

In this remarkably prescient piece of analysis, Morin argues that as fashion steps down from its 'olympian' mountain to engage with mass culture, it lends mass clothing a kind of gloss and glamour. It promises the expression of individuality through mass manufacture; it allows for ordinary people to copy stars and celebrities. Far from a trivial adjunct, fashion is key to the functioning of modern consumerist society.

In this environment, film and fashion become more closely linked, with designers pleased to see their clothing promoted by stars both in film and on the red carpet. The first designer dress in film, Givenchy's uncredited design of Audrey Hepburn's stunning black-and-white ball dress in *Sabrina* (Wilder, 1954) (uncredited because Edith Head, costume designer at Paramount, was able to insist she got the credit for all costume design at the studio) had by the 1980s mutated into significant product placement. Costuming had devolved into a combination of designing, renting and shopping, in part because of diminishing budgets for costume departments.

The fashion film takes the logic of product placement one step further as 'the film's function as a shop window is not secondary to its story.'[32] Rather, it is a film that 'could easily be watched minus the soundtrack, to better appreciate the clothing.'[33] While earlier films such as *Sabrina* or *Rear Window* can be defined a posteriori as fashion films by their fans, for Hilary Radner what distinguishes the twenty-first-century fashion film is its self-conscious play upon the attraction of fashion and style for potential audiences. 'While costume serves to highlight character', Radner continues, 'fashion refers neither to character nor to clothing per se, but to a set of objects defined by specific discourses generated from an array of sources.'[34] The sources that demarcate objects as belonging to the world of fashion include fashion shows, newspapers, television reportage and programming, and (arguably) most importantly women's fashion magazines such as *Vogue* and *Harper's Bazaar*. Fashion then is deployed in contrast with the idea prevalent in film costume design that costume should be expressive of character, but is displayed for its own sake, as a pleasure independent of narrative drive and more dependent on notions of attraction and spectacle. It delivers and promotes the idea of high end couture fashion as a pleasure that is accessible beyond the extremely wealthy elite who could possibly purchase the goods, and creates a series of synergies between films and the more massified end of the couture market (handbags and in particular perfume). The twenty-first-century fashion film cultivates a viewer sensibility that is receptive to couture as relevant, pleasurable and enticing (rather than irrelevant, restrictive and alienating, as a more traditional Marxist/ feminist approach may argue). Indeed, one could even argue that the fashion film plays a didactic role, training the viewer in how to distinguish a Manolo from a Louboutin: a kind of knowledge and connoisseurship we see prominently on display in *The Bling Ring*.

In the case of *The Bling Ring*, the dynamics of the fashion film are disrupted as the film becomes a meta-reflection on the dynamics of the fashion industry itself: in particular, its relentless promotion of consumerist desire and self-centred narcissism. The fashion film showcases fashion, through various devices such as montage sequences, on-screen fashion shows, makeovers and transformations. It underlines the importance of fashionable clothes to a feminine sense of the self and defines high fashion as more than pleasurable: it makes the outfits worn by celebrities and the ability to imitate them desirable and indeed even necessary for self-fulfilment. In some ways, *The Bling Ring* performs an auto-critique, as it showcases the glamour and appeal of celebrity clothing in a similar way to fashion film, but spirals into a void of meaningless repetition that finishes in either vapid self-promotion or harsh retributive punishment. The very logic of fashion and consumerism itself – that one can never be too fashionable, or have too much – becomes obscene in the face of overwhelming excess. Visual and narrative repetitions operate at a structural level in the film, showing how the teens and the celebrities they emulate/copy are never satisfied but driven by an insatiable desire.

The teens of *The Bling Ring* further demonstrate how the alleged individuality and difference of fashion becomes subsumed into a system that reproduces fixed images of acceptable feminine bodies: the physical resemblance between the girls of the group testifies to the pervasive influence of celebrity culture, the bodies and the images it produces. Coppola shows us a hectic montage of archive photographs of Paris Hilton, Lindsay Lohan, Audrina Patridge, Rachel Bilson and Megan Fox, who embody a type of femininity characterised by long glossy hair, high-heeled shoes, over-sized sunglasses and slim trousers or short dresses to showcase slender legs. This is a femininity that can be easily replicated as it demands the production of the self as nothing more than a branded image. Delphine Letort, in her lively and engaging analysis of the film, explains that the film 'abounds with scenes of dressing that point out the performative dimension of gender.'[35] While Marc, the only boy in the group, wears high heels or puts on lipstick for the private amusement of his girlfriends, and keeps the shoes he steals under his bed, the girls' selection of clothes and shoes from Hilton's closet is predictable, and for public display in nightclubs and via social media. For girls, branded goods and a suitable body to display them are pre-requisites for a standardised performance of the feminine.

As for *Marie Antoinette*, that film also offers a reflexive take on the fashion film, here through setting up a dialogue between 'costume' and 'fashion'. It makes use of period setting and design, and the more traditional sense that costume can be read as expressive of Marie Antoinette's character and preoccupations, with the fashion film's desire to showcase desirable designer goods. It thus sets up costume and fashion on a collision course in the text itself; as we read the costume for what it can tell us about the historic Marie Antoinette, her life and her times, the jarring notes of fashion objects that are deliberately iconic and spectacular draw our attention instead to fashion as contemporary visual pleasure. What I mean by this is that costume is understood as transparent and authentic; an attempt to transcribe the past into the present without comment or opinion, whereas fashion deliberately introduces concepts of style, individuality, subjectivity and modernity. Through turning a costume film into a fashion picture, Coppola comments – through the devices of look and style – on how Marie Antoinette's image is part of a mediated and ever-changing concept of teen girlhood and its duties, demands, pleasures and pitfalls.

As cinematographer Lance Acord explains, the ambition was to make a film that while authentic in its setting (Versailles) and aspects of its look (period costumes) does not evoke the pastness of painting and portraiture, but the freshness and vivacity of a lived present moment.

> 'Our obsession from the start was to try and be the exact opposite of the costume film', says Lance Acord. 'Historical works often refer to paintings from the period. We got as far away as possible' [...] A few days

away from editing, does she [Sofia] think she's got the film she wanted? 'It's still hard to say. Sometimes I feel discouraged and I think we're just making one more costume film, something like a BBC TV series [...] everything will come together with the editing and the music, but I think it'll be unique and a little strange.'[36]

Such a comment, produced as it is in French newspaper coverage of the film's shooting, prior to the film's release, can be understood as part of a global marketing campaign to position the film as different from costume drama in order to underline its appeal for the target market of 16–25-year-olds; we can see for example a similar comment in Columbia Picture's production notes, quoting Coppola to the effect that she wanted to avoid making a dry period piece à la Masterpiece Theatre.[37] Spinnaker, the digital marketing agency, was commissioned by Sony to create a marketing campaign which targeted youth-oriented social networking sites such as Pizco, Get Lippy and Refresh. The aim of the campaign was to 'encompass [...] the aspirational nature of today's youth culture and the decadency of the period in which *Marie Antoinette* is set' and third party sites were chosen 'to speak to our specific target group of students and young fashion-conscious teenagers.'[38] Nor is it surprising that a fashion-led film attempted to target a teen market; teens of all social classes are among the most significant consumers, spending over $170 billion in 2007 in the United States – more than the budget of the state of Texas. Total U.S. teen spending exceeds the GNP of smaller countries such as Finland, Norway, or Greece, with the bulk of that money (33%) spent on clothes. In general, clothes top the list of items purchased by female adolescents, with twice as many female as male teens purchasing fashion items.[39] In this context, Coppola's decision to highlight Marie Antoinette as a teen girl able to indulge in fashionable clothes, hair and make-up with her good female friends without the annoying impositions of parents or school would seem a canny marketing move able to mould her as an aspirational figure for the contemporary teen market as much as a feminist revision demonstrating the youth and naivety of an unfairly maligned figure.

Despite this market-led insistence on its status as fashion film, *Marie Antoinette* does in some ways conform to the demands of the costume film in which generally speaking, costume is used to indicate period setting and great attention is paid to the detail and style of beautiful clothes from past eras. In classic costume films such as *Howards End* (Ivory, 1992) and *Sense and Sensibility* (Lee, 1995), according to Stella Bruzzi, 'the major designer effort is to signal the accuracy of the costumes and to submit them to the greater framework of historical and literary authenticity.'[40] *Marie Antoinette*'s costumes, designed by renowned costume designer

Milena Canonero, who won the Oscar for her work on this film, conform to this requirement: they were carefully researched and meticulously made and 'the costumes were correctly cut' and the 'the quality of the materials' was 'absolutely of the period in question'.[41] Furthermore, Canonero and Coppola work together to make costume one of the key drivers of the narrative in the film, which is again a much more conventional use of clothing than the fashion's film insistence on its qualities of spectacle, attraction and opulent display. Clothes communicate to us the complexities of Marie Antoinette's social position, her relation to her courtiers, and the state of her erotic and internal life through 'shifts in style, color, cut, coiffure, accessories, jewelry, headgear and even necklines'.[42]

However, Canonero goes on to explain that was there was also a process of reinterpretation of the period, which was to be found 'in the colors, the coordination with the make-up and the hair – that is where I took liberties.' Thus Canonero retains the spirit of historical authenticity while at the same time introducing contemporary touches that offer new perspectives on life at Versailles, and it is precisely by bringing together the authentic and the artificial, the period and the contemporary that Coppola offers us something different to the standard costume film and its cousin the historical biopic, and makes over Marie Antoinette as a contemporary fashion icon.[43]

Coppola's decidedly irreverent and sketchy approach to as significant a historical event as the French Revolution caused great controversy when *Marie Antoinette* was released: it was infamously booed at the press screening at the 2006 Cannes film festival (equally repeated across media reporting the booing is Coppola's admirably sanguine comment that 'it's better to get a reaction...than a mediocre response').[44] A decade on, Coppola's postmodern approach that privileges emotion, interiority and femininity over objectivity, exteriority and masculinity has generated generous scholarly reassessment that recognises the film's ambition and scope as it insists on the need to understand history from a personal perspective as the precondition for any engagement with the past (in other words, it reveals the myth of the 'objective' view). Coppola gives us the tone and feel, the sensibility, of how we might imagine the decadent luxury of eighteenth-century Versailles not despite but *because* of the decision to feature contemporary designer goods, a post-punk pop soundtrack and a range of natural accents. In particular, Diana Diamond, Jacki Willson and Heidi Brevik-Zender engage with Coppola's use of clothing and the complex dialogue between past and present images of femininity its use sustains. While the emphasis of their accounts necessarily varies, all of them read the clothes as promoting female agency, creativity and rebellion. Their interpretations all engage with the status of *Marie Antoinette* as a film about fashion, even if they do not explicitly make this claim. They all demonstrate that Coppola uses fashion to comment on the richly creative yet darkly restricted nature of contemporary girlhood, including her own complex position of speaking from a place of professional compromise.

Le Petit Trianon is marked in the film as the space for Marie Antoinette to find her creative resources and to indulge in the senses; the nearest she can come to experiencing Coppola's ability to make a world. We see Louis XVI handing Marie Antoinette a key to her new abode as they are stood outside it, and then cut to a tracking shot through the pale blue doors to a tableaux of Marie Antoinette with four musicians seated around her playing gentle guitar music. The tracking shot brings us slowly into the room where she is sitting, gradually allowing us into this intimate space. The shot lasts 30 seconds, slowing the pace of the film, and introduces a series of images lasting some 3 minutes that emphasise the senses as we see Marie Antoinette picking a clover; a close-up on her hand brushing through grasses; a field of flowers, studded with pink and yellow; her little toddler daughter feeding a lamb and picking a daisy; and a party drifting on the boating lake, Marie Antoinette's hand trailing in the water. The film cuts back to the monolithic Versailles and we hear Count Mercy explaining to an upset couple that Marie Antoinette isn't entertaining formally at present. We cut back to him explaining to Marie Antoinette that she has caused problems, to which she replies, 'but this is my escape from protocol'; her light pink curls and the large pink feathered fern by her ear amply make the point too.

Christina Lane and Nicole Richter read the more relaxed atmosphere of Le Petit Trianon as a kind of metaphor for Coppola's relationship to mainstream film culture. The bedroom – the place that should be private – has become the place of all too public humiliation and interest (first, for her failure to conceive; second, nearly killing her by crowding her while she was giving birth to her daughter). Marie Antoinette thus escapes to a less excessive and more natural form of life, finding herself away from the excessive interest of a version of celebrity culture.

> Le Petit Trianon becomes a metaphor for Coppola's position within the industry; it is a space that is connected to a larger institutional structure but one that is privileged, self-sustaining, and somewhat contained within the more imposing configuration of the royal quarters. Versailles [...] is governed by a repressive protocol that is perhaps as every bit as limiting to female power as Hollywood when it comes to women's filmmaking. [...]Unlike Marie, however, Coppola's approach to style suggests that she is much more informed and knowing.[45]

For Diana Diamond, the film makes Marie Antoinette into a contemporary fashion icon, and she documents how the film inspired a range of consumer products, from the relatively mass-market perfume from the teen fashion line Juicy Couture, to John Galliano's masquerade and bondage collection for Dior, that featured hoop-skirted Marie Antoinette gowns printed with tableaux of the queen's life (including her execution by guillotine, a gory finish Coppola's film avoids). Kirsten Dunst also featured in costume, her hair piled high, on the cover of the September 2006 issue of *Vogue*, signalling the synergies the film set up between its portrayal of the historic Marie Antoinette and contemporary fashion industries (and that were part of its intense marketing at a young fashion-conscious audience as I discuss above). Furthermore, she argues that the film itself showcases fashion as 'the nexus for expressing female desire and empowerment, a route to female bonding, and a signifier of the unconscious wishes, conflicts and desires of the wearer.'[46]

Jacki Willson also examines important resonances between Coppola's film and contemporary performances of femininity. She compares Coppola's strategy of revisiting an imaginary eighteenth century to create Marie Antoinette as knowing spectacle to contemporary burlesque performances by Imogen Kelly and Gwendolen Lamour. Kelly dresses up as Marie Antoinette and performs a striptease, before spreading cake and cream over her body. Lamour performs an interpretation of Jean-Honoré Fragonard's painting *The Swing*, completed in 1767. Willson concludes that

> when we [...] watch Kirsten Dunst lounging around in her cinematic rooms in *Marie Antoinette*, or Imogen Kelly in her impossibly tall wig riotously stripping in a grotesque gastronomic orgy of food, or Gwendoline Lamour smiling, winking and stripping nonchalantly on her swing, we understand that this visual feast has significance. Like the young woman swinging in Fragonard's painting, in these performances there is a liberating sense of independence and authorship [...] this is performative painting which brings feminised spaces to life, performing historical images to extricate, or at least emphasize, the real from within the mythologised [...] These images [...] are given new contemporary meaning by real women actually inserting their own bodies into the frame, bringing to life the indolence and insouciance of the imagery.[47]

For Heidi Brevik-Zender, what is particularly significant about *Marie Antoinette* and its deployment of fashion is how this permits engagement with Walter Benjamin's theorisation of fashion and its relation to modernity. As she explains, fashion works as a theoretical tool to think about the very nature of modern life for both Benjamin and Coppola. Although they may appear to have little in common, they both interpret media-driven, commodity cultures through the lens of fashion. She comments that 'fashion is a crucial signifier that enables Benjamin to articulate the temporal instability that is, for him, constitutive of modernity; fashion is also a vital tool used by Coppola to overlap her life with the modern Marie Antoinette that she creates in her film.'[48] For Brevik-Zender, Coppola's film is consistent with Benjamin's understanding of fashion as a 'transhistorical manifestation that draws from the past even as it looks to the future in its representation of the present.'[49] For Benjamin, fashion is dialectical, as it reconfigures old styles into new looks, bringing together the oldest and the newest. It thus functions as the perfect metaphor for modernity itself, as it too relies on the expression of dialectical tensions. For Brevik-Zender, the film's opening image 'captures the transhistorical modernity' of fashion.[50] The film begins with the harsh, dissonant chords of Gang of Four's 'Natural's Not In It' (1979) before credits appear in hot pink lettering. The viewer is then confronted with an image of Kirsten Dunst in the title role, dressed in white undergarments, with a huge feather in her hair. White is the colour of the French royal family; but these are intimate clothes rather than State finery. She is lying back on a pale-blue period chaise longue, lazily dipping her finger into a piece of cake while a maid, clothed in a black-and-white outfit that looks more like a nineteenth-century chamber maid's costume than that of a Versailles lady-in-waiting, places a shoe on her foot. Dunst stares directly into the camera, breaking the fourth wall, and winks at the viewer, inviting us to enjoy the confrontation of periods and styles in the mix of music, food, fashion and setting (see Fig 4.2).[51] The transformative potential of fashion is also hinted at, as the maid seems to be about to dress the princess, and thus the image could soon change again.

Marie Antoinette thus exists in a moment of sartorial tension that is neither past nor future but on the threshold between both: the present time itself. In this moment Coppola forces together late 1970s punk music, which was already retroactive with the film's 2006 debut, and Dunst's polyvalent white garments, producing a disquieting, explosive tension.[52]

Conclusion: High Heels

An excellent example of how Coppola twists transparent costume into spectacular fashion, and what precisely might be at stake in this, is her use of the shoe in this film. While the infamous 'joke' lavender Converse trainer placed among the dainty heels in the shoe montage[53] (discussed in chapter 3) clearly lets us know

Fig. 4.2. Marie Antoinette stares at the camera

we're watching a reconstruction of the past, the use of shoes in general is part of what Rosalind Galt accurately diagnoses as 'a deliberately anachronistic discourse on the shoe as commodity fetish.'[54] The significance of designer shoes as indicative of postfeminist reclamation of female empowerment through consumption has been thoroughly established through the *Sex and the City* TV and movie franchise, especially in season 6, episode 9, paradigmatically entitled 'A Woman's Right to Shoes' (and which included a sequence filmed at the Manolo Blahnik store in Manhattan). Furthermore, the series did a lot to make the shoe designer Manolo Blahnik more well-known, as his designs were featured (alongside those of Jimmy Choo) throughout the 94 episodes of the TV series and in both films in the franchise.[55] The designer brands become unofficial partners, keen to lend clothing in a mutually beneficial move that increases the films' clothing budgets and gets them exposure. The show's costume designer, Patricia Field, explains the synergistic relation between designers and the programme, and the importance of shoes to the show's look.

> In the beginning, designers were cooperative, but now we have huge access, especially when it comes to the couture. The designers are great to us. Sarah Jessica [Parker] is like a supermodel, and for her to wear the clothing on the show is important to the designers [...] The foot is a very good place to work the sexy look, and we've got all the girls in high heels now [...] The success of [Sarah Jessica] in heels really convinced everybody that none of the characters should wear clunky shoes or flats.[56]

At costume designer Milano Canonero's suggestion, Blahnik was invited to design the special shoes for *Marie Antoinette*'s montage sequence set to Bow Wow Wow's 'I Want Candy': fur-lined, feather-trimmed, jewel-encrusted, they reference contemporary ideas of shoes as fulfilments of feminine fantasy and agency, and are designed to be read in a similar way to the shoes in *Sex and the City*, accorded close-ups and finally even story-lines of their own. Clearly, Blahnik has the skill to exactly reproduce shoes of the type and style worn by the historic Marie Antoinette. However, while 'the spectacular collection of Manolo Blahnik shoes takes its inspiration from the multicolored satin slippers trimmed with bows and jewels that are featured in portraits of Marie Antoinette [...] these are clearly hybrids, with anachronistic stiletto heels.'[57]

The shoes add then to the contemporary look and feel of the film, but also its modernity in Brevik-Zender's understanding of the term: the dialectical tension between old and new which is key to the truly fashionable. In particular, their stiletto heels, the site of their newness, emphasise the fetishistic aspect of Marie Antoinette's relationship to fashion, with this highly (over determinedly) phallic signifier occurring at the very moment in the film where Marie Antoinette has been humiliated by her failure to consummate her relationship with her husband. Rather, she ushers the phallic object into an overtly feminine world as she giggles with her girlfriends. Coppola wittily suggests the possible sexual overtones of this female bonding as an overhead shot of a pink pastry with a bright pink raspberry at its centre is clearly suggestive of a breast (see Fig 4.3). A series of jump cuts of

Fig. 4.3. The pastries that Marie Antoinette serves resemble breasts

lipsticked mouths biting into the sugared pastries combine the pleasures of sex, eating and fashion into a potentially queer sensory overload outside of the bedroom with its emphasis on heterosexual reproduction.

Furthermore, stiletto heels have their own complex sets of cultural meanings which Coppola activates by appending them to eighteenth-century style slippers. Lee Wright argues that the stiletto heel is an object which is 'seen as being exclusively female.'[58] In fact, this exclusivity has been in place only since the nineteenth century, when the heel was discontinued as part of male dress code: in the 1670s, Louis XIV issued an edict that only members of his court could wear red heels, and a 1701 portrait by Hyacinthe Regaud shows Louis in a fine pair of white shoes with bright red heels and buckles. However, by the 1950s stilettos were firmly established as part of 'women's culture' and were seen as a rebellious expression of freedom and glamour against domestic drudgery. They were a means by which younger women could mediate their collective and individual identities in relation to both their predecessors and one another. The stiletto is the icon of the daughter searching for an identity away from that of the mother, and its power lies in its evocation of differences within feminine identity. It is a negotiation via the body of a more liberated femininity.

If we can see Coppola's entire filmography as a negotiation between private and public, image and voice, production and consumption, fashion comes to be some of these very structuring tensions as it is simultaneously an individually worn item designed to signal a particular identity, and an institutional system that works to massify production and deny individuality; a system based on look and image that attempts to allow girls and women to articulate a voice; a system that encourages (over)expenditure and consumption but also enables female creativity and productive industry, from costume designers, to fashion editors, to models, to girls putting together outfits for a night out with friends. Through foregrounding fashion, Coppola centralises without resolving the dilemma of her films, which asks how a female voice expressing feminine desire and girls' identities avoids the traps of essentialism, homogeneity and being subsumed back into the dynamics of male looking and masculine power. That she poses these complex questions through devices dismissed as trivial and frivolous aligns her with her cinematic portrayal of Marie Antoinette herself, not so much ignoring the public power play of politics at Versailles as realising the limits on her agency and creating an alternative universe in Le Petit Trianon based in image, sensuality and ephemera.

The anachronistic stiletto acts as a perfect metaphor for the paradoxes and contradictions of Coppola's postfeminist auteurship. If, as Wright argues, the stiletto is an icon of liberation, it is certainly a fraught one, as it is harmful both in terms of stereotypes of elegant femininity and painful health problems for the feet. Of course, it is its badness which makes it such an exquisite emblem of rebellion. This is the double-bind of Coppola's cinema of girlhood. Her girls offer up images of liberation from maternal bonds; they offer us a sympathetic enjoyment of, indeed revelling in, images of gorgeous sensual beauty, favouring mood and tone over narrative and action. But they do so within strictly confined worlds, where the very experience and enjoyment of femininity comes barbed with a corollary of pain. Coppola's liberated girls can pleasurably linger over objects of desire, such as shoes; what they can't do is grow up and mature into adult women who can express resistance through politics. They remain rebellious teens, their angers and frustrations able to be managed and dismissed in a system that tells them if they are unhappy, it's because they want the wrong things, not that the wrong things are being demanded of them.

Conclusion: The Agency of Authorship

In her article on female authorship, Catherine Grant throws down a challenge: what exactly are the feminist objectives of studying women's cinema within an authorial framework? To begin to answer this question, she traces the history of feminist engagement with the question of the female auteur director, admirably surveying the contributions to the field by Claire Johnston, Kaja Silverman and Judith Mayne. She traces how all three critics insist on the need to pay attention to the gender of the auteur and its political value, but also become tangled up in questions of authority, agency and voice.[1]

Johnston begins by insisting on the political necessity of examining the output of female directors as 'the image of woman in the cinema has been an image created by men.' She seeks out alternative images offered within Hollywood by directors such as Dorothy Arzner and Ira Lupino, claiming that they both used various strategies to 'articulate critiques of prevailing sexist ideology.'[2] For Johnston, auteurism is useful because of its interpretive potential. Following Peter Wollen's classic discussion of Howard Hawks, she argues for the auteur as the organising principle of the unconscious structure of the film; the author's intentions are thus founded within their psychoanalytic history, creating a network of obsessions outside of their control, but which can be uncovered by the critic. As Grant explains, this leaves us with a series of rather intractable problems: why is it the director, rather than say the costume designer or star, who imprints the film with their unconscious motivations and desires? If the deep structure of the film emanates from the unconscious, is there any point to raising awareness for other women directors of how they may wish to intervene *consciously* to change representations of women? How does one explain the paradox between the passive director, unable to control the meaning of their film, and the expert critic/spectator, able to tease out networks of obsessions?

Silverman also insists on the political necessity of attending to the output of female directors for the feminist critic, arguing that 'the gendered positions of libidinal desire' enunciated in the film be read according to the biographical gender of the director because 'it is clearly not the same thing, socially or politically, for a woman to speak with a female voice as it is for a man to do so, and vice versa.'[3] Despite this appeal to society and politics, for Silverman, the feminist critic's task is to understand the film itself as an enunciative discourse, with the director inscribed discursively into the text. As with Johnston, for Silverman too there is 'a psychoanalytic pattern of energy cathexis' in authorship. She remains more interested in the psychoanalytic dynamics at work in the text, and between text and spectator, than with the relation between the female authorial voice inside and outside of the film text and how their relation is understood: it remains difficult to deduce how 'the fact of female authorship' gives a particular inflection to 'the representation of female desire.'[4]

For Judith Mayne, 'central to a theorising of female authorship in the cinema is an expanded definition of textuality attentive to the complex network of intersections, distances and resistances of "woman" to "women."' While Grant explains that Mayne retains a structuralist suspicion of biography, so that her study of Arzner privileges textual signatures over questions of authority and agency, she nevertheless does attend to how Arzner chooses to present relations between women on screen, positing that her 'evidently lesbian persona' may on some level inform her preoccupations. For Grant, while she praises the brilliance of Mayne's formalist reading, there remains a problem. If Johnston too easily slips between determinism and voluntarism, and Silverman brackets off the historical auteur entirely, then Mayne's 'methodology combined close textual analysis [...] with a largely asserted, and at times metaphorical, correspondence with hazily sketched, authorial "personae"'. She concludes that Mayne needs the historical, and implicitly the biographical, to 'play a greater part in her self-consciously non-universalising desire for "local" analysis of films by women.'[5] Grant concludes that the feminist project for examining female authorship is one that attends to the still urgent need for greater female representation on film, and rather than understanding the film as pure essence, focuses on how the auteur works as an anchoring point between the fictional world of the text and its own social and historical outside. Accordingly, she calls for an extended understanding of what it is legitimate to theorise when considering female authorship: 'not just the films and 'facts' of a director's life, but also interviews, film reviews, and academic studies'[6]: a broad array of cultural texts that allow us to begin the grasp the many mediations at work in the fashioning of the auteur.

The great power of auteur study is that it takes us back to the principle of specificity in the world of texts, so that 'far from consolidating the notion of a universal or a unitary subject, the retracing of the work to its author is a working back to historical, cultural and political embeddedness.'[7] Indeed, the work of the politically aware critic demands attention to the embeddedness of the text, its conditions of production, which operate within networks of economic, cultural and social capital acquired differently by different subjects. These subjects have direct and reflexive, if not entirely intentional and determining, relations to the cultural texts they help to produce.

Sofia Coppola provides an ideal case-study for this understanding of the feminist purpose in examining the work of the female auteur. The question of her own agency is placed under erasure from the very fact of her name, and how it signals her position as daughter of a famous film director. Her first appearance on film, as a baby boy, in her father's film, crystallises how her biographical, biological and cinematic origins remain forever intertwined with those of her father. It is the question of her agency, how this can be expressed, and what it means to speak from the position of daughter, which demands to be theorised. Coppola as auteur acts out, exposes, glamorises, the role of girl/daughter: equally, however, this is a role she occupies through an accident of birth, and which will also inform the psychoanalytic energies of her work. Her films allow us to map a complex constellation of girlhood, understood as a political, social, cultural, affective and aesthetic state; both knowing interventions within, and unconscious responses to, contemporary girl culture.

There is one last paradox in this question of girlhood, agency and voice that I wish to discuss by way of conclusion. In March 2014, *Variety* reported that Sofia Coppola had been lined up to direct Working Title's *Little Mermaid* adaptation, with Caroline Thompson working on the script.[8] The Hans Christian Anderson fairy-tale is a twist on the coming-of-age story in which a 15-year-old mermaid undergoes painful rites-of-passage in order to try and win the heart of a prince. She has her tongue cut out in exchange for a potion from a sea-witch; the potion allows her to swap her tail for a pair of legs in order to become human. Walking remains painful, and her feet bleed; she cannot speak and has to try and seduce the prince through grace, charm and beauty. She fails, dies and is condemned to a life as foam on the sea, for mermaids have no souls. As such, it offers ripe thematic material that chimes with Coppola's authorial preoccupations of girls' adolescence, rites and rituals, coming-of-age, pain and death. Indeed, Noah Gittell in *The Atlantic* argues that

> the producers of the film deserve props not (only) for choosing a woman director, but for choosing the perfect director for the story they're going to tell [...]She's not a political filmmaker per se, but the world that she depicts is one in which women are oppressed – not necessarily by men, but by cultural myths. Whether portraying a strictly traditional monarchy (*Marie Antoinette*), a fame- and image-obsessed society (*The Bling Ring*), or the all-American horny teenager (*The Virgin Suicides*), Coppola's films rebel against a world that dictates the rules for women and then punishes them for playing by them. *The Little Mermaid* follows the exact same template, but takes the punishment even further.[9]

Gittell reads this unmade film, with an as yet undecided script, through an auteurist template, based on his knowledge of the story, illustrating the impact and significance of Coppola's films and their positioning as the product of auteurist agency. How ironic, then, that by June 2015, Coppola had been dropped from the project, over 'creative differences'; most likely, speculates *Variety*, her unwillingness to agree to Chloe Moretz as star (Moretz remains attached to the project; the script is now being re-written by Richard Curtis).[10] Partly this speaks to the chequered production histories that characterise many Hollywood projects, and is hardly unique to female directors. However, in a film that potentially foregrounds how girls routinely lose their voices when they attempt to fashion the world to their desires, it seems paradoxical at least that Coppola lost this opportunity to express herself.

So inviting however, is this meeting of Coppola's girl auteur persona and this material, that the Youtube channel Funny or Die made a two minute imaginary spoof trailer for a Coppola *Little Mermaid*.[11] The clip layers references to various Coppola motifs, shots and ideas, borrowing in particular from *Lost in Translation*, *Somewhere* and *The Bling Ring* while basing its characters' names and styling on the Disney version of the story, *The Little Mermaid* (Clements and Musker, 1989). Against strident chords, and following an underwater shot of bubbles in water, we see a shot of mermaid's tail and bottom that mimics the opening shot of *Lost in Translation*. We cut from Ariel alone in her bedroom, on her mobile phone, to a shot of Prince Eric floating in the pool at the 'Shellteau Marmont'. We break to black screen credits flashing in bright pink neon that this is a film made by Sofia Coppola, then adding a further credit saying that this is the daughter of Francis Ford Coppola. We then return to Eric in the pool on his yellow lilo. He wears a cast on his arm that Ariel signs; underneath she writes 'I can't speak'. We see flashes of the logos from various film festival screenings and awards (Cannes, Venice, Toronto, Telluride,

Tribeca) before cutting back to Ariel in her bedroom, waggling her feet and legs. This frenetic section cuts to the rhythm of a contemporary sounding track; the lyrics proclaim, 'I'm swimming in the ocean blue with my tits out', as if we were back in the Japanese strip club where Charlotte and Bob listen to Peaches' 'Fuck the Pain Away'. We then see Ariel and Eric in bed, Ariel eating ice-cream; Eric says 'there's something fishy about you'. We watch them at karaoke; then we see them embrace back at the Shellteau swimming pool, and Ariel leans in to whisper something in Eric's ear. 'You said literally nothing', he comments, and she nods, putting paid to the speculation about what Bob may have said to Charlotte at the end of *Lost in Translation*. The final shot of the montage has them side-by-side on sun loungers at the Shellteau, referencing Johnny and Cleo's day hanging out in *Somewhere*; Ariel flips her tail and the clip finishes. The soundtrack moves from the laid back reprise of the Strokes to hard, dissonant rock; the credit sequence promises music from at least 20 different artists. While Gittell chooses to emphasise the serious political and thematic underpinnings of her filmic explorations of girlhood, Funny or Die take an affectionate and more light-hearted approach to a Coppola aesthetic that emphasises music, tone, mood and affect. Even though Coppola never got to make the *Little Mermaid*, the mere fact that her name was attached to the project makes it available for cultural work under the sign of her authorship, and the story is filtered through her sensibility. Whether brilliantly funny like Funny or Die's imaginary Coppola trailer, or politically analytical like Gittell, both interventions articulate her authorship as a piece of shared cultural understanding and exchange. The Coppola girl now exists within the cultural imaginary, even if Coppola herself is not present to direct her.

Notes

1 Sofia Coppola: Postfeminist [d]au[gh]te[u]r?

1. Simone de Beauvoir, *The Second Sex* (New York: Vintage, 1989), 267.
2. Hilary Radner, *Neo-Feminist Cinema: Girly Film, Chick Flicks and Consumer Culture* (New York: Routledge, 2011), 6.
3. Sofia Coppola, qtd in Kristin Hohenadel, 'French Royalty as Seen by Hollywood Royalty', *New York Times* September 10, 2006.
4. See Molly Haskell, *From Reverence to Rape: The Treatment of Women in the Movies* (New York: New English Library, 1974); Marjorie Rosen, *Popcorn Venus: Women, Movies and the American Dream* (New York: Coward, McCann and Geoghegan, 1973); Laura Mulvey, 'Visual Pleasure and Narrative Cinema', *Screen* 16:3 (Autumn 1975), 6–18; Claire Johnston, 'Women's Cinema as Counter-Cinema', in Claire Johnston, ed. *Notes on Women's Cinema* (London: SEFT, 1975).
5. Laura Mulvey, 'British Feminist Film Theory's Female Spectators: Presence and Absence', *Camera Obscura* 20/21 (1989), 68–81 (p.72).
6. For further discussion of contemporary women's filmmaking, see Sue Thornham, *What if I had been the Hero? Investigating Women's Cinema* (London: BFI, 2012).
7. For further definition of 'chick' postfeminism (and its distinction from its less common sisters, academic postfeminism and grrrl postfeminism), see Chris Holmlund, 'Postfeminism from A to G', *Cinema Journal* 44:2 (2005), 116–121.
8. Rosalind Gill, *Gender and the Media* (Cambridge: Polity Press, 2007), 250–251.
9. Hilary Radner, *Neo-Feminist Cinema*, 3.
10. The term Conglomerate Hollywood comes from Thomas Schatz, and is used to describe the contemporary situation where, following series of acquisitions and mergers, 'Hollywood' effectively means a coherently integrated system of six global mass media conglomerates, fashioned by the globalisation of markets, the conglomeration of firms and the fragmentation of audiences. Hollywood's 'Big Six' (News Corporation, General Electric, Sony, Time Warner, Viacon and Disney) own and control all of the United States' big studios and all of the United States' big television networks. As Schatz notes, Hollywood has now 'effected the strategic integration of their film and film and TV operations in the U.S., by far the world's richest and most robust media market, as well as their collective domination of the global media marketplace.' Thomas Schatz, 'New Hollywood, New Millennium', in Warren Buckland, ed. *Film Theory and Contemporary Hollywood Movies* (New York: Routledge, 2009). Rob Schaap explains that film, especially watched on cinema screens, is of relatively little importance to the parent conglomerate business, and they have effectively become loss leaders to permit franchising and merchandising. The most successful films are those aimed at young male audiences – every billion dollar film released between 1999 and 2007 was based on children's literature, had an adolescent male protagonist, sufficiently bizarre

supporting characters to support games and action-figures, and offered fantastic spectacle and extensive animation, but never anything that might jeopardise a PG rating (hence the chaste relationships portrayed). Marketers research potential audiences intensively, attempting to appeal as broadly as possible. Schaap summarises as follows: 'females go to see films that address them as male and older audiences go to see films that address them as youngsters, but in either case does the reverse significantly apply. Clearly, the quadrant most disadvantaged by the cruel logic of demography is the mature female, those over 25.' While some films (such as Nancy Meyer's 'older bird' romcoms or the *Sex and the City* franchise) do get made, the demographic remains under-represented and those films that are addressed to them glorify consumption. See Rob Schaap, 'No Country For Old Women: Gendering Cinema in Conglomerate Hollywood', in Hilary Radner and Rebecca Stringer, eds *Feminism at the Movies: Understanding Gender in Contemporary Popular Cinema* (New York and Oxford: Routledge, 2011), 151–162.

11. Hilary Radner, *Neo-Feminist Cinema*, 4.
12. Catherine Driscoll, *Girls: Feminine Adolescence in Popular Culture and Theory* (New York: Columbia University Press, 2002), 9.
13. Sarah Projansky, 'Mass Magazine Cover Girls: Some Reflections on Postfeminist Girls and Postfeminism's Daughters', in Diane Negra and Yvonne Tasker, eds *Interrogating Postfeminism: Gender and the Politics of Popular Culture* (Durham, NC: Duke University Press, 2007), 40–72 (p. 42).
14. Ibid, 44.
15. Diane Negra and Yvonne Tasker, 'Introduction: Feminist Politics and Postfeminist Culture', in Negra and Tasker, eds *Interrogating Postfeminism*, 17.
16. Jean-Max Colard, 'Robert Mapplethorpe par Sofia Coppola: une belle surprise', *Les Inrockuptibles* 13 December 2011. All translations my own unless otherwise stated.
17. Lynn Hirschberg, 'The Coppola Smart Mob', *New York Times*, August 31 2003 and Anon, 'Sofia Coppola', *Les Inrockuptibles*, http://www.lesinrocks.com/artiste/sofia-coppola/.
18. See Sue Thornham, *What if I Had Been the Hero?*, 2.
19. Sam Adams, 'Does Sofia Coppola have a problem with privilege or do her critics?', *Indiewire*, http://blogs.indiewire.com/criticwire/does-sofia-coppola-have-a-problem-with-privilege-or-do-her-critics.
20. Peter Vonder Haar, 'Marie Antoinette', *Film Threat* October 2006, http://www.filmthreat.com/indexphp?section=reviews&Id=9379 and Dana Stevens, 'Queen Bees, Sofia Coppola and Marie Antoinette Have A Lot in Common', *Slate* October 2006, http://www.slate.com/id/2151855.
21. Caitlin Yuneun Lewis, 'Cool Postfeminism: The Stardom of Sofia Coppola', in Diane Negra and Su Holmes, eds *In the Limelight and Under the Microscope: The Form and Functions of Female Celebrity* (London and New York: Continuum, 2011), 174–198 (p. 180).
22. Todd Kennedy, 'Off with Hollywood's Head: Sofia Coppola as Feminine Auteur', *Film Criticism* 35:1 (Fall 2010), 37–59 and Amy Woodworth, 'A Feminist Theorization of Sofia Coppola's Postfeminist Trilogy', in Marcelline Block, ed. *Situating the Feminist Gaze and Spectatorship in Postwar Cinema* (Newcastle: Cambridge Scholars Press, 2008), 138–167.
23. Todd Kennedy, 'Off with Hollywood's Head', 37.

24. Amy Woodworth, 'Feminist Theorization', 142.

25. Ibid,155.

26. Lucy Bolton, *Film and Female Consciousness: Irigaray, Cinema and Thinking Women* (Basingstoke: Palgrave, 2011), esp. 95–127 and Diana Diamond, 'Sofia Coppola's *Marie Antoinette*: Costumes, Girl Power and Feminism', in Adrienne Munich, ed. *Fashion and Film* (Bloomington and Indianapolis: Indiana University Press, 2011), 203–231.

27. Bree Hoskin, 'Playground Love: Landscape and Longing in Sofia Coppola's *The Virgin Suicides*', *Literature/Film Quarterly* 35:3 (July 2007), 214–225 (223).

28. Alice Marwood and danah boyd, 'To See and Be Seen: Celebrity Practice on Twitter', *Convergence: The International Journal of Research into New Media Technologies* 17: 2 (2010), 139–158 (139).

29. Ibid, 140.

30. Ana Moya, 'Neo-Feminism In-Between: Female Cosmopolitan Subjects in Contemporary American Film', in Joel Gwynne and Nadine Muller, eds *Postfeminism and Contemporary Hollywood Cinema* (Basingstoke: Palgrave, 2013), 13–26.

31. Vito Zaggario, 'Their Voyage to Italy: New Hollywood Film Artists and the theme of "Nostalgia"', in Giuliana Muscio, Joseph Sciorra, Giovanni Spagnoletti and Anthony Julian Tamburri, eds *Mediated Ethnicity: New Italian-American Cinema* (New York: John D Calandra Italian-American Institute, 2010), 117–126.

32. The following websites have dedicated Sofia Coppola fansites, and both seem to target a young female audience: http://rookiemag.com/tag/sofia-coppola/ and http://www.iwantto-beacoppola.com/.

33. Chantal Akerman, 'Chantal Akerman on Jeanne Dielman', *Camera Obscura* 2 (1977), 118–119.

34. Teresa de Lauretis, 'Rethinking Women's Cinema: Aesthetics and Feminist Theory', in Patricia Erens, ed. *Issues in Feminist Film Criticism* (Bloomington and Indianapolis: Indiana University Press, 1990), 292–311 (p. 297).

35. Amy Woodworth, 'Feminist Theorization', 145.

36. Most notable in this context are the attacks carried out by Mary Richardson against 'The Toilet of Venus' (the Rokeby Venus) at the National Gallery, March 1913 and the actions of Annie Briggs, Lillian Forrester and Evelyn Manesta in Manchester City Art Gallery, April 1913, where they attacked some 13 paintings in protest against the imprisonment and ill treatment of Emmeline Pankhurst. Suffragette Ethel Smyth summarised the position as follows: 'there is to me something hateful, sinister, sickening in this heaping up of art treasures, this sentimentalising over the beautiful, while the desecration and ruin of bodies of women and little children by lust, disease, and poverty are looked upon with indifference.' Anon, 'Wonder Women', Manchester City Art Gallery, http://www.manchestergalleries.org/the-collections/wonder-women/ (link no longer working).

37. Geoff King, *Lost in Translation* (Edinburgh: Edinburgh University Press, 2010), 11.

38. Laura Mulvey, 'Visual Pleasure', 69.

39. Pam Cook, 'Portrait of a Lady', *Sight and Sound* November 2006, 36–40 (38).

40. Hilary Radner, *Neo-feminist Cinema*, 197.

41. Qtd in A.O. Scott, 'Evanescent Trees and Sisters in an Enchanted 1970s Suburb', *New York Times* April 20, 2000.

42. Timothy Corrigan, 'The Commerce of Auteurism: A Voice without Authority', *New German Critique* 49 (Winter 1990), 43–57 (44).

43. Lynn Hirschberg, 'Sofia Coppola's Guide to Paris', *New York Times* September 24, 2006.

44. Richard Dyer, *Stars* (London: BFI, 2nd edition 1998).

45. Su Holmes and Diane Negra, 'Introduction', in Negra and Holmes, eds *In the Limelight and Under the Microscope: The Form and Functions of Female Celebrity* (London and New York: Continuum, 2011), 1–16 (13).

46. Su Holmes and Sean Redmond, 'Editorial', *Celebrity Studies* 1:1 2010, 1–10 (7).

47. Graeme Turner, *Understanding Celebrity* (London: Sage, 2004), 92.

48. Holmes and Negra, 'Introduction', 2.

49. Harriet Quick, 'An Oscar, An It Bag, Marc Jacobs on Speed Dial', *Red* July 2013, 56–63.

50. Jean-Luc Godard, *Arts* April 1959, np.

51. Qtd in Antoine de Baecque and Serge Toubiana, *François Truffaut: A Biography* Trans. Catherine Temerson (New York: Knopf, 1999), 110.

52. Lynn Hirschberg, 'The Coppola Smart Mob.'

53. Kennedy also discusses the film's casting of Peter Bogdanovitch, an important figure from the 1970s New Hollywood who was influential in importing French auteur theory to Hollywood, worked as both director and film critic, and defended Orson Welles as a misunderstood cinematic genius. She casts him as the principal of RLS junior high. Kennedy argues that the film asks us to mock him as he punishes Kate for some minor infraction. Equally, we could see the pettiness of his actions as a nod to the ultimately arbitrary nature of social power and rules and the system which gives adult males the right to control the behaviour of those younger or of a different gender. Todd Kennedy, 'Off with Hollywood's Head', 43.

54. Ibid', 43.

55. Ibid, 43.

56. Christina Lane and Nicole Richter, 'The Feminist Poetics of Sofia Coppola: Spectacle and Self-Consciousness in *Marie Antoinette* (2006)', in Radner and Stringer, eds *Feminism at the Movies*, 189–202. In October 2013, James Schamus was replaced by Peter Schlessel as parent company Universal absorbed distributor FilmDistrict and reorganised its operation in London, New York and Los Angeles; an excellent indicator of the ways Focus is very much part of Conglomerate Hollywood despite its 'specialty film' focus.

57. Geoff King, *Lost in Translation*, 13–30.

58. Ibid, 12.

59. Christina Lane and Nicole Richter, 'Feminist Poetics', 191–92.

60. Qtd in R Barton Palmer, 'Some Thoughts on New Hollywood's Multiplicity: Sofia Coppola's Young Girl Trilogy', in Claire Perkins and Constantine Verevis, eds *Film Trilogies: New Critical Approaches* (Basingstoke: Palgrave, 2012), 35–54 (50–51).

61. Amy Woodworth, 'Feminist Theorization.'

62. R Barton Palmer, 'Sofia Coppola's Young Girls Trilogy', 40–41.

63. Ibid, 42.

64. Ibid, 53.

65. For further discussion of Coppola's film as authorial trilogy, and how this inserts her films into a particular kind of postfeminist authorship, see Fiona Handyside, 'Girlhood,

Postfeminism and Contemporary Female Art-House Authorship: The "Nameless Trilogies" of Sofia Coppola and Mia Hansen-Løve', *Alphaville: Journal of Screen and Film Media* 10 Winter 2015, http://www.alphavillejournal.com/Issue10/HTML/ArticleHandyside.html.

66. Anna Rogers, 'Sofia Coppola', *Senses of Cinema* November 2007, http://sensesofcinema.com/2007/great-directors/sofia-coppola/.

67. Pam Cook, 'Sofia Coppola', in Yvonne Tasker, ed. *Fifty Contemporary Film Directors* (Oxford and London: Routledge, 2nd edition 2011), 126–134 (130).

68. Sarah Projansky, 'Mass magazine cover girls', 44.

69. Jeffrey Sconce, 'Irony, Nihilism, and the new American "smart" film', *Screen* 43:4 (Winter 2002), 349–369 (350).

70. Ibid, 351.

71. Ibid, 352.

72. Ibid, 355.

73. Available to watch at http://www.youtube.com/watch?v=XeeVKfRGl3I.

74. Anna Rogers, 'Sofia Coppola'.

75. David Bordwell, 'The Art Cinema as Mode of Film Practice', in Catherine Fowler, ed. *The European Cinema Reader* (London and New York: Routledge, 2002), 94–102 (96).

76. See for example Manohla Dargis's comment that 'the princess lived inside a bubble, and it's from inside that bubble that Ms. Coppola tells her story. Thus [...she] ignores what's best about Marie Antoinette's story. She doesn't seem to realise that what made this spoiled, rotten woman worthy of attention was the role she played in a bloody historical convulsion.' Manohla Dargis, 'Under the Spell of Royal Ritual', *New York Times* May 25 2006. In a riposte published on the same day, A.O. Scott claims conversely that 'though it depicts a confectionary reality in which appearance matters above all, *Marie Antoinette* is far from superficial, and though it is often very funny, it is much more than a fancy-dress pastiche. Seen from the inside, Marie's gilded cage is a realm of beauty and delight, but also of loneliness and alienation [...and] a movie about a long-dead historical figure [...] feel[s] so personal, so genuine, so knowing.' A. O. Scott, 'Holding Up a Mirror to Hollywood', *New York Times* May 25 2006.

77. Angela McRobbie, *The Aftermath of Feminism: Gender, Culture and Social Change* (London: Sage, 2009), 29.

78. Kristin Hohenadel, 'French Royalty as Seen by Hollywood Royalty', *New York Times* September 10, 2006.

79. Pam Cook, 'Sofia Coppola', 128.

80. Lynn Hirschberg, 'The Coppola Smart Mob', *New York Times* August 31 2003.

81. Elvis Mitchell, 'An American in Japan making a connection', *New York Times* 12 September 2003.

82. Geoff King, *Lost in Translation*, 116.

83. Ibid, 50.

84. Lynn Hirschberg, 'The Coppola Smart Mob'. Coppola divorced Jonze and is now married to Thomas Mars from French electronic band Phoenix. The band has a cameo role in *Marie Antoinette* where we see them playing music for Marie Antoinette as she relaxes at the Petit Trianon.

85. Pam Cook, 'Sofia Coppola', 131.

86. Hilary Radner, *Neo-Feminist Cinema*, 2.

87. For a reading of Charlotte as flaneuse, see Amy Murphy, 'Traces of the Flâneuse. From *Roman Holiday* to *Lost In Translation*', *Journal of Architectural Education*, 2006, 33–42.

88. Kathleen Rowe Karlyn, *Unruly Girls, Unrepentant Mothers: Redefining Feminism on Screen* (Austin, TX: University of Texas Press, 2011), 77.

89. Ibid, 78–80.

2 Luminous Girlhoods: Sparkle and Light in Coppola's Films

1. Marnina Gonick, Emma Renold, Jessica Ringrose and Lisa Weems, 'Rethinking Agency and Resistance: What Comes After Girl Power?', *Girlhood Studies* 2:2 (Winter 2009), 1–9 (1).

2. Amy Larocca, 'Lost and Found', *New York Magazine,* http://nymag.com/nymetro/shopping/fashion/12544/.

3. Sofia Coppola, 'Sofia Coppola Interviews the Sisters Behind her New Favorite Film', *The New York Times* 17 August 2015, http://www.nytimes.com/2015/08/17/t-magazine/alice-alba-rohrwacher.html.

4. Antonia Fraser describes the historic document as follows: 'The entire royal family signed in the appropriate order, first of all "Louis" for the King, then "Louis Auguste" neatly and precisely written by the Dauphin. But the third signature, "Marie Antoinette Josephe Jeanne" had a large blot on the first "J": the first of these blots – were they careless or nervous – that would blight Marie Antoinette's correspondence with her mother. Furthermore her signature began to slope markedly downwards on "ette" after the half-word "Antoine" as though the Dauphine had not quite accustomed herself to her new signature.' Antonia Fraser, *Marie Antoinette: The Journey* (London: Weidenfield and Nicholson, 2001), 83.

5. Janet Staiger, 'Authorship Approaches', in David Gerstner and Janet Staiger, eds *Authorship and Film* (London and New York: Routledge, 2002), 27–60 (49).

6. Tiqqun, *Preliminary Materials for a Theory of the Young Girl* Trans. Ariana Reines (Los Angeles, CA: Semiotext(e), 2012), 36.

7. Felicity Colman, 'Hit me Harder: The Transversality of Becoming-Adolescent', *Woman: A Cultural Review* 16:3 (2005), 356–371 (357).

8. It is interesting in the context of the former to consider Antonia Fraser's comment in her biography of Marie Antoinette that was the basis for Coppola's screenplay that the loss of her attendants would have been more far more painful for the princess than the process of being stripped to her underwear for the removal of her Austrian wedding clothes. 'You did not have to be the Francophile who found the Dauphine "a thousand times more charming" in her new attire, to realise that parting from her faithful suite was a good deal more painful [...] than the formal divestment. She had, after all, been treated as a doll, to be dressed up in this and that at the adults' whim since childhood.' *Marie Antoinette*, 71.

9. Alison Winch, *Girlfriends and Postfeminist Sisterhood* (Basingstoke: Palgrave, 2013), 10.

10. Ibid, 13.

11. Ibid, 12.

12. Meanwhile, the internet site Vulture.com suggests in its acerbically entertaining review that *Marie Antoinette* too can sustain direct comparison to *Mean Girls*. 'It is a high school

movie transplanted to Versailles. This makes Dunst's Antoinette the Cady Heron of eighteenth-century France, though she never gets to apologise to a Baroque Tina Fey and start a new life as an everybody. In Coppola's re-reading, like in *Mean Girls*, our heroine is a victim of unfamiliar social situations, of wanting to please, and crucially of her basic teenage desire to be cool. She wears ridiculous clothes because everyone else does. She goes to parties because she has status to maintain. Like all popular girls in movies, Marie Antoinette gets punished for these instincts; since this is based on history, she gets decapitated. But the film makes clear that Antoinette did not create her own circumstances, and it allows her – in my favorite scene, with a Dunst eye-roll that deserves its own Oscar, or at least a GIF Wall – to call the court rituals "ridiculous." She goes along with things because she has to, and then she gets swept up in the consequences. What else was she supposed to do?, the movie suggests, which is absurd in terms of historical responsibility but makes a remarkable amount of sense to anyone who has ever been or known a tenth-grade girl.' Amanda Dobbins, 'In Defense of Coppola's *Marie Antoinette*', *Vulture Devouring Culture* June 18 2013, http://www.vulture.com/2013/06/defense-of-sofia-coppolas-marie-antoinette.html

13. Laurent Rigoulet, 'Versailles tendance Coppola', *Télérama* 22 June 2005.

14. Anna Backman Rogers offers a fascinating and insightful reading of gossip as part of court ritual in her analysis of this sequence. See Anna Backman Rogers, 'The Historical Threshold: Crisis, Ritual and Liminality in Sofia Coppola's *Marie Antoinette*', *Relief* 6:1 (2012), 80–97 (89–90), http://www.revue-relief.org/index.php/relief/article/view/762/802.

15. Later in the film, Coppola will suggest that the phrase 'let them eat cake' was invented in order to attack Marie Antoinette, a reading she draws from her source text, Antonia Fraser's sympathetic biography of the queen.

16. Felicity Colman, 'Hit me Harder: The Transversality of Becoming-Adolescent', 361.

17. Richard Prince, 'Sofia Coppola', *Interview*, http://www.interviewmagazine.com/film/sofia-coppola/#_

18. Judith Jack Halberstam, in Elizabeth Freeman, ed. 'Theorising Queer Temporalities: A Roundtable Discussion', *GLQ: A Journal of Lesbian and Gay Studies* 13: 2–3 (2007), 177–195 (186).

19. Ibid, 186.

20. I am thinking here both of such activities as the 'pink stinks' campaign (www.pinkstinks.co.uk) and the long standing association in youth and cultural studies of boys rather than girls with resistant subcultures.

21. Judith Jack Halberstam, 'Oh Bondage Up Yours! Female Masculinity and the Tomboy', in Steve Bruhm and Natasha Hurley, eds *Curiouser: On the Queerness of Children* (Minneapolis: University of Minnesota Press, 2014), 191–214 (194).

22. Felicity Colman, 'Hit me Harder: The Transversality of Becoming-Adolescent', (367–7).

23. Marnina Gonick, Emma Renold, Jessica Ringrose and Lisa Weems, 'Rethinking Agency and Resistance', 1.

24. Sarah Projansky, *Spectacular Girls: Media Fascination and Celebrity Culture* (New York: New York University Press, 2014), 2.

25. Carol Dyhouse, *Girl Trouble: Panic and Progress in the History of Young Women* (London: Zed, 2013), 7.

26. Sarah Projansky, *Spectacular Girls*, 11.

27. Frances Gateward and Murray Pomerance, eds, *Sugar, Spice and Everything Nice: Cinemas of Girlhood* (Detroit, MI: Wayne State University Press, 2002).

28. Kathleen Rowe Karlyn, *Unruly Girls, Unrepentant Mothers: Redefining Feminism on Screen* (Austin, TX: University of Texas Press, 2011), 21.

29. There exists what Jennifer Baumgardner and Amy Richards call 'a veritable cottage industry […] forced out of the fertile soil of girls' failing self-esteem.' *Manifesta: Young Women, Feminism and the Future* (New York: Farrar, Straus and Giroux, 2000), 179. Self-help books for parents specifically tackle the problems associated with raising girls, covering a multitude of topics such as self-esteem, educational achievement and consumerism. Mary Pipher's *Reviving Ophelia: Saving the Selves of Adolescent Girls* (New York: Random House, 1994) was a *New York Times'* best-seller for several months. More recent books include Australian 'child-care guru' Steve Biddulph's *Raising Girls* (London: Harper Collins, 2013)which he promoted on Tuesday 22 January 2013 on BBC Radio 4 Woman's Hour arguing that 'girls are in trouble in a world that seems bent on poisoning their confidence and trashing their lives.' There is also continuation of a long standing suspicion of the kind of media girls enjoy consuming, with what I would call 'Princess Panic' books: Peggy Orenstein, *Cinderella Ate My Daughter: Dispatches from the Front Lines of the New Girlie-Girl Culture* (New York: Harper Collins, 2011), Jennifer Harstein, *Princess Recovery: A Guide to Raising Strong, Empowered Girls Who Can Create their Own Happily Ever Afters* (Avon, MA: Adams Media, 2011) and Rebecca C. Hains, *The Princess Problem: Guiding Our Girls Through the Princess Obsessed Years* (Naperville, Illinois: Sourcebooks, 2014). In terms of government policy and intervention, the UK government commissioned no fewer than 3 reports on young people and sexualisation between 2009 and 2011: David Buckingham's *The Impact of the Commercial World*, Linda Papadopoulos's *Sexualisation of Young People* review and Reg Bailey's *Letting Children be Children: Report of an Independent Review of the Commercialisation and Sexualisation of Childhood*. What is particularly interesting to note here is that these reports were produced under different government regimes: Labour for the first two and a Conservative/Liberal Democrat Coalition for the second, and yet despite this change, there is no difference whatsoever in the focus of anxiety about young people, commerce and sex. Nor is this moral panic about girlhood confined to the Anglo-American world which tends to dominate analysis by feminist girls' media studies scholars such as Projansky, Driscoll and Gonick. As Danielle Hipkins's important work has demonstrated, for example, the figure of the velina, or television showgirl, 'has become a shorthand for moral corruption and cultural decay which prominent thinkers and writers within Italy itself seem overly hasty to endorse.' See '"Whore-ocracy": Show Girls, the Beauty Trade-Off, and Mainstream Oppositional Discourse in Italy', *Italian Studies* 66:3, (2011), 413–30 (414).

30. Quoted in Carol Dyhouse, *Girl Trouble*, 223.

31. Anita Harris, *Future Girl: Young Women in the Twenty-First Century* (London: Routledge, 2004), 2.

32. Tiqqun, *Preliminary Materials for a Theory of the Young Girl* 15–17. I think the 'girling' of the Pope is in reference to Pope Francis having a twitter feed (PopeFrancis@Pontiflex) and an Instagram account (@Franciscus); his softening of the image of the Vatican; his description of faith as a 'party to which everyone is invited.'

33. Sarah Projansky, *Spectacular Girls*, 5–6.

34. Ibid, 6.

35. Ibid, 7.

36. Angela McRobbie, 'Top Girls: Young Women and the Postfeminist Sexual Contract', *Cultural Studies* 21:4–5 (2007), 718–737.

37. Ibid, 732.

38. Mary Celeste Kearney, 'Sparkle: Luminosity and post-girlpower media', *Continuum: Journal of Media and Cultural Studies* 29:2 (2015), 263–273 (265) [italics in original].

39. Ibid, 263.

40. Ibid, 264.

41. Monica Swindle, 'Feeling Girl, Girling Feeling: An Examination of Girl as Affect', *Rhizomes* 22 (2011), http://www.rhizomes.net/issue22/swindle.html.

42. Richard Prince, 'Sofia Coppola', *Interview*, http://www.interviewmagazine.com/film/sofia-coppola/.

43. Anita Harris, *Future Girl*.

44. Marnina Gonick, 'Between "Girl-Power" and "Reviving Ophelia": Constituting the Neoliberal Girl Subject', *NWSA Journal* 18:2 (2006), 1–23.

45. Ibid, 22.

46. Jacki Willson, *Being Gorgeous: Feminism, Sexuality and the Pleasures of the Visual* (London: I.B.Tauris, 2014), 54.

47. Barbara Risman quoted by Swindle, 'Feeling Girl'.

48. Anna Backman Rogers, *American Independent Cinema: Rites of Passage and the Crisis Image* (Edinburgh: Edinburgh University Press, 2015), 24–42.

49. Olivier Davenas, *Teen! Cinéma de l'adolescence* (Paris: Moutons électriques, 2013), 22.

50. Tavi Gevinson, 'Girls with Power and Mystique: An Interview with Sofia Coppola', *Rookie* 17 June 2013, http://www.rookiemag.com/2013/06/sofia-coppola-interview/2/

51. Lucy Bolton, *Film and Female Consciousness: Irigaray, Cinema and Thinking Women* (Basingstoke: Palgrave, 2011), 95–127.

52. Ibid, 120.

53. For a long discussion of Jacobs's style, see Amy Larocca, 'Lost and Found', *New York magazine*, http://nymag.com/nymetro/shopping/fashion/12544/.

54. Themarcjacobs, *Instagram*, https://instagram.com/p/4iFNEOGJCd/

55. The advertisements can be watched online: Daisy at https://www.youtube.com/watch?v=dcyR7PFi-14 and Daisy Trio at https://www.youtube.com/watch?v=s0enWUED3Fo

56. Coppola has an original photo print of the Eggleston image on display in her townhouse in Manhattan. See Lynn Hirschberg, 'Girls on Film', *W Magazine* June 2013, http://www.wmagazine.com/people/celebrities/2013/06/sofia-coppola-director-the-bling-ring-with-emma-watson.

57. Elizabeth Holmes, 'Perfume Bottles Gone Wild', *The Wall Street Journal* 7 June 2012, http://www.wsj.com/news/articles/SB10001424052702303753904577450312917322948.

58. For more on film stars and perfume, see my analysis of Catherine Deneuve's advertisements for Chanel in Fiona Handyside, 'Belle toujours: Deneuve as Fashion icon', in Lisa

Downing and Sue Harris, eds *From Perversion to Purity: The Stardom of Catherine Deneuve* (Manchester: Manchester University Press, 2007), 161–179.

59. Dhani Mau, 'Marc Jacobs is Coming Out with Another Daisy Perfume', *Fashionista* 7 May 2014, http://fashionista.com/2014/05/marc-jacobs-daisy-dream.

60. Elizabeth Wissinger, 'Always on Display: Affective Production in the Modeling Industry', in Jean Clough and Jean Halley, eds *The Affective Turn: Theorising the Social* (Durham: Duke University Press, 2007), 231–260 (236).

61. Gabrielle Ivinson and Emma Renold, 'Valley Girls: Re-theorising bodies and agency in a semi-rural post-industrial locale', *Gender and Education* 25:6 (2013), 704–721 (721).

62. Catherine Driscoll, *Girls*, 203–234.

63. Ibid, 225.

64. First Time Fest Q&A panel March 2013, Anon, 'Exclusive: Sofia Coppola and Ed Lachman talk "Virgin Suicides" at FTF screening', *The Examiner.com*, http://www.examiner.com/article/exclusive-sofia-coppola-and-ed-lachman-talk-virgin-suicides-at-ftf-screening.

65. Philippe Azoury, 'Etoiles mystérieuses', *Les Inrockuptibles* 1 August 2000.

66. Tavi Gevinson, 'Girls with Power and Mystique', *Rookie*, http://www.rookiemag.com/2013/06/sofia-coppola-interview/.

67. Catherine Driscoll, *Girls*, 216.

68. See for example, Anon, 'The Sofia Coppola Look Book', *New York magazine* October 2012, http://nymag.com/thecut/2012/10/sofia-coppola-look-book.html; Cristina Perez, 'Three Things I Learned about Style from Sofia Coppola's Totally Understated Chic', *Glamour* May 16 2013, http://www.glamour.com/fashion/blogs/dressed/2013/05/sofia-coppolas-understated-chi; Lee Radziwill and Sofia Coppola, 'On Protecting Privacy', *New York Times Magazine* May 30 2013, http://tmagazine.blogs.nytimes.com/2013/05/30/in-conversation-lee-radziwill-and-sophia-coppola-on-protecting-privacy/.

69. Kate Donnelly, 'Sofia's Juicy Red Valentine', *New York Times magazine* February 12 2015, http://tmagazine.blogs.nytimes.com/2015/02/12/sofia-coppola-red-wine/

70. Richard Prince, 'Sofia Coppola', *Interview,* http://www.interviewmagazine.com/film/sofia-coppola/.

71. It seems that Anne Billson from *The Daily Telegraph* unwittingly got the point when she rather snottily described the film's poster. She commented that its Sub Comic Caption Bold font in solid black with white outline is 'reminiscent of the piping on a chavvy tracksuit' and criticised it for having 'the most boring Hollywood background possible (ye gods that might as well be Torquay).' Anne Billson, 'The Bling Ring: is this the ugliest movie poster ever?', *The Daily Telegraph* 10 May 2013, http://www.telegraph.co.uk/culture/film/10048804/The-Bling-Ring-is-this-the-ugliest-movie-poster-ever.html.

72. Jackie Stacey, *Star-Gazing: Hollywood Cinema and Female Spectatorship* (Oxford and New York: Routledge, 1994), 178.

73. Charles Eckert, 'The Carol Lombard in Macy's Window', in Christine Gledhill, ed. *Stardom: Industry of Desire* (London: Routledge, 1991), 30–39.

74. Mary Ann Doane, 'The Economy of Desire: The Commodity Form in/of Cinema,' *Quarterly Review of Film and Video* 11, 1989, 22–33 (31–32).

75. See especially Rachel Moseley, *Growing Up with Audrey Hepburn: Text, Audience, Resonance* (Manchester: Manchester University Press, 2003).

76. James Breen, 'In brief: Breakfast at Tiffany's', *Sight and Sound* Winter 1961–2, 38.

77. Chantal Cornut-Gentille D'Arcy, 'Who's Afraid of the Femme Fatale in *Breakfast at Tiffany's*? Exposure and Implications of a Myth', in Chantal Cornut-Gentille D'Arcy and José García Landa, eds *Gender, I-deology: Essays on Theory, Fiction and Film* (Amsterdam: Rodopi, 1996), 371–385 (374).

78. For discussion of this, see in particular Diane Negra, *What a Girl Wants: Fantasizing the Reclamation of the Self in Postfeminism* (London: Routledge, 2009).

79. Emma Renold and Jessica Ringrose, 'Regulation and Rupture: Mapping Tween and Teenage Girls' Resistance to the Heterosexual Matrix', *Feminist Studies* 9:3 (2008), 313–338 (314).

80. Ibid, 319.

81. Clélia Cohen and Jacky Goldberg, 'Princesse du cool', *Les Inrockuptibles* 5 January 2011.

82. First Time Fest Q&A panel March 2013. Anon, 'Exclusive: Sofia Coppola and Ed Lachman talk "Virgin Suicides" at FTF screening'.

83. Geoff King, *Lost in Translation* (Edinburgh: Edinburgh University Press, 2010), 11.

84. Sofia Coppola, 'Summer Talks: *The Bling Ring*', Film Society of Lincoln Centre, New York, June 10 2013, http://www.filmlinc.org/daily/summer-talks-sofia-coppola-on-the-bling-ring/.

85. Heather Warren-Crow, *Girlhood and the Plastic Image* (Dartmouth: University Press of New England, 2014), 10.

86. Vicky Lebeau, *Childhood and Cinema* (London: Reaktion, 2008), 4.

87. Heather Warren-Crow, *Girlhood and the Plastic Image*, 10.

88. Ibid, 8.

89. Ibid, 17.

90. First Time Fest Q&A panel March 2013.

91. Cynthia Fuchs, 'The Virgin Suicides', *Pop Matters*, http://www.popmatters.com/review/virgin-suicides2/.

92. Anna Backman Rogers, *American Independent Cinema*, 30, 34; Olivier Davenas, *Teen*, 22.

93. Vicky Lebeau, *Childhood and Cinema*, 91.

94. Ibid, 104–105.

95. Ibid, 110.

96. Leslie Parris, ed. *The Pre-Raphaelites* (London: Tate, 1984), 96–98.

97. Colin McCabe, *Godard: Images, Sounds, Politics* (London: BFI, 1980), 96–98.

98. Anna Backman Rogers, *American Independent Cinema*, 32.

99. Martine Beugnet, *Cinema and Sensation: French Film and the Art of Transgression* (Edinburgh: Edinburgh University Press, 2007), 136.

100. Richard Dyer, *White: Essays on Race and Culture* (London and New York: Routledge, 1997).

101. See Meagan Hatcher-Mays, 'How Sofia Coppola Whitewashed *The Bling Ring*', *Jezebel* 20 June 2013, http://jezebel.com/how-sofia-coppola-whitewashed-the-bling-ring-514020537; Muna Mire and Isabelle Nastasia, 'Sofia Coppola and the Unbearable Whiteness of *The Bling Ring*' *mic.com* 4 July 2013, http://mic.com/articles/52649/sofia-coppola-and-the-unbearable-whiteness-of-the-bling-ring; Jorge Rivas, 'The Immigrant You Won't See in Sofia Coppola's *Bling Ring*', *Colorlines* 13 June 2013, http://www.color-lines.com/articles/immigrant-you-wont-see-sofia-coppolas-bling-ring.

102. John Hiscock, 'Sofia Coppola Interview: "The Bling Ring isn't my world."' *The Daily Telegraph* 4 July 2013, http://www.telegraph.co.uk/culture/film/10126910/Sofia-Coppola-interview-The-Bling-Ring-isnt-my-world.html.

103. Alexander Fury, 'Milan Fashion Week: Donatella Versace on sex and why she'd rather be a feminist than a muse', *The Independent* 19 September 2013, http://www.independent.co.uk/life-style/fashion/features/milan-fashion-week-donatella-versace-on-sex-and-why-shed-rather-be-a-feminist-than-a-muse-8824528.html.

104. See for example her comment to *The Daily Telegraph*: 'She's not showbusiness at all; she always looked at it from a distance. She's not one for being the centre of attention: she likes to be quiet and on the side. "I don't ever yell on the set, and people wonder why, when my dad is so loud. But I get my demeanour from my mom. She's great at observing those strange, funny, telling little details."' Anon, 'LA Confidential: Sofia Coppola Interview', *The Daily Telegraph* 6 December 2010, http://www.telegraph.co.uk/culture/film/filmmakersonfilm/8176308/LA-confidential-Sofia-Coppola-interview.html.

105. Stephen Gundle, *Glamour: A History* (Oxford: Oxford University Press, 2008), 15.

106. Raka Shome, *Diana and Beyond: White Femininity, National Identity, and Contemporary Media Culture* (Urbana, Chicago and Springfield: University of Illinois Press, 2014), 27.

107. Richard Dyer, *White*, 78.

108. Masafumi Monden, 'Contemplating in a Dreamlike Room: *The Virgin Suicides* and the Aesthetic Imagination of Girlhood', *Film, Fashion and Consumption* 2:2 (June 2013), 139–158 (153).

109. Gabrielle Ivinson and Emma Renold, 'Valley Girls', 720.

110. Heather Warren-Crow, *Girlhood and the Plastic Image*, 15–16.

111. Robert Latham, *Consuming Youth: Vampires, Cyborgs and the Cultures of Consumption* (Chicago: University of Chicago Press, 2004), 140.

112. Anita Harris, *Future Girl*.

113. Heather Warren-Crow, *Girlhood and the Plastic Image*, 19.

114. Helen Pilinovsky, 'Body as Wonderland: Alice's Graphic Iteration in *Lost Girls*', in Christopher Hollingsworth, ed. *Alice Beyond Wonderland: Essays from the 21ˢᵗ Century* (Iowa: Iowa University Press, 2009), 175–198 (182).

115. Lewis Carroll, *Alice in Wonderland and Through the Looking-Glass* (London: Dean and Son, abridged edition, nd), 30.

116. Ibid, 31.

3 'There's No Place Like Home!' The Exploded Home as Postfeminist Chronotope

1. Mikhail Bakhtin, cited in Vivian Sobchack, 'Lounge Time: Postwar crisis and the chronotope of film noir', in Nick Browne, ed. *Refiguring American Film Genres: History and Theory* (Berkeley and LA: University of California Press, 1998), 129–170, (150).

2. Kristin Hohenadel, 'French Royalty as seen by Hollywood Royalty', *New York Times* September 10 2006, http://www.nytimes.com/2006/09/10/movies/moviesspecial/10hohe.html?pagewanted=all.

3. Mark Olsen, 'The Directors: Sofia Coppola takes a floor at the Chateau Marmont', *Los Angeles Times* October 31 2010, http://articles.latimes.com/2010/oct/31/entertainment/la-ca-sneaks-somewhere-20101031. Indeed, Coppola's connection to the hotel merges the personal and the professional and her interests in fashion, photography and film, in ways that are typical of Coppola's celebrity auteur persona and its intermedial construction. As well as hosting her 21st birthday party, the Chateau was also the location for a photo shoot for *W* magazine promoting her MilkFed clothing line in 1994, and she even remembers being sung to in the lobby as a child.

4. Kristin Hohenadel, 'French Royalty as seen by Hollywood Royalty'.

5. Ibid.

6. Anon, 'Scene of the crime interview with Paris Hilton', *The Bling Ring* DVD Studiocanal, 2013.

7. Lee Radziwill, 'In conversation: Lee Radziwill and Sofia Coppola, on Protecting Privacy', *The New York Times* May 30 2013, http://tmagazine.blogs.nytimes.com/2013/05/30/in-conversation-lee-radziwill-and-sophia-coppola-on-protecting-privacy/.

8. Ibid.

9. Chris Rojek, *Celebrity* (London: Reaktion, 2001), 20.

10. Michael Holmquist, glossary to Bakhtin, *The Dialogic Imagination: 4 Essays* Trans. Caryl Ermerson (Austin, TX: University of Texas Press, 1982), 425–426.

11. Vivian Sobchack, 'Lounge Time', 149–150.

12. Ibid, 151.

13. Ibid,151.

14. Lee Wallace, *Lesbianism, Cinema, Space: The Sexual Life of Apartments* (London: Routledge, 2011), 3.

15. Michael V. Montgomery, *Carnivals and Commonplaces: Bakhtin's Chronotope, Cultural Studies, and Film* (New York: Peter Lang, 1993), 91.

16. Jonathan Shia, 'Somewhere', *The Last Magazine* December 29 2010, https://thelast-magazine.com/somewhere/.

17. Sharon Lin Tay, *Women on the Edge: Twelve Political Film Practices* (New York: Palgrave, 2009), 134.

18. Rebecca Munford and Melanie Waters, *Feminism and Popular Culture: Investigating the Postfeminist Mystique* (London: I.B.Tauris, 2014), 72.

19. See Diane Negra, *What a Girl Wants: Fantasizing the Reclamation of the Self in Postfeminism* (London, Routledge, 2009) and Joanne Hollows, '"Can I Go Home Yet?" Feminism, Postfeminism and Domesticity', in Joanne Hollows and Rachel Moseley, *Feminism in Popular Culture* (Oxford: Berg, 2006), 97–118.

20. Rebecca Munford and Melanie Waters, *Feminism and Popular Culture*, 119.

21. Nathan Lee, 'Pretty Vacant: The Radical Frivolity of Sofia Coppola's *Marie Antoinette*', *Film Comment* September-October 2006, 24–26.

22. Ibid.

23. Lynn Porter, 'Bahktin's Chronotope: Time and Space in *A Touch of the Poet* and *More Stately Mansions*', *Modern Drama* 34:3 (Fall 1991), 369–382 (370).

24. P. Adams Sitney, *Vital Crises in Italian Cinema: Iconography, Stylistics, Politics* (Oxford: Oxford University Press, 2nd edition 2013).

25. Belinda Smaill, 'Sofia Coppola: Reading the Director', *Feminist Media Studies* 13:1 (2013), 148–162.

26. Patrice Petro, *Aftershocks of the New: Feminism and Film History* (New Brunswick: Rutgers University Press, 2002), 93.

27. Quoted in J.M.Tyree, 'Searching for *Somewhere*', *Film Quarterly* 64:4 (Summer 2011), 16.

28. Ivone Margulies, 'A Matter of Time: Jeanne Dielman, 23, Quai du commerce, 1080 Bruxelles', *Criterion*, https://www.criterion.com/current/posts/1215-a-matter-of-time-jeanne -dielman-23-quai-du-commerce-1080-bruxelles.

29. Ibid.

30. Nathan Lee, 'Pretty Vacant', 26.

31. Anna Backman Rogers, 'The Historical Threshold: Crisis, Ritual and Liminality in Sofia Coppola's *Marie Antoinette* (2006)', *Relief* 6:1 (2012), http://www.revue-relief.org/index.php/relief/article/view/762/802.

32. Ibid.

33. Antonia Fraser, *Marie Antoinette*, 90.

34. Anna Backman Rogers, 'The Historical Threshold'.

35. The term guerrilla here refers to both the strategy for obtaining this footage and its resulting style (the two are obviously linked). As Geoff King explains, street sequences were shot in an impromptu manner with a small crew and handheld camera, without any crowd control or official permissions (very different from standard studio procedure where streets are closed off and crowds are provided by professional extras). The aim was to shoot in a flexible, mobile style that was both a practicality for a low-budget production and a central contribution to the fleeting impression created of the texture of the city. Geoff King, *Lost in Translation* (Edinburgh: Edinburgh University Press, 2010), 11–12.

36. Marlow Stern, 'Sofia Coppola discusses *Lost in Translation* on its 10th Anniversary', *The Daily Beast* 9 December 2013, http://www.thedailybeast.com/articles/2013/09/12/sofia-coppola-discusses-lost-in-translation-on-its-10th-anniversary.html.

37. According to Homay King, this is a funeral service, although there is nothing in the film to make this explicit, and is an interpretation which depends on extra-textual knowledge. Homay King, *Lost in Translation: Orientalism, Cinema, and the Enigmatic Signifier* (Durham and London: Duke University Press, 2010), 166.

38. Homay King, *Lost in Translation*, 161–170.

39. Lucy Bolton, *Film and Female Consciousness: Irigaray, Cinema and Thinking Women* (London Palgrave, 2011), 111.

40. Homay King, *Lost in Translation*, 163.

41. Lucy Bolton, *Film and Female Consciousness*, 127.

42. Laurent Berlant, 'Intimacy: A Special Issue', *Critical Inquiry* 24:2 (Winter 1998), 281–288 (283).

43. Ibid, 286.

44. Lauren Berlant, *The Female Complaint: The Unfinished Business of Sentimentality in American Culture* (Durham: Duke University Press, 2008), 6.

45. Ibid.

46. Samiha Matin, 'Private Femininity, Public Femininity: Tactical Aesthetics in the Costume Film', in Christine Gledhill, ed. *Gender Meets Genre in Postwar Cinemas* (Urbana, Chicago and Springfield: University of Illinois Press, 2012), 96–110 (99) [my italics].

47. Benedict Anderson, *Imagined Communities: Reflections on the Origins and Spread of Nationalism* (London: Verso, 1983).

48. Ibid, 20.

49. Sarah Projansky, *Spectacular Girls: Media Fascination and Celebrity Culture* (New York: New York University Press, 2014). See chapter 2 for further discussion of Projansky.

50. Anon, 'LA Confidential: Sofia Coppola Interview', *The Daily Telegraph* 6 December 2010, http://www.telegraph.co.uk/culture/film/filmmakersonfilm/8176308/LA-confidential-Sofia-Coppola-interview.html.

51. Julianne Pidduck, *Contemporary Costume Film: Space, Place and the Past* (London: BFI, 2004), 54.

52. Ibid.

53. Diane Negra, *What a Girl Wants*, 5.

54. Gaston Bachelard, *The Poetics of Space* Trans. Maria Jolas (Boston, MA: Beacon Press, 1994), 7.

55. Ibid, xxxii.

56. Ibid, xxxiii.

57. This shot was suggested to Coppola by Savides when he saw the location they would be using and realised he could use a camera set-up from across the street. Partly the shot allows the film to find new ways to show us similar events – teens robbing houses – and thus serves the function of providing additional visual interest, but the shot also enriches the dominant theme of outside and inside. As the production schedule fell behind, the shot was dropped and Savides fought hard for its reinstatement, saying they had to get that shot. Coppola explains 'I'm so glad because that is one of my favourite shots.' Sofia Coppola, 'Summer Talks: The Bling Ring', Film Society at the Lincoln Center, 10 June 2013, http://www.film-linc.org/daily/summer-talks-sofia-coppola-on-the-bling-ring/.

58. Coppola credits her sound designer Richard Beggs with the subtlety of this mix, saying they decided together not to have music and allow natural sounds to dominate. 'Sofia Coppola, 'Summer Talks: The Bling Ring', Film Society at the Lincoln Center, 10 June 2013, http://www.filmlinc.org/daily/summer-talks-sofia-coppola-on-the-bling-ring/.

59. Bree Hoskin, 'Playground Love: Landscape and Longing in Sofia Coppola's *The Virgin Suicides', Literature/Film Quarterly* 35:3 (2007), 214–221 (215).

60. Sigmund Freud, 'The Uncanny', *Art and Literature 14: The Penguin Freud Library* Trans. and ed. James Strachey (Harmondsworth: Penguin, 1990), 112–173 (117).

61. 'Scene of the crime interview with Paris Hilton', *The Bling Ring* DVD Studiocanal, 2013

62. Louise J. Kaplan, *Female Perversions: The Temptations of Madame Bovary* (Harmondsworth: Penguin, 1993), 34.

63. Robert Stoller, *Observing the Erotic Imagination* (New Haven and London: Yale University Press, 1985), 155.

64. 'Why was that? Yeah, he [Roman] shot the whole "I Want Candy" montage and he just saw that there [the trainers] and put it in for me for fun. He just shot a bunch of stuff and left that in for fun because he thought I would like it, and then when I was editing we decided to leave it in.' Todd Gilchrist, 'Interview: Sofia Coppola', *IGN* 17 October 2006, http://uk.ign.com/articles/2006/10/17/interview-sofia-coppola.

65. Rebecca Munford and Melanie Waters, *Feminism and Popular Culture*, 135–136.

66. Ibid, 20.

67. Ibid, 20.

68. Bree Hoskin, 'Playground Love', 214.

69. Wendy Haslem, 'Neon Gothic: *Lost in Translation*', *Senses of Cinema* April 2004, http://sensesofcinema.com/2004/feature-articles/lost_in_translation/.

70. Ibid.

71. For Heidi Brevik-Zender, Coppola's insistence on Marie Antoinette's conscious acknowledgement of the camera's presence, repeated later in the film when she glances at the camera while crying over a letter from her mother berating her for her failure to conceive children, recalls reality television and the way it permits audiences to share in the characters' deepest mortifications while enjoying the role of voyeur. See Heidi Brevik-Zender, 'Let them wear Manolos: Fashion, Walter Benjamin, and Sofia Coppola's *Marie Antoinette*', *Camera Obscura* 78 26:3 (2011), 1–33.

72. Bree Hoskin, 'Playground Love', 215.

73. Rebecca Munford and Melanie Waters, *Feminism and Popular Culture*, 122.

74. Robynn Stilwell, 'Vinyl Communion: The Record as Ritual Object in Girls' Rite-of-Passage Films', in Phil Powrie and Robynn Stilwell, eds *Changing Tunes: The Use of Pre-Existing Music in Films* (Aldershot: Ashford, 2006), 152–167 (156).

75. Ibid, 158.

76. Richard Prince, 'Sofia Coppola', *Interview magazine,* http://www.interviewmagazine.com/film/sofia-coppola/#_.

77. Ina Rae Hark, 'Movie-Going, "Home-Leaving" and the Problematic Girl Protagonist of the *Wizard of Oz*', in Frances K. Gateward and Murray Pomerance, eds *Sugar, Spice and Everything Nice: Cinemas of Girlhood* (Detroit, MI: Wayne State University Press, 2002), 25–38 (25).

78. Ibid, 28.

4 Dressing Up and Playing About: Costume and Fashion

1. Leslie W Rabine, 'A Woman's Two Bodies: Fashion Magazines, Consumerism and Feminism', in Shari Benstock and Suzanne Ferriss, eds, *On Fashion* (New Brunswick: Rutgers University Press), 59–75 (67).

2. Todd Gilchrist, 'Interview: Sofia Coppola', *IGN* 17 October 2006, http://uk.ign.com/articles/2006/10/17/interview-sofia-coppola?page=3.

3. The idea of having your own clothing line came to Coppola through her involvement with Kim Gordon's X Girl range; X-Girl stores were among the first to stock Milk Fed clothing in the 1990s in the States. Coppola explains that Gordon made her realise she could just launch a collection without needing masses of experience or skill (when she helped Kim Gordon

put on her Soho show and realised Gordon didn't know how to sew!) See Merle Ginsberg, 'Launching Sofia', *W* September 1994, http://www.wmagazine.com/fashion/1994/09/sofia-coppola-milk-fed/photos. While this could (almost) be seen as part of a 'DIY' culture that aligns itself with grrrls and zines, the celebrity fashion line is now far more corporate and widespread, such as Sienna Miller's Twenty8Twelve, Sarah Jessica Parker's Bitten and Justin Timberlake's William Rast.

4. See for example *Vogue* Italia Dec 1992; *Vogue* Paris Dec 2004; *Stylist* (UK) June 2013; *Red* (UK)July 2013; *Vogue* Australia August 2013; *High Class* (Paraguay) October 2013; *Vogue* Italia February 2014.

5. Caitlin Yuneun-Lewis, 'Cool Postfeminism: The Stardom of Sofia Coppola', Diane Negra and Su Holmes, eds *In the Limelight and Under the Microscope: The Form and Functions of Female Celebrity* (London and New York: Continuum, 2011), 174–198.

6. Pam Cook, 'An American in Paris: Sofia Coppola and the new auteurism', Melbourne University workshop, 25 September 2013, Unpublished paper quoted with kind permission of Pam Cook.

7. Caitlin Yuneun-Lewis, 'Cool Postfeminism: The Stardom of Sofia Coppola', 175.

8. Ibid.

9. Maureen Orth, *The Importance of Being Famous: Behind the Scenes of the Celebrity-Industrial Complex* (New York: Henry Holt, 2004).

10. Evgenia Peretz, 'Something About Sofia', *Vanity Fair* 553 September 2006, 237. This quotation is considered so central to the Coppola auteur persona in its defiant defence of fashion and desire to overcome the binary of frivolity and depth central to patriarchal dismissal of 'women's issues' that it is reproduced on the Internet Movie Database's Sofia Coppola page as one of her 'key quotes'.

11. Given his commitment to this 'profundity of the superficial' as opposed to the 'superficiality of profundity', it is intriguing that Rohmer directed a history film that stands sustained comparison with Coppola's *Marie Antoinette*. Rohmer made a film about the French Revolution from the perspective of a foreign aristocratic female, Grace Elliott, with his 2001 film *L'Anglaise et le duc*. While Coppola uses the devices of playful anachronism to destroy the illusion of historical mimesis and emphasise the distance between us and the historic Versailles, Rohmer uses digital technology to encrust his actors into painted backdrops that show us how we can only ever experience history as mediated representation. Both films align their representational politics – undermining the illusion of an objective look at the past – with an attention to issues of gender and nationality.

12. Fabrice Ziolkowski, 'Comedies and Proverbs: An Interview with Eric Rohmer', *Wide Angle* 5:1 (1982), 62–67 (63).

13. Tania Modleski, *The Women Who Knew Too Much: Hitchcock and Feminist Theory* (London: Routledge, 2nd edition 2005), 73.

14. Juliet Ash and Elizabeth Wilson, 'Introduction', in Juliet Ash and Elizabeth Wilson, eds *Chic Thrills: A Fashion Reader* (London: Harper Collins, 1992), xi–xvii, (xii).

15. Alexandra Warwick and Dani Cavallaro, *Fashioning the Frame: Boundaries, Dress and the Body* (Oxford: Berg, 1998), 7, emphasis in original.

16. The bright blue bow tied at Marie Antoinette's neck, an exaggerated version of that found in a portrait of Marie Antoinette by Elisabeth Vigée-Lebrun, could also be read

as a premonition of Marie Antoinette's ultimate fate. Although Coppola avoids show-ing us Marie Antoinette's death at the guillotine, the dainty strip of satin around Marie Antoinette's neck at the moment she is handed over to the French court foreshadows the queen's decapitation by drawing our attention to the place where her head will be severed from her body. Caroline Weber further confirms this reading of the significance of the ribbon when she makes note of the morbid fashion that sprang up following the queen's decapitation for young aristocratic women to wear a thin red ribbon tied around their necks as if to anticipate their possible fates. Caroline Weber, *Queen of Fashion: What Marie Antoinette Wore to the Revolution* (New York: Picador, 2006), 9.

17. Kennedy Fraser, 'Kirsten Dunst: Teen Queen', *Vogue* September 2006.

18. Christina Lane and Nicole Richter, 'The Feminist Poetics of Sofia Coppola: Spectacle and Self-Consciousness in *Marie Antoinette* (2006)', in Hilary Radner and Rebecca Stringer, eds *Feminism at the Movies: Understanding Gender in Contemporary Popular Cinema* (London: Routledge, 2011), 189–202 (195).

19. Diana Diamond, 'Sofia Coppola's *Marie Antoinette*: Costumes, Girl Power and Feminism', in Adrienne Munich, ed *Fashion in Film* (Bloomington and Indianapolis: Indiana University Press, 2011), 203–231 (221).

20. Ibid.

21. Ilya Parkins, 'Building a Feminist Theory of Fashion', *Australian Feminist Studies* 23:58 (2008), 501–515 (511).

22. Linda M. Scott, *Fresh Lipstick: Redressing Fashion and Feminism* (New York: Palgrave, 2005), 2–3.

23. Ibid, 3.

24. Ibid, 52.

25. Parkins, 'Building a Feminist Theory of Fashion', 511.

26. Within the logic of the films' storyworlds, so dominated by the girls' perspective, of course, the mother does not *need* fashion to express herself as her voice is so dominant. In *Marie Antoinette*, the main character-voice that has narrative power is that of Marie Antoinette's mother, who interrupts Marie Antoinette's life at Versailles with letters, read in voice-over, that remind Marie Antoinette of her duty to bear children. As Richter and Lane suggest, the fact that the mother is played by the iconic Marianne Faithfull gives an ironic twist to her power, as Faithfull has the status of rugged survivor of many challenges. 'Feminist Poetics', 196. There is a similar dynamic in *The Bling Ring*; when Nicki is interviewed by Kate from *Vanity Fair* she twice interrupts her mother in the space of 30 seconds in order to express herself. The perception, at least for Nicki, is of her mother's dominant voice.

27. Pamela Church Gibson, 'Redressing the Balance: Patriarchy, Postmodernism and Feminism', in Stella Bruzzi and Pamela Church Gibson, eds *Fashion Cultures: Theory, Exploration and Analysis* (London: Routledge, 2001), 231.

28. Parkins, 'Building a Feminist Theory of Fashion', 512.

29. Ibid, 512.

30. Hilary Radner, *Neo-Feminist Cinema: Girly Films, Chick Flicks and Consumer Culture* (London: Routledge, 2011), 134.

31. Edgar Morin, *L'Esprit du temps* (Paris: Grasset, 1962), 192–4.

32. Hilary Radner, *Neo-feminist Cinema*, 135.

33. Ibid.
34. Ibid.
35. Delphine Letort, 'The Cultural Capital of Sofia Coppola's *The Bling Ring* (2013): Branding Feminine Celebrity in Los Angeles', *Celebrity Studies* 2015, http://www.tandfonline.com/doi/abs/10.1080/19392397.2015.1119657.
36. Laurent Rigoulet, 'Versailles tendance Coppola', *Télérama* 22 June 2005.
37. *Marie Antoinette* production notes available online at www.visualhollywood.com/movies/marieantoinette/notes.pdf. As Pam Cook explains, Masterpiece Theatre is a television drama series that airs on PBS. A high proportion of its programing is quality period drama.
38. Danielle Long, 'Sony Targets social networking sites for *Marie Antoinette*', *Marketing Magazine* 20 October 2006, http://www.marketingmagazine.co.uk/article/599673/sony-targets-social-networking-sites-marie-antoinette.
39. Diana Diamond, 'Sofia Coppola's *Marie Antoinette*', 225–226.
40. Stella Bruzzi, *Undressing Cinema: Clothing and Identity at the Movies* (London: Routledge, 1997), 34.
41. Diana Diamond, 'Sofia Coppola's *Marie Antoinette*', 213.
42. Ibid.
43. There has been a good deal of scholarship on *Marie Antoinette* and its revision of the historical biopic, much of which is beyond the scope of this chapter. See Dennis Bingham, *Whose Lives are they Anyway? The Biopic as Contemporary Film Genre* (Pescataway, NJ: Rutgers University Press, 2010), 361–376; Pam Cook, 'History in the Making: Sofia Coppola's *Marie Antoinette* and the New Auteurism', in Tom Brown and Belen Vidal, eds *The Biopic in Contemporary Film Culture* (London: Routledge, 2014), 212–226; Elizabeth A. Ford and Deborah C. Mitchell, *Royal Portraits in Hollywood: Filming the Lives of Queens* (Lexington: University Press of Kentucky, 2009). Marie Antoinette has been the subject of several historical literary biographies, including Antonia Fraser's *Marie Antoinette: The Journey* (London: Weidenfield and Nicholson, 2001) which was optioned by Coppola in 2001 and the rights finally bought as filming began in 2005. Fraser received a 'based on' credit. When she first optioned the book (on the advice of her mother), Coppola wrote to Fraser, saying she liked her account as it is 'the best one…full of life, not a dry historical drama.' Coppola stayed in touch with Fraser as she developed her screenplay, emailing her for various pieces of advice and information through 2001–2002, prior to the filming of *Lost in Translation*. Fraser, whose daughter, Natasha, was an extra in the film, also visited the set several times while filming was taking place. For a most entertaining account of the Fraser/Coppola collaboration, see Antonia Fraser, 'Sofia's Choice', *Vanity Fair* October 31 2006, http://www.vanityfair.com/news/2006/11/fraser200611. Fraser's biography is sympathetic to the queen, and most notable for its desire 'not to allow the sombre tomb to make its presence felt too early. The elegiac should have its place as well as the tragic, flowers and music as well as revolution and counter-revolution' (xvii). The resonance of flowers and especially music with contemporary teen girl cultures are of course enhanced in Coppola's film and link back to the aesthetics of girlhood she uses as I discuss in chapter 2. Coppola initially optioned French historian Evelyne Lever's volume *Marie Antoinette: The Last Queen of France*, which appeared in English translation in 2000. Lever also receives a historical advisor credit on the film, along with French historian Jacques-Charles Gaffiot.

44. Mark Brown, 'Coppola Film Booed', *The Guardian* Thursday 25 May 2006, http://www.the-guardian.com/world/2006/may/25/film.cannes2006.

45. Christina Lane and Nicole Richter, 'Feminist Poetics', 200.

46. Diana Diamond, 'Sofia Coppola's *Marie Antoinette*', 206–208.

47. Jacki Willson, *Being Gorgeous: Feminism, Sexuality and the Pleasure of the Visual* (London: I.B.Tauris, 2015), 75.

48. Heidi Brevik-Zender, 'Let them wear Manolos: Fashion, Walter Benjamin, and Sofia Coppola's *Marie Antoinette*', *Camera Obscura* 78 26:3 (2011), 1–33 (2).

49. Ibid, 3.

50. Ibid, 12.

51. I discuss in chapter 1 the significance of iconoclasm. There is iconoclasm going on in this image too, as it deliberately destroys any notion of an authentic picture of royal femininity and also suggests the dauphine's affinity to a courtesan as she is dressed in her underwear (just like a prostitute she is valued only for her sexual organs – in this case her womb). Coppola reworks iconic art historical references here too. Edouard Manet's *Olympia*, a classic representation of a prostitute, was greeted with howls of outrage and incomprehension when it was first displayed at the Paris salon of 1865. This was partly because Olympia while presented invitingly to the viewer stares back defiantly at him; an attitude imitated here by Coppola's Marie Antoinette. Through acknowledging the gaze of the male viewer, Olympia forces the art-critic to acknowledge (if only unconsciously) his voyeuristic impulses when perusing art, as 'his picture [...] quotes from the social vocabulary of the Courtesan and the pictorial vocabulary of the Nude, but only in order to equivocate them both, forcing a recognition that the body of the woman in the painting cannot be recuperated into the comfortable space of either; reminding the male viewer that he had, in his own primitive way, actually got the point he wished to ignore when, in his guise as nineteenth century art critic, he described the body as 'dirty', 'unwashed', 'greasy'; namely, that Olympia comes from the streets, and that the happy charade prettifying the money/sex exchange could be accomplished only by a retreat into bad faith, by literally averting one's eyes.' Christopher Prendergast, *Paris and the Nineteenth Century* (Oxford: Blackwell,1992), 138.

52. Heidi Brevik-Zender, 'Let them eat Manolos', 13.

53. For Brevik-Zender, the Converse adds further layers to the 'transhistorical' use of fashion in the film, as the trainer dates from the 1920s, and is now an established fashion classic. Ibid, 13.

54. Rosalind Galt, *Pretty: Film and the Decorative Image* (New York: Columbia University Press, 2011), 22.

55. Hilary Radner, *Neo-feminist Cinema*, 155.

56. Amy Sohn, *Sex and the City: Kiss and Tell* (New York: Pocket Books, 2004), 68–69.

57. Diana Diamond, 'Sofia Coppola's Marie Antoinette', 219.

58. Lee Wright, 'Objectifying Gender: The Stiletto Heel', in Malcom Barnard, ed. *Fashion Theory: A Reader* (London: Routledge, 2007), 247–258, (250).

Conclusion: The Agency of Authorship

1. Catherine Grant, 'Secret Agents: Feminist Theories of Women's Film Authorship', *Feminist Theory* 2:1 (April 2001), 113–130.
2. Ibid, 115.
3. Ibid, 119.
4. Ibid, 121.
5. Ibid, 126–7.
6. Ibid, 127.
7. Ibid, 128.
8. Justin Kroll, 'Sofia Coppola to Direct Universal and Working Title's *Little Mermaid*', *Variety* March 18 2014, http://variety.com/2014/film/news/sofia-coppola-to-direct-universal-and-working-titles-little-mermaid-1201137793/.
9. Noah Gittell, '*The Little Mermaid*'s Twisted, Sofia-Coppola-esque Origins', *The Atlantic* 21 March 2014, http://www.theatlantic.com/entertainment/archive/2014/03/-em-the-little-mermaid-em-s-twisted-sofia-coppola-esque.
10. Justin Kroll, 'Chloe Moretz to star in *Little Mermaid* for Working Title; Richard Curtis to Pen Script', *Variety* 6 November 2015, http://variety.com/2015/film/news/chloe-moretz-little-mermaid-1201579228/.
11. Fuuny or Die, 'Sofia Coppola's Little Mermaid'.13 May 2014. https://www.youtube.com/watch?v=YPT4bdo1kZw.

Bibliography

Adams, Sam. 'Does Sofia Coppola have a problem with privilege or do her critics?', *Indiewire*, <http://blogs.indiewire.com/criticwire/does-sofia-coppola-have-a-problem-with-privilege-or-do-her-critics>. Accessed 31 May 2016.

Adams Sitney, P. *Vital Crises in Italian Cinema: Iconography, Stylistics, Politics* (Oxford: Oxford University Press, 2nd edition 2013).

Akerman, Chantal. 'Chantal Akerman on Jeanne Dielman', *Camera Obscura* 2 (1977).

Anderson, Benedict. *Imagined Communities: Reflections on the Origins and Spread of Nationalism* (London: Verso, 1983).

Anon, 'Exclusive: Sofia Coppola and Ed Lachman talk "Virgin Suicides" at FTF screening', *The Examiner.com*, <http://www.examiner.com/article/exclusive-sofia-coppola-and-ed-lachman-talk-virgin-suicides-at-ftf-screening>. Accessed 31 May 2016.

———, 'LA Confidential: Sofia Coppola Interview', *The Daily Telegraph* 6 December 2010, <http://www.telegraph.co.uk/culture/film/filmmakersonfilm/8176308/LA-confidential-Sofia-Coppola-interview.html>. Accessed 31 May 2016.

———, 'Marie Antoinette Press Book', <www.visualhollywood.com/movies/marieantoinette/notes.pdf>. Accessed 31 May 2016.

———, 'Sofia Coppola', *Les Inrockuptibles*, <http://www.lesinrocks.com/artiste/sofia-tauris>

———, 'The Sofia Coppola Look Book', *New York magazine* October 2012, <http://nymag.com/thecut/2012/10/sofia-coppola-look-book.html>. Accessed 31 May 2016.

———, 'Wonder Women', Manchester City Art Gallery, <http://www.manchestergalleries.org/the-collections/wonder-women>. Link no longer working.

Ash, Juliet and Elizabeth Wilson, 'Introduction', in Juliet Ash and Elizabeth Wilson, eds *Chic Thrills: A Fashion Reader* (London: Harper Collins, 1992), xi–xvii.

Azoury, Philippe, 'Etoiles mystérieuses', *Les Inrockuptibles* 1 August 2000.

Bachelard, Gaston, *The Poetics of Space* Trans. Maria Jolas (Boston, MA: Beacon Press, 1994).

Backman Rogers, Anna, 'The Historical Threshold: Crisis, Ritual and Liminality in Sofia Coppola's *Marie Antoinette*', *Relief* 6:1 (2012), 80–97, <http://www.revue-relief.org/index.php/relief/article/view/762/802>. Accessed 31 May 2016.

———, *American Independent Cinema: Rites of Passage and the Crisis Image* (Edinburgh: Edinburgh University Press, 2015).

de Baecque, Antoine and Serge Toubiana, *François Truffaut: A Biography* Trans. Catherine Temerson (New York: Knopf, 1999).

Bakhtin, Mikhail, *The Dialogic Imagination: 4 Essays* Trans. Caryl Ermerson (Austin, TX: University of Texas Press, 1982).

Barton Palmer, R., 'Some Thoughts on New Hollywood's Multiplicity: Sofia Coppola's Young Girl Trilogy', in Claire Perkins and Constantine Verevis, eds *Film Trilogies: New Critical Approaches* (Basingstoke: Palgrave, 2012), 35–54.

Bibliography

Baumgardner, Jennifer and Amy Richards, *Manifesta: Young Women, Feminism and the Future* (New York: Farrar, Straus and Giroux, 2000).

de Beauvoir, Simone, *The Second Sex* Trans. H.M. Parshley (New York: Vintage, 1989).

Berlant, Lauren, 'Intimacy: A Special Issue', *Critical Inquiry* 24:2 (Winter 1998), 281–288.

——, *The Female Complaint: The Unfinished Business of Sentimentality in American Culture* (Durham: Duke University Press, 2008).

Beugnet, Martine, *Cinema and Sensation: French Film and the Art of Transgression* (Edinburgh: Edinburgh University Press, 2007).

Biddulph, Steve, *Raising Girls* (London: Harper Collins, 2013).

Billson, Anne, 'The Bling Ring: is this the ugliest movie poster ever?', *The Daily Telegraph* 10 May 2013, <http://www.telegraph.co.uk/culture/film/10048804/The-Bling-Ring-is-this-the-ugliest-movie-poster-ever.html>. Accessed 31 May 2016.

Bingham, Dennis, *Whose Lives are they Anyway? The Biopic as Contemporary Film Genre* (Pescataway, NJ: Rutgers University Press, 2010).

Bolton, Lucy, *Film and Female Consciousness: Irigaray, Cinema and Thinking Women* (Basingstoke: Palgrave, 2011).

Bordwell, David, 'The Art Cinema as Mode of Film Practice', in Catherine Fowler, ed. *The European Cinema Reader* (London and New York: Routledge, 2002), 94–102.

Breen, James, 'In brief: Breakfast at Tiffany's', *Sight and Sound* Winter 1961–2.

Brevik-Zender, Heidi, 'Let them wear Manolos: Fashion, Walter Benjamin, and Sofia Coppola's *Marie Antoinette*', *Camera Obscure* 78 26:3 (2011), 1–33.

Brown, Mark, 'Coppola Film Booed', *The Guardian* Thursday 25 May 2006, <http://www.the-guardian.com/world/2006/may/25/film.cannes2006>. Accessed 31 May 2016.

Bruzzi, Stella, *Undressing Cinema: Clothing and Identity at the Movies* (London: Routledge, 1997).

Carroll, Lewis, *Alice in Wonderland and Through the Looking-Glass* (London: Dean and Son, abridged edition, nd [1865]).

Church Gibson, Pamela, 'Redressing the Balance: Patriarchy, Postmodernism and Feminism', in Stella Bruzzi and Pamela Church Gibson, eds *Fashion Cultures: Theory, Exploration and Analysis* (London: Routledge, 2001), 350–360.

Cohen, Clélia and Jacky Goldberg, 'Princesse du cool', *Les Inrockuptibles* 5 January 2011.

Colard, Jean-Max, 'Robert Mapplethorpe par Sofia Coppola: une belle surprise', *Les Inrockuptibles* 13 December 2011.

Colman, Felicity, 'Hit me Harder: The Transversality of Becoming-Adolescent', *Woman: A Cultural Review* 16:3 (2005), 356–371.

Cook, Pam, 'Portrait of a Lady', *Sight and Sound* November 2006, 36–40.

——, 'Sofia Coppola', in Yvonne Tasker, ed. *Fifty Contemporary Film Directors* (Oxford and London: Routledge, 2nd edition 2011), 126–134.

——, 'An American in Paris: Sofia Coppola and the new auteurism', Melbourne University workshop, 25 September 2013, Unpublished paper quoted with kind permission of Pam Cook.

——, 'History in the Making: Sofia Coppola's *Marie Antoinette* and the New Auteurism', in Tom Brown and Belen Vidal, eds *The Biopic in Contemporary Film Culture* (London: Routledge, 2014), 212–226.

Bibliography

Coppola, Sofia, 'Summer Talks: *The Bling Ring*', Film Society of Lincoln Centre, New York, June 10 2013, <http://www.filmlinc.org/daily/summer-talks-sofia-coppola-on-the-bling-ring>. Accessed 31 May 2016.

———, 'Sofia Coppola Interviews the Sisters Behind her New Favorite Film', *The New York Times* 17 August 2015, <http://www.nytimes.com/2015/08/17/t-magazine/alice-alba-rohrwacher.html>. Accessed 31 May 2016.

Cornut-Gentille D'Arcy, Chantal, 'Who's Afraid of the Femme Fatale in *Breakfast at Tiffany's*? Exposure and Implications of a Myth', in Chantal Cornut-Gentille D'Arcy and José García Landa, eds *Gender, I-deology: Essays on Theory, Fiction and Film* (Amsterdam: Rodopi, 1996), 371–385.

Corrigan, Timothy, 'The Commerce of Auteurism: A Voice without Authority', *New German Critique* 49 (Winter 1990), 43–57.

Dargis, Manohla, 'Under the Spell of Royal Ritual', *New York Times* May 25 2006.

Davenas, Olivier, *Teen! Cinéma de l'adolescence* (Paris: Moutons électriques, 2013).

Diamond, Diana, 'Sofia Coppola's Marie Antoinette: Costumes, Girl Power and Feminism', in Adrienne Munich, ed *Fashion and Film* (Bloomington and Indianapolis: Indiana University Press, 2011), 203–231.

Doane, Mary Ann, 'The Economy of Desire: The Commodity Form in/of Cinema,' *Quarterly Review of Film and Video* 11, 1989, 22–33.

Dobbins, Amanda, 'In Defense of Coppola's Marie Antoinette', *Vulture Devouring Culture* June 18 2013, <http://www.vulture.com/2013/06/defense-of-sofia-coppolas-marie-antoinette.html>. Accessed May 31 2016.

Donnelly, Kate, 'Sofia's Juicy Red Valentine', *New York Times magazine* February 12 2015, <http://tmagazine.blogs.nytimes.com/2015/02/12/sofia-coppola-red-wine/>. Accessed 31 May 2016.

Driscoll, Catherine, *Girls: Feminine Adolescence in Popular Culture and Theory* (New York: Columbia University Press, 2002).

Dyer, Richard, *Stars* (London: BFI, 2nd edition 1998).

———, *White: Essays on Race and Culture* (London and New York: Routledge, 2007).

Dyhouse, Carol, *Girl Trouble: Panic and Progress in the History of Young Women* (London: Zed books, 2013).

Eckert, Charles, 'The Carol Lombard in Macy's Window', in Christine Gledhill, ed. *Stardom: Industry of Desire* (London: Routledge, 1991).

Ford, Elizabeth A. and Deborah C. Mitchell, *Royal Portraits in Hollywood: Filming the Lives of Queens* (Lexington, KY: University Press of Kentucky, 2009).

Fraser, Antonia, *Marie Antoinette: The Journey* (London: Weidenfield and Nicholson, 2001).

———, 'Sofia's Choice', *Vanity Fair* October 31 2006, <http://www.vanityfair.com/news/2006/11/fraser200611>. Accessed 31 May 2016.

Fraser, Kennedy, 'Kirsten Dunst: Teen Queen', *Vogue* September 2006.

Freud, Sigmund, 'The Uncanny', *Art and Literature 14: The Penguin Freud Library* Trans. and ed. James Strachey (Harmondsworth: Penguin, 1990).

Fuchs, Cynthia, 'The Virgin Suicides', *Pop Matters*, <http://www.popmatters.com/review/virgin-suicides2>. Accessed 31 May 2016.

Fury, Alexander, 'Milan Fashion Week: Donatella Versace on sex and why she'd rather be a feminist than a muse', *The Independent* 19 September 2013, <http://www.independent.co.uk/life-style/fashion/features/milan-fashion-week-donatella-versace-on-sex-and-why-shed-rather-be-a-feminist-than-a-muse-8824528.html>. Accessed 31 May 2016.

Galt, Rosalind, *Pretty: Film and the Decorative Image* (New York: Columbia University Press, 2011).

Gateward, Frances and Murray Pomerance, eds *Sugar, Spice and Everything Nice: Cinemas of Girlhood* (Detroit, MI: Wayne State University Press, 2002).

Gevinson, Tavi, 'Girls with Power and Mystique: An Interview with Sofia Coppola', *Rookie* 17 June 2013, http://www.rookiemag.com/2013/06/sofia-coppola-interview/2. Accessed 31 May 2016.

Gilchrist, Todd. 'Interview: Sofia Coppola', *IGN* 17 October 2006, <http://uk.ign.com/articles/2006/10/17/interview-sofia-coppola>. Accessed 31 May 2016.

Gill, Rosalind, *Gender and the Media* (Cambridge: Polity Press, 2007).

Ginsberg, Merle, 'Launching Sofia', *W Magazine* September 1994.

Gittell, Noah, 'The Little Mermaid's Twisted, Sofia-Coppola-esque Origins', *The Atlantic* 21 March 2014.

Godard, Jean-Luc, *Arts* April 1959.

Gonick, Marnina, 'Between "Girl-Power" and "Reviving Ophelia": Constituting the Neoliberal Girl Subject', *NWSA Journal* 18:2 (2006), 1–23.

——, Emma Renold, Jessica Ringrose and Lisa Weems, 'Rethinking Agency and Resistance: What Comes After Girl Power?', *Girlhood Studies* 2:2 (Winter 2009), 1–9.

Grant, Catherine, 'Secret Agents: Feminist Theories of Women's Film Authorship', *Feminist Theory* 2:1 (April 2001), 113–130.

Gundle, Stephen, *Glamour: A History* (Oxford: Oxford University Press, 2008).

Hains, Rebecca, C. *The Princess Problem: Guiding Our Girls Through the Princess Obsessed Years* (Naperville, IL: Sourcebooks, 2014).

Halberstam, Judith Jack, in Elizabeth Freeman, ed. 'Theorising Queer Temporalities: A Roundtable Discussion', *GLQ: A Journal of Lesbian and Gay Studies* 13: 2–3 (2007), 177–195.

——, 'Oh Bondage Up Yours! Female Masculinity and the Tomboy', in Steve Bruhm and Natasha Hurley, eds *Curiouser: On the Queerness of Children* (Minneapolis, MN: University of Minnesota Press, 2014), 191–214.

Handyside, Fiona, 'Belle toujours: Deneuve as Fashion icon', in Lisa Downing and Sue Harris, eds *From Perversion to Purity: The Stardom of Catherine Deneuve* (Manchester: Manchester University Press, 2007), 161–179.

——, 'Girlhood, Postfeminism and Contemporary Female Art-House Authorship: The "Nameless Trilogies" of Sofia Coppola and Mia Hansen-Løve', *Alphaville: Journal of Screen and Film Media* 10 Winter 2015, <http://www.alphavillejournal.com/Issue10/HTML/ArticleHandyside.html>. Accessed 31 May 2016.

Harris, Anita, *Future Girl: Young Women in the Twenty-First Century* (London: Routledge, 2004).

Harstein, Jennifer, *Princess Recovery: A Guide to Raising Strong, Empowered Girls Who Can Create their Own Happily Ever Afters* (Avon, MA: Adams Media, 2011).

190

Bibliography

Haskell, Molly, *From Reverence to Rape: The Treatment of Women in the Movies* (New York: New English Library, 1974).

Haslem, Wendy, 'Neon Gothic: Lost in Translation', *Senses of Cinema* April 2004, <http://sensesof-cinema.com/2004/feature-articles/lost_in_translation>. Accessed 31 May 2016.

Hatcher-Mays, Meagan, 'How Sofia Coppola Whitewashed The Bling Ring', *Jezebel* 20 June 2013, <http://jezebel.com/how-sofia-coppola-whitewashed-the-bling-ring-514020537>. Accessed 31 May 2016.

Hipkins, Danielle, '"Whore-ocracy": Show Girls, the Beauty Trade-Off, and Mainstream Oppositional Discourse in Italy', *Italian Studies* 66:3, (2011), 413–30.

Hirschberg, Lynn, 'The Coppola Smart Mob', *New York Times*, August 31 2003.

——, 'Sofia Coppola's Guide to Paris', *New York Times* September 24 2006.

——, 'Girls on Film', *W Magazine* June 2013, <http://www.wmagazine.com/people/celebri-ties/2013/06/sofia-coppola-director-the-bling-ring-with-emma-watson>. Accessed 31 May 2016.

Hiscock, John, 'Sofia Coppola Interview: "The Bling Ring isn't my world."' *The Daily Telegraph* 4 July 2013, <http://www.telegraph.co.uk/culture/film/10126910/Sofia-Coppola-interview-The-Bling-Ring-isnt-my-world.html>. Accessed 31 May 2016.

Hohenadel, Kristin, 'French Royalty as Seen by Hollywood Royalty', *New York Times* September 10, 2006, <http://www.nytimes.com/2006/09/10/movies/moviesspecial/10hohe.html?pagewanted=all>. Accessed 31 May 2016.

Hollows, Joanne, '"Can I Go Home Yet?" Feminism, Postfeminism and Domesticity', in Joanne Hollows and Rachel Moseley, eds *Feminism in Popular Culture* (Oxford: Berg, 2006), 97–118.

Holmes, Elizabeth, 'Perfume Bottles Gone Wild', *The Wall Street Journal* 7 June 2012, <http://www.wsj.com/news/articles/SB10001424052702303753904577450312917322948>. Accessed 31 May 2016.

Holmes, Su and Sean Redmond, 'Editorial', *Celebrity Studies* 1:1 2010, 1–10.

——, and Diane Negra 'Introduction', in Negra and Holmes, eds *In the Limelight and Under the Microscope: The Form and Functions of Female Celebrity* (London and New York: Continuum, 2011), 1–16.

Holmlund, Chris, 'Postfeminism from A to G', *Cinema Journal* 44:2 (2005), 116–121.

Hoskin, Bree, 'Playground Love: Landscape and Longing in Sofia Coppola's *The Virgin Suicides*', *Literature/Film Quarterly* 35:3 (July 2007), 214–225.

Ivinson, Gabrielle and Emma Renold, 'Valley Girls: Re-theorising bodies and agency in a semi-rural post-industrial locale', *Gender and Education* 25:6 (2013), 704–721.

Jacobs, Marc, Themarcjacobs, *Instagram* <https://instagram.com/p/4iFNEOGJCd/>. Accessed 31 May 2016.

Johnston, Claire, 'Women's Cinema as Counter-Cinema', in Claire Johnston, ed. *Notes on Women's Cinema* (London: SEFT, 1975).

Kaplan, Louise J., *Female Perversions: The Temptations of Madame Bovary* (Harmondsworth: Penguin, 1993).

Kearney, Mary Celeste, 'Sparkle: Luminosity and post-girlpower media', *Continuum: Journal of Media and Cultural Studies* 29:2 (2015), 263–273.

Kennedy, Todd, 'Off with Hollywood's Head: Sofia Coppola as Feminine Auteur', *Film Criticism* 35:1 (Fall 2010), 37–59.

King, Geoff, *Lost in Translation* (Edinburgh: Edinburgh University Press, 2010).

King, Homay, *Lost in Translation: Orientalism, Cinema, and the Enigmatic Signifier* (Durham, NC and London: Duke University Press, 2010).

Kroll, Justin, 'Sofia Coppola to Direct Universal and Working Title's *Little Mermaid*', *Variety* March 18 2014, <http://variety.com/2014/film/news/sofia-coppola-to-direct-universal-and-working-titles-little-mermaid-1201137793/>. Accessed 31 May 2016.

——, 'Chloe Moretz to star in *Little Mermaid* for Working Title; Richard Curtis to Pen Script', *Variety* 6 November 2015, <http://variety.com/2015/film/news/chloe-moretz-little-mermaid-1201579228/>. Accessed 31 May 2016.

Lane, Christina, and Nicole Richter, 'The Feminist Poetics of Sofia Coppola: Spectacle and Self-Consciousness in Marie Antoinette (2006)', in Radner and Stringer, eds *Feminism at the Movies: Understanding Gender in Contemporary Popular Cinema* (New York and Oxford: Routledge, 2011), 189–202.

Larocca, Amy, 'Lost and Found', *New York Magazine,* <http://nymag.com/nymetro/shopping/fashion/12544>. Accessed 31 May 2016.

Latham, Robert, *Consuming Youth: Vampires, Cyborgs and the Cultures of Consumption* (Chicago: University of Chicago Press, 2004).

de Lauretis, Teresa 'Rethinking Women's Cinema: Aesthetics and Feminist Theory', in Patricia Erens, ed. *Issues in Feminist Film Criticism* (Bloomington and Indianapolis, IN: Indiana University Press, 1990), 292–311.

Lebeau, Vicky, *Childhood and Cinema* (London: Reaktion, 2008).

Lee, Nathan, 'Pretty Vacant: The Radical Frivolity of Sofia Coppola's *Marie Antoinette*', *Film Comment* September–October 2006, 24–26.

Letort, Delphine, 'The Cultural Capital of Sofia Coppola's *The Bling Ring* (2013): Branding Feminine Celebrity in Los Angeles', *Celebrity Studies* 2015, <http://www.tandfonline.com/doi/abs/10.1080/19392397.2015.1119657>. Accessed 31 May 2016.

Long, Danielle, 'Sony Targets social networking sites for Marie Antoinette', *Marketing Magazine* 20 October 2006, <http://www.marketingmagazine.co.uk/article/599673/sony-targets-social-networking-sites-marie-antoinette>. Accessed 31 May 2016.

McCabe, Colin, *Godard: Images, Sounds, Politics* (London: BFI, 1980).

McRobbie, Angela, 'Top Girls: Young Women and the Postfeminist Sexual Contract', *Cultural Studies* 21:4–5 (2007), 718–737.

——, *The Aftermath of Feminism: Gender, Culture and Social Change* (London: Sage, 2009).

Margulies, Ivone, 'A Matter of Time: Jeanne Dielman, 23, Quai du commerce, 1080 Bruxelles', *Criterion,* <https://www.criterion.com/current/posts/1215-a-matter-of-time-jeanne-dielman-23-quai-du-commerce-1080-bruxelles>. Accessed 31 May 2016.

Marwood, Alice and danah boyd, 'To See and Be Seen: Celebrity Practice on Twitter', *Convergence: The International Journal of Research into New Media Technologies* 17: 2 (2010), 139–158 (139).

Matin, Samiha, 'Private Femininity, Public Femininity: Tactical Aesthetics in the Costume Film', in Christine Gledhill, ed. *Gender Meets Genre in Postwar Cinemas* (Urbana, Chicago and Springfield, IL: University of Illinois Press, 2012), 96–110.

Mau, Dhani, 'Marc Jacobs is Coming Out with Another Daisy Perfume', *Fashionista* 7 May 2014, <http://fashionista.com/2014/05/marc-jacobs-daisy-dream>. Accessed 31 May 2016.

Bibliography

Mire, Muna, and Isabelle Nastasia, 'Sofia Coppola and the Unbearable Whiteness of The Bling Ring' *mic.com* 4 July 2013, <http://mic.com/articles/52649/sofia-coppola-and-the-unbearable-whiteness-of-the-bling-ring>. Accessed 31 May 2016.

Mitchell, Elvis, 'An American in Japan making a connection', *New York Times* 12 September 2003.

Modleski, Tania, *The Women Who Knew Too Much: Hitchcock and Feminist Theory* (London: Routledge, 2nd edition 2005).

Monden, Masafumi, 'Contemplating in a Dreamlike Room: *The Virgin Suicides* and the Aesthetic Imagination of Girlhood', *Film, Fashion and Consumption* 2:2 (June 2013), 139–158.

Montgomery, Michael V., *Carnivals and Commonplaces: Bakhtin's Chronotope, Cultural Studies, and Film* (New York: Peter Lang, 1993).

Morin, Edgar, *L'Esprit du temps* (Paris: Grasset, 1962).

Moseley, Rachel, *Growing Up with Audrey Hepburn: Text, Audience, Resonance* (Manchester: Manchester University Press, 2003).

Moya, Ana, 'Neo-Feminism In-Between: Female Cosmopolitan Subjects in Contemporary American Film', in Joel Gwynne and Nadine Muller, eds *Postfeminism and Contemporary Hollywood Cinema* (Basingstoke: Palgrave, 2013), 13–26.

Mulvey, Laura, 'Visual Pleasure and Narrative Cinema', *Screen* 16:3 (Autumn 1975).

——, 'British Feminist Film Theory's Female Spectators: Presence and Absence', *Camera Obscura* 20/21 (1989), 68–81.

Munford, Rebecca and Melanie Waters, *Feminism and Popular Culture: Investigating the Postfeminist Mystique* (London: I.B.Tauris, 2014).

Murphy, Amy, 'Traces of the Flâneuse. From Roman Holiday to Lost In Translation', *Journal of Architectural Education*, 2006, 33–42.

Negra, Diane, *What a Girl Wants? Fantasizing the Reclamation of the Self in Postfeminism* (Oxford and New York: Routledge, 2009).

———, 'Introduction: Feminist Politics and Postfeminist Culture', in Negra and Tasker, eds *Interrogating Postfeminism: Gender and the Politics of Popular Culture* (Durham, NC: Duke University Press, 2007), 1–26.

Olsen, Mark, 'The Directors: Sofia Coppola takes a floor at the Chateau Marmont', *Los Angeles Times* October 31 2010, <http://articles.latimes.com/2010/oct/31/entertainment/la-ca-sneaks-somewhere-20101031>. Accessed 31 May 2016.

Orenstein, Peggy, *Cinderella Ate My Daughter: Dispatches from the Front Lines of the New Girlie-Girl Culture* (New York: Harper Collins, 2011).

Orth, Maureen, *The Importance of Being Famous: Behind the Scenes of the Celebrity-Industrial Complex* (New York: Henry Holt, 2004).

Parkins, Ilya, 'Building a Feminist Theory of Fashion', *Australian Feminist Studies* 23:58 (2008), 501–515.

Parris, Leslie, ed. *The Pre-Raphaelites* (London: Tate, 1984).

Peretz, Evgenia, 'Something About Sofia', *Vanity Fair* 553 September 2006.

Perez, Cristina, 'Three Things I Learned about Style from Sofia Coppola's Totally Understated Chic', *Glamour* May 16 2013.

Petro, Patrice, *Aftershocks of the New: Feminism and Film History* (New Brunswick, NJ: Rutgers University Press, 2002).

Pidduck, Julianne, *Contemporary Costume Film: Space, Place and the Past* (London: BFI, 2004).

Pilinovsky, Helen, 'Body as Wonderland: Alice's Graphic Iteration in Lost Girls', in Christopher Hollingsworth, ed. *Alice Beyond Wonderland: Essays from the 21st Century* (Iowa, IA: Iowa University Press, 2009), 175–198.

Pipher, Mary, *Reviving Ophelia: Saving the Selves of Adolescent Girls* (New York: Random House, 1994).

Porter, Lynn, 'Bahktin's Chronotope: Time and Space in A Touch of the Poet and More Stately Mansions', *Modern Drama* 34:3 (Fall 1991), 369–382.

Prendergast, Christopher, *Paris and the Nineteenth Century* (Oxford: Blackwell, 1992).

Prince, Richard, 'Sofia Coppola', *Interview*, <http://www.interviewmagazine.com/film/sofia-coppola/#>. Accessed 31 May 2016.

Projansky, Sarah, 'Mass Magazine Cover Girls: Some Reflections on Postfeminist Girls and Postfeminism's Daughters', in Diane Negra and Yvonne Tasker, eds *Interrogating Postfeminism: Gender and the Politics of Popular Culture* (Durham, NC: Duke University Press, 2007), 40–72.

——, *Spectacular Girls: Media Fascination and Celebrity Culture* (New York: New York University Press, 2014).

Quick, Harriet, 'An Oscar, An It Bag, Marc Jacobs on Speed Dial', *Red* July 2013, 56–63.

Rabine, Leslie W., 'A Woman's Two Bodies: Fashion Magazines, Consumerism and Feminism', in Shari Benstock and Suzanne Ferriss, eds *On Fashion* (New Brunswick, NJ: Rutgers University Press), 59–75.

Radner, Hilary, *Neo-Feminist Cinema: Girly Film, Chick Flicks and Consumer Culture* (New York: Routledge, 2011).

Radziwill, Lee and Sofia Coppola, 'On Protecting Privacy', *New York Times Magazine* May 30 2013, <http://tmagazine.blogs.nytimes.com/2013/05/30/in-conversation-lee-radziwill-and-sophia-coppola-on-protecting-privacy>. Accessed 31 May 2016.

Rae Hark, Ina, 'Movie-going, "Home-Leaving," and the Problematic Girl Protagonist of *The Wizard of Oz*', in Gateward and Pomerance, eds *Sugar, Spice and Everything Nice: Cinemas of Girlhood* (Detroit, MI: Wayne State University Press, 2002), 25–38.

Renold, Emma and Jessica Ringrose, 'Regulation and Rupture: Mapping Tween and Teenage Girls' Resistance to the Heterosexual Matrix', *Feminist Studies* 9:3 (2008), 313–338.

Rigoulet, Laurent, 'Versailles tendance Coppola', *Télérama* 22 June 2005.

Rivas, Jorge, 'The Immigrant You Won't See in Sofia Coppola's *Bling Ring*', *Colorlines* 13 June 2013, <http://www.colorlines.com/articles/immigrant-you-wont-see-sofia-coppolas-bling-ring>. Accessed 31 May 2016.

Rogers, Anna, 'Sofia Coppola', *Senses of Cinema* November 2007, <http://sensesofcinema.com/2007/great-directors/sofia-coppola>. Accessed 31 May 2016.

Rojek, Chris. *Celebrity* (London: Reaktion, 2001).

Rosen, Marjorie, *Popcorn Venus: Women, Movies and the American Dream* (New York: Coward, McCann and Geoghegan, 1973).

Rowe Karlyn, Kathleen, *Unruly Girls, Unrepentant Mothers: Redefining Feminism on Screen* (Austin, TX: University of Texas Press, 2011).

Bibliography

Schaap, Rob, 'No Country for Old Women: Gendering Cinema in Conglomerate Hollywood', in Radner and Stringer, eds *Feminism at the Movies: Understanding Gender in Contemporary Popular Cinema* (New York and Oxford: Routledge, 2011), 151–162.

Schatz, Thomas, 'New Hollywood, New Millennium', in Warren Buckland, ed. *Film Theory and Contemporary Hollywood Movies* (New York: Routledge, 2009).

Sconce, Jeffrey, 'Irony, Nihilism, and the new American "smart" film', *Screen* 43:4 (Winter 2002), 349–369.

Scott, A.O., 'Evanescent Trees and Sisters in an Enchanted 1970s Suburb', *New York Times* April 20, 2000.

——, 'Holding Up a Mirror to Hollywood', *New York Times* May 25 2006.

Scott, Linda M., *Fresh Lipstick: Redressing Fashion and Feminism* (New York: Palgrave, 2005).

Shia, Jonathan, 'Somewhere', *The Last Magazine* December 29 2010. <https://thelast-magazine.com/somewhere/>. Accessed 31 May 2016.

Shome, Raka, *Diana and Beyond: White Femininity, National Identity, and Contemporary Media Culture* (Urbana, Chicago and Springfield, IL: University of Illinois Press, 2014).

Smaill, Belinda, 'Sofia Coppola: Reading the Director', *Feminist Media Studies* 13:1 (2013), 148–162.

Sobchack, Vivian, 'Lounge Time: Postwar crisis and the chronotope of film noir', in Nick Browne, ed. *Refiguring American Film Genres: History and Theory* (Berkeley and Los Angeles, CA: University of California Press, 1998), 129–170.

Sohn, Amy, *Sex and the City: Kiss and Tell* (New York: Pocket Books, 2004).

Stacey, Jackie, *Star-Gazing: Hollywood Cinema and Female Spectatorship* (Oxford and New York: Routledge, 1994).

Staiger, Janet, 'Authorship Approaches', in David Gerstner and Janet Staiger, eds *Authorship and Film* (London and New York: Routledge, 2002), 27–60.

Stern, Marlow, 'Sofia Coppola discusses *Lost in Translation* on its 10th Anniversary', *The Daily Beast* 9 December 2013, <http://www.thedailybeast.com/articles/2013/09/12/sofia-coppola-discusses-lost-in-translation-on-its-10th-anniversary.html>. Accessed 31 May 2016.

Stevens, Dana, 'Queen Bees, Sofia Coppola and Marie Antoinette Have A Lot in Common', *Slate* October 2006, <http://www.slate.com/id/2151855>. Accessed 31 May 2016.

Stilwell, Robynn, 'Vinyl Communion: The Record as Ritual Object in Girls' Rite-of-Passage Films', in Phil Powrie and Robynn Stilwell, eds *Changing Tunes: The Use of Pre-Existing Music in Films* (Aldershot: Ashford, 2006), 152–167.

Stoller, Robert, *Observing the Erotic Imagination* (New Haven and London: Yale University Press, 1985).

Swindle, Monica, 'Feeling Girl, Girling Feeling: An Examination of Girl as Affect', *Rhizomes* 22 (2011), <http://www.rhizomes.net/issue22/swindle.html>. Accessed 31 May 2016.

Tay, Sharon Lay, *Women on the Edge: Twelve Political Film Practices* (New York: Palgrave, 2009).

Thornham, Sue, *What if I had been the Hero? Investigating Women's Cinema* (London: BFI, 2012).

Tiqqun, *Preliminary Materials for a Theory of the Young Girl* Trans. Ariana Reines (Los Angeles, CA: Semiotext(e), 2012).

Turner, Graeme, *Understanding Celebrity* (London: Sage, 2004).

Tyree, J.M., 'Searching for Somewhere', *Film Quarterly* 64:4 (Summer 2011).

Vonder Haar, Peter, 'Marie Antoinette', *Film Threat* October 2006.

Wallace, Lee, *Lesbianism, Cinema, Space: The Sexual Life of Apartments* (London: Routledge, 2011).

Warren-Crow, Heather, *Girlhood and the Plastic Image* (Dartmouth, NH: University Press of New England, 2014).

Warwick, Alexandra and Dani Cavallaro, *Fashioning the Frame: Boundaries, Dress and the Body* (Oxford: Berg, 1998).

Weber, Caroline, *Queen of Fashion: What Marie Antoinette Wore to the Revolution* (New York: Picador, 2006).

Willson, Jacki, *Being Gorgeous: Feminism, Sexuality and the Pleasures of the Visual* (London: I.B.Tauris, 2014).

Winch, Alison, *Girlfriends and Postfeminist Sisterhood* (Basingstoke: Palgrave, 2013).

Wissinger, Elizabeth, 'Always on Display: Affective Production in the Modeling Industry', in Jean Clough and Jean Halley, eds *The Affective Turn: Theorising the Social* (Durham: Duke University Press, 2007), 231–260.

Woodworth, Amy, 'A Feminist Theorization of Sofia Coppola's Postfeminist Trilogy', in Marcelline Block, ed. *Situating the Feminist Gaze and Spectatorship in Postwar Cinema* (Newcastle: Cambridge Scholars Press), 138–167.

Wright, Lee, 'Objectifying Gender: The Stiletto Heel', in Malcom Barnard, ed. *Fashion Theory: A Reader* (London: Routledge, 2007), 247–258.

Yuneun Lewis, Caitlin, 'Cool Postfeminism: The Stardom of Sofia Coppola', in Diane Negra and Su Holmes, eds *In the Limelight and Under the Microscope: The Form and Functions of Female Celebrity* (London and New York: Continuum, 2011), 174–198.

Zaggario, Vito, 'Their Voyage to Italy: New Hollywood Film Artists and the theme of "Nostalgia"', in Giuliana Muscio, Joseph Sciorra, Giovanni Spagnoletti and Anthony Julian Tamburri, eds *Mediated Ethnicity: New Italian-American Cinema* (New York: John D Calandra Italian-American Institute, 2010), 117–126.

Ziolkowski, Fabrice, 'Comedies and Proverbs: An Interview with Eric Rohmer', *Wide Angle* 5:1 (1982), 62–67.

Filmography

Akerman, Chantal. *Jeanne Dielman, 23 quai du Commerce, 1080 Bruxelles*. 1976.

_____. *La Captive*. 2000.

Anderson, Wes. *Rushmore*. 1998.

Andrews, Mark, Brenda Chapman and Steve Purcell. *Brave*. 2012.

Anon, 'Scene of the crime interview with Paris Hilton', *The Bling Ring* DVD Studiocanal, 2013.

Antonioni, Michelangelo. *L'Avventura*. 1960.

_____. *La Notte*. 1961.

_____. *L'Eclisse*. 1962.

Ball, Alan. *Six Feet Under*. 2001–2005.

Baskin, Alex, Kathleen French and Douglas Ross. *The Real Housewives of Beverly Hills* [TV series] (2010–).

De Bon, Jan. *Speed*. 1994.

Breillat, Catherine. *A Ma Soeur*. 2001.

Buck, Chris and Jennifer Lee. *Frozen*. 2013.

Cameron, James. *Titanic*. 1997.

Cherry, Marc. *Desperate Housewives*. [TV series]. 2004–2012.

Clements, Ron and John Musker. *The Little Mermaid*. 1989.

Coppola, Francis Ford. *The Godfather*. 1972.

_____. *Apocalypse Now*. 1979.

_____. *Rumblefish*. 1983.

_____. *The Godfather Part Three*. 1990.

Coppola, Sofia. *Lick the Star* [short]. 1998.

_____. *The Virgin Suicides*. 1999.

_____. *Lost in Translation*. 2003.

_____. *Marie Antoinette*. 2006.

_____. *Somewhere*. 2010.

_____. *The Bling Ring*. 2013.

_____. 'Daisy' [TV advertisement]. <https://www.youtube.com/watch?v=dcyR7PFi-14>. Accessed 31 May 2016.

_____. 'Daisy Trio' [TV advertisement]. <https://www.youtube.com/watch?v=s0enWUED3Fo>. Accessed 31 May 2016.

Correll, Rich, Barry O'Brien and Michael Poyres. *Hannah Montana*. [TV series]. 2006–2011.

Cottrell, William, David Hand et al. *Snow White and the Seven Dwarves*. 1937.

Costa-Gavras. *Z*. 1969.

Dee, Rees. *Pariah*. 2011.

Edwards, Blake. *Breakfast at Tiffany's*. 1961.

Fellini, Federico. *La Dolce Vita*. 1960.

Fleming, Victor. *Gone with the Wind*. 1939.

_____. *The Wizard of Oz*. 1939.

Foley, Jerry. *The Late Show with David Letterman*. [TV series]. 13 February 2004.

Frankel, David. *The Devil Wears Prada*. 2006.

Frears, Stephen. *High Fidelity*. 2000.

Funny or Die. 'Sofia Coppola's Little Mermaid'. 13 May 2014. https://www.youtube.com/watch?v=YPT4bdo1kZw

Godard, Jean-Luc and Gorin, Jean-Pierre. *Tout va bien*. 1974.

Hitchcock, Alfred. *Rear Window*. 1954.

Ivory, James. *Howards End*. 1992.

Jonze, Spike. *Being John Malkovitch*. 1999.

Kaplan, Jonathan. *Over the Edge*. 1979.

King, Michael P. *Sex and the City: the Movie*. 2008.

Kreigman, Mitchell. *Clarissa Explains it All* [TV series]. 1991–1994.

Kubrick, Stanley. *Lolita*. 1962.

Lee, Ang. *Sense and Sensibility*. 1995.

_____. *Ice Storm*. 1997.

Lean, David. *Dr Zhivago*. 1965.

Luketic, Robert. *Legally Blonde*. 2001.

Lyne, Adrian. *Foxes*. 1980.

Maguire, Sharon. *Bridget Jones' Diary*. 2001.

Malick, Terence. *Badlands*. 1973.

Marshall, Garry. *Pretty Woman*. 1990.

Ortega, Kenny. *High School Musical*. 2006.

De Palma, Brian. *Carrie*. 1976.

Polanski, Roman. *Chinatown*. 1974.

Resnais, Alain. *Last Year at Marienbad/L'Année Dernière à Marienbad*. 1961.

Rohmer, Eric. *Pauline à la plage/ Pauline at the Beach*. 1983.

_____. *Les Nuits de la pleine lune/ Full Moon in Paris*. 1984.

_____. *L'Anglaise et le duc/ The Lady and the Duke*. 2001.

Ross, Gary. *The Hunger Games*. 2012.

Savage, Stephanie and Josh Schwartz. *Gossip Girl* [TV series]. 2007–2012.

Scott, Ridley. *Blade Runner*. 1982.

_____. *Thelma and Louise*. 1991.

Star, Darren. *Sex and the City*. [TV series].1998–2004.

Truffaut, François. *The 400 Blows/Les 400 Coups*. 1959.

Varda, Agnès. *Cléo from 5 to 7/Cléo de 5 à 7*. 1962.

Di Villo, Adam. *The Hills*. [TV series]. 2006–2010.

Waters, Mark. *Mean Girls*. 2004.

Weiner, Matthew. *Mad Men*. [TV series]. 2007–2015.

Wilder, Billy. *Sabrina*. 1954.

_____. *The Seven Year Itch*. 1955.

Winick, Gary. *Bride Wars*. 2009.

Wise, Robert. *The Sound of Music*. 1965.

Zwigoff, Terry. *Ghost World*. 2001.

Index

Index